D1216532

A PURPOSE FOR *EVERYTHING*

To John B. Cobb, Jr

A
PURPOSE FOR
EVERYTHING

Religion in a Postmodern Worldview

CHARLES BIRCH

TWENTY-THIRD PUBLICATIONS
Mystic, Connecticut

North American Edition 1990

Twenty-Third Publications
185 Willow Street
P.O. Box 180
Mystic CT 06355
(203) 536-2611

Originally published in Australia in 1990 as *On Purpose* by the new South Wales University Press, Kensington, New South Wales, Australia.

ISBN 0-89622-453-8
Library of Congress Catalog Card Number 90-70991

Contents

Till Darwin came to earth upon a year
To show the evolution how to steer.
They mean to tell us, though, the omnibus
Had no real purpose till it got to us.

Never believe it. At the very worst
It must have had the purpose from the first
To produce purpose as the fitter bred:
We were just purpose coming to a head.

Robert Frost, 'Accidentally On Purpose'

Acknowledgements

I am greatly indebted to Clive Cossley, David Griffin and John Haught who read an early version of the manuscript and who provided me with much helpful criticism and many ideas to better tie together the meaning of purpose developed in successive chapters. I thank Peter Farleigh who kept me in touch with a younger generation and Warwick Fox who kept me posted on deep ecology and ecophilosophy in general. I am deeply indebted to John Cobb who helped me to interpret process thought with fewer mistakes than would otherwise have been the case. He encouraged me from the beginning to attempt to produce a book on process thought that might be accessible to the lay person unfamiliar with the terminology that tends to be associated with it.

Extract from the poetry of R P Dickey reprinted with the permission of the Ohio University Press, Athens. Extracts from the poetry of Robert Frost reprinted with the permission of Jonathan Cape Ltd, London. Extracts from the poetry of T S Eliot reprinted with the permission of Faber and Faber Ltd, London. Extract from the poetry of Henry Reed reprinted with the permission of The Royal Literary Fund, London.

Introduction

In this phase of human history there is widespread conflict between our conception of ourselves and our conception of the world. We see ourselves as beings that are conscious, that are rational, have free will and are purposive. But we see the world as consisting of mindless, meaningless, totally determined physical bits and pieces that are non-purposive. A society that lives with this dichotomy is operating out of a profound error that is destroying much that is worthwhile both in ourselves and in the world.

The general picture most of us have about the world is derived from Newton's mechanics of the seventeenth century. The man in the street, whether he knows it or not, still lives in Newton's world. A lot has changed since then, but the general picture for most of us hasn't. In classical Newtonian mechanics, once the initial conditions and the force laws are given, everything is calculable for ever before and after. The system is governed completely by the laws of mechanics and of conservation of energy. It is totally determined. It has no freedom.

By contrast, any human situation is quite different. Imagine a city street in which pedestrians and traffic are milling around. The flows of traffic and the movements of any pedestrian cannot be predicted using the laws of mechanics. If a pedestrian tries to cross the road against the traffic lights he may meet an oncoming vehicle; the driver applies brakes and there is an accident. Newton's laws are no help at all in describing that system. The situation is utterly dependent upon the decision of the pedestrian to cross the street at the wrong time and the decision of the driver to try to stop his vehicle. Planets, solar systems, atoms and molecules seem helpless slaves to the forces that push them around. Human beings are also pushed around. But most of us recognise something else in ourselves—some degree of freedom to choose what we do. Purposes determine a great deal about our lives.

Although this example has a modern ring to it, there is nothing really new about the problem it presents, which is: How is it that freedom and purpose that determine so much about us arise in a world that seems to run entirely on mechanical laws? The issue of two kinds of cause, mechanical ones and purposive ones, was set before his fellow Athenians by Socrates in 399 BC as he sat in prison contemplating his death. Today it is the central issue in the battle between science and religion. It is also the central issue in the relationship of modern human beings to their environment. Whether we are aware of it or not, most of the problems of the modern world revolve around this dichotomy between ourselves and the world.

Some people have resolved the dichotomy by contending that what we think is our freedom to choose different purposes is a gigantic illusion. Our destiny is determined as much as that of the solar system or the atoms that compose it. We are cogs in a mechanical universe. If we think like that it logically follows that we can legitimately treat other people as cogs in a machine. To do that is to manipulate people. Bertrand Russell (1968) warned against the dangers of encouraging people to see themselves and others as cogs in a machine-like world. He suggested this had already reached the point where people might be tempted to pray like cogs:

> Almighty and most merciful Machine, we have erred and strayed from thy ways like lost screws; we have put in those nuts which we ought not to have put in, and we have left out those nuts which we ought to have put in, and there is no cogginess in us. (pp. 57–8)

The picture of the universe as a gigantic contrivance and ourselves as small contrivances or machines is now beleaguered on several fronts. It is challenged by modern physics, modern biology and by frontier thinking in theology and philosophy. But the news has not yet reached the headlines. One objective of this book is to help to put it there. It could change our view of ourselves and the world and the way we live in the world.

The science and the philosophy that have promoted the view of a largely mechanistic man in a completely mechanistic universe are today in the same predicament as Baron Munchhausen's horse. During a wintry ride through Poland, Munchhausen was overtaken by darkness on a desolate snowy expanse. After tying his horse to what appeared to be a tree stump, he fell asleep in the snow drifts. The next morning Munchhausen was astonished to awaken in a churchyard and to discover his horse hanging from the top of a steeple. The snow, which had covered all but the church spire, had melted, gently lowering the baron to the ground but leaving his mount suspended precariously from the steeple. Science and philosophy and a deal of Christian theology were once securely tethered to the sturdy edifice of Newtonian mechanics. The universe was a machine. God, if God existed, was the mechanic who made the machine. God operated by the mechanical means of pushing things around through miracle and catastrophe. What was once thought to be solid ground has melted away, leaving these concepts dangling precariously above the abyss.

The mechanical images no longer fit. They are giving way to quite a different image of the universe and ourselves. This discovery is being made simultaneously by a science, a philosophy and a theology as yet little known. Its new images are no longer mechanical: they are organic and ecological. The universe turns out to be less like a machine and more like a life. This constitutes a new revolution in science, philosophy and theology in our time.

The name of this way of thinking, which provides the framework of this book, is process thought. The greatest exponent of this position is Alfred North Whitehead (1861–1947), who is probably the greatest polymath of this century. For most of his life he was a mathematician, teaching first at Cambridge University where one of his students was Bertrand Russell. Later he was Professor of Mathematics in the University of London. It was there that he collaborated with Bertrand Russell for ten years to produce *Principia Mathematica*, a treatise on symbolic logic. At the age of sixty Whitehead moved across the Atlantic to accept an invitation to become a professor of philosophy at Harvard University, where he remained for the rest of his life. From then onwards the thoughts of these two men diverged. Russell became a leading exponent of a materialistic philosophy, yet sensitive to human values. Whitehead rejected materialism and the dominant interpretation of science which was mechanism for what he called an organic view of the universe. Russell said that either life is matter-like or matter is life-like and chose the former, while Whitehead chose the latter. Whitehead introduced Russell at a lecture at Harvard as follows: 'Bertie says that I am muddle-headed. But I think that he is simple-minded.' In quoting this remark Hartshorne (1970a) says:

> Here, in unsurpassably succinct form, is one of the great contrasts between philosophers. There are those who would be clear (and even neat and witty) at almost any cost, including that of vastly over-simplifying things. There are those who would above all be adequate to the richness and many-sidedness of reality, even if they cannot always be neat and clear in their account of it. (p. 69)

From time to time in this book the contrast between these two positions becomes apparent.

For Whitehead, the universe is not made of bits of stuff that can be understood as particles or atoms. The entities that make up the universe, from protons to people, are events or processes. Hence the title of his greatest work, *Process and Reality*. Far from thinking of billiard balls as symbols of reality, Whitehead takes human experience as the event or process that points to the nature of all individual entities, from protons to people. Or, as Cobb and Griffin (1976) say: 'Process philosophy sees human experience as a high-level exemplification of reality in general' (p. 13). All individual entities such as protons and atoms resemble human experience in the sense of taking account of their environment without being totally determined by it. All have subjectivity and responsiveness. Their response is purposive, even if unconsciously so. This is their self-determination.

What I have called 'taking account of' can also be called, more technically, an 'internal relation'. Most of Western thought about relations has focused on 'external' relations. A relation is external when it does not affect the nature of the things related. For example, a pen lying on the table is thought to be unaffected by that location. It is thought to be the same, unchanged pen when I pick it up. The relations to the table and to my hand are changed, but the pen is not. An 'internal' relation is different. It is part of the entity that is related. For example, my seeing the pen is part of my experience now. If I were not seeing the pen, the experience would be different. Hence, my relation to the pen is internal to my experience. Since the pen is not significantly affected, we can say that the relation is external to the pen.

Whitehead thought that internal relations are of primary importance in the world. They are constitutive of all the truly individual entities that make up the world. These are all momentary-unit events or, in Whitehead's technical language, 'actual occasions' or 'occasions of experience'. At the molecular level there are such actual occasions moment by moment in the molecules of the pen. But the pen as a whole is an aggregate of such occasions, so that the receptivity and activity that take place at the molecular level do not appear. The pen seems to have only external relations to its environment. On the other hand, an electron is a succession of actual occasions, and so is the flow of experience that can be identified as a human person.

Each occasion, each succession of occasions, that constitute each individual entity can be thought of as a minute organism. Each organism is internally related to other such organisms. This binds them together in larger organisms such as animals, and since these are internally related to one another as well, larger groupings too have an organic character. It is obvious why Whitehead called his philosophy the philosophy of organism. Biology, he said, was the study of large organisms and physics was the study of small organisms.

I have introduced here more of Whitehead's technical terms than I use in the rest of this book, and henceforth I use only the term individual entity to refer to the truly individual entities such as protons and people. What are not individual entities are assemblages of these and are called aggregates.

Because of his emphasis on internal relations as constitutive of all individual entities in the universe, Whitehead is the ecological philosopher *par excellence*. We and all individual entities are literally 'members one of another'. This makes his philosophy ever more relevant to our day.

Whitehead believed that this view of reality made sense of relativity theory, quantum mechanics and the theory of biological evolution as well as human social phenomena. It illuminated the mind–body problem, the evolution of the living from so-called non-living, the nature of time, the relations of God and the world and many other issues.

This is a bad time for polymaths—those who attempt to embrace all reality and delete the boundaries between disciplines. There are many reasons for this. One is the scepticism of all philosophy and all religion. Another is the belief by experts and technocrats that all the problems of the world will be solved by science and technology; we are still in the grip of the modern worldview. But Whitehead's approach is no mere flight of fancy into the stratosphere of thought. 'The true nature of discovery,' he said, 'is like the flight of an aeroplane. It starts from the ground of particular observation; it makes a flight in the thin air of imaginative generalisation; and it again lands for renewed observation rendered acute by rational interpretation.' (1978 p. 5). The adequacy of this view, as of any other, depends upon the extent to which it provides a comprehensive interpretation of things.

There are many references in this book to the writings of Charles Hartshorne. He was an assistant of Whitehead at Harvard,

since when he has become the leading process philosopher. I
became familiar with Hartshorne's work through one of my first
teachers, Professor W. E. Agar, Professor of Zoology in the University of Melbourne, who had written a book (Agar 1943) relating
his understanding of biology and Whitehead's philosophy. In addition to advising me to read Whitehead he urged me to read as much
of Hartshorne as I could. That led eventually to my enjoying a
lifelong friendship with Professor Hartshorne both in the U.S.A.
and on his visits to Australia. His seminal contribution to process
philosophy is commemorated in the twentieth volume of The Library of Living Philosophers, which is devoted to his thought (Hahn
1990).

The application of process thought to theology is known as
process theology. Whitehead taught that just as all the minute mo-
mentary organisms, or actual occasions, are internally related to
others, so also God is internally related to the world and the world
is internally related to God. Indeed, it is God's presence in the
occasion that enables it to be something more than the determined
outcome of the past. It is God's presence that gives it the possibility
of free responsiveness without determining just what the response
will be. It is God's presence that introduces life. In a very important
sense God is the Life of the world.

God, for process theology, is not the external maker of the
world. God is, instead, the Spirit that breathes life into the creatures
and calls the higher organism to the more abundant life of love.
There is no compulsion or control here, only gift and persuasion.
God is not before all creation but with all creation. Process theology
is thus a thoroughgoing incarnational theology standing in strong
contrast to the triumphalist, dualistic, monarchical and patriarchal
God of much classical theology. Its central affirmation can be found
in biblical thought and in the meeting of biblical with Greek
thought, as in the writings of the early Christian fathers. And, as
with the thought of many of these early innovators, it is a developing
theology. It recognises that a living vital religion cannot remain
static. It has to grow, just as science has to grow. Today growing
points are along the frontiers of modern science, in relation to other
religions and to the economic and political problems of our time.

A leading exponent of process theology is a nonpareil of theology today, John Cobb, to whom this book is dedicated. To him I
owe a debt of friendship and a dialogue across the years which has
enabled me to see what I did not see before, to find the world a

richer place and to invest the word God with a new depth of meaning. Recently Professor Cobb (1985) wrote:

> Process theology has taken as its situation the decline of credibility of Christian belief in the modern world. It has concluded that much of this loss has been due to formulations of faith that are not worthy of credence, and it has undertaken to provide more credible statements of what the Christian believes. This is not a mere game. There are millions of people who have rejected the Christian faith because of its incredibility, and the doubt and confusion of those who remain are often painful. Often the pain that is addressed is that of process theologians themselves. (p. 128)

As a teacher for most of my life I know the pain of the youth who discovers that the simplistic formulations of the faith into which he or she was initiated are no longer credible. The serious students I have known want to experience life in its fullness and seek an understanding of that experience. They are not finding it in the formulations of tradition. They find, instead, the world produced by the older notion of the credible is in shambles, intellectually, politically, socially and ecologically. Some are discovering there are alternative ways of expressing the depth of human experience and the relation of God to life. When depth of experience and depth of meaning go hand in hand a new vividness is added to experience which T. S. Eliot expressed thus:

> We had the experience but missed the meaning.
> And approach to the meaning restores the experience
> In different form.

I am not a materialist. The prime reason is that I have had experiences which materialism cannot explain. Secondly, I know too much about matter from modern physics to be a materialist. Thirdly, as a biologist I have come to realise that the urge to live is as basic to life as are DNA molecules. I recognise it in myself and fellow humans, I recognise it also in the rest of the individual entities of creation. Because I find materialism incredible I look for an alternative view that will be true to my profoundest feelings and to the understanding I find from modern science.

The notion of, and the need for, integrity is the root meaning of the word religion—*religare*, to bind together. As the chasm between our inner intentions and outer acts, our pretensions and our

practice, deepens, so does our hunger for wholeness. And wholeness includes a sense of at-one-ment with ourselves and the rest of
the universe. When personal integrity falls apart, we become vulner-
able to whatever solution is presented to us by countless sects and
movements that parade their wares. The principal reason why
people turn to astrology and kindred superstitions is that they lack
in their own lives spiritual resources to cope with serious personal
problems. Some become fanatics of religion, obsessed by what I
heard the German novelist Gunter Grass describe as 'religious
dementia'. Others become anti-religious.

Today I sense a deep need for a coherent faith that can meet
our deep need for integrity of mind, spirit and body and that relates
deeply to the new meanings being discovered by science and other
aspects of culture. My hope is that this book may contribute to that
quest.

The viewpoint of this book accords with what is becoming
known as a postmodern worldview in the sense used by Griffin
(1988). The term itself, as Griffin points out, witnesses to a growing
dissatisfaction with modernity and to the sense that the modern age
has not only had a beginning but can have an end as well.
Postmodernism challenges modernism which can be said to have
begun with seventeenth-century mechanism, petrified with
eighteenth-century rationalism, nineteenth-century positivism and
twentieth-century nihilism. As contrasted with the modern
worldview which is sustained more by habit than conviction and
which has promoted ecological despoliation, militarism, anti-
feminism and disciplinary fragmentation, the postmodern
worldview is postmechanistic and ecological in its view of nature,
postreductionist in its view of science, postanthropocentric in its
view of ethics and economics, postdiscipline in relation to knowledge and postpatriarchal and postsexist in relation to society.
Postmodernism is not a call back to the premodern but a creative
synthesis of the best of the modern, premodern and new concepts in
the forefront of holistic thinking.

More specifically the vision of this book is what Cobb (1988)
has called a postmodern *ecological* worldview. The word 'ecological'
is added because of the emphasis on relationships in the development of postmodern thought that has been influenced by process
philosophy and in particular the thought of A.N. Whitehead. As
Cobb points out there is only one other ecological worldview and

that is deep ecology, based on the writings of the Norwegian philosopher Arne Naess (1989).

The central symbol of ecological thinking in this book is purpose. It has become the central problem for contemporary thought because of the mismatch in modernism between how we think of ourselves and how we think and act in relation to the rest of the world. The book commences with purpose in human life. Without purpose our lives wither. It proceeds to ask the question of whether purpose has any meaning in nonhuman life. If not there is a profound gap between ourselves and the rest of nature. Finding purpose in nature we proceed to the question as to whether life is an exception in the universe. Is the universe machinery and nothing else? If that is the case there is a profound gap between all life and the universe from which it has sprung. Finding purpose pervasive throughout the individual entities of the universe, we ask what permanent value has the whole of the evolution of the cosmos from cosmic evolution through biological evolution to social evolution. The question forces itself upon us because of the inevitable eventual demise of our planet and the universe as we know it. There are only two answers to this question. Either we and the rest of the creation have no permanent value or else we may say that there is a cosmic life, a divine life, able to appropriate and retain as experiences in its life our lesser lives and that of other individuals of creation. Either we and the rest live for what transcends ourselves or we live without ultimate meaning and ultimate purpose. The final chapters are concerned with the implications of this postmodern ecological worldview for society today. The reformation of modernism into postmodernism involves a radical transformation of science, religion and culture that constitutes a revolution even greater than the Scientific Revolution and the Enlightenment.

> Let knowledge grow from more to more,
> But more of reverence in us dwell;
> That mind and soul, according well,
> May make one music as before,
> But vaster. . .
>
> Alfred Lord Tennyson, *In Memoriam A.H.H.*

CHAPTER 1

Purpose in Human Life

He who has a why to live can bear with almost any how.

Friedrich Nietzsche

Without interest and passion nothing great has ever happened in history.

G. W. F. Hegel

If there is much unhappiness among today's student body, the reason is not material hardship, but the lack of trust that makes it too difficult for the individual to give his life a meaning.

Werner Heisenberg (in Wilber 1984 p. 43)

The most powerful influence in human life is neither the environment in which we happen to be brought up, the genes we were bequeathed from our parents at birth, nor all the slings and arrows of fate, no matter how tragic and harrowing their effects may be. We blame our lack of zest for life on to anything but ourselves. As Cassius said:

> The fault, dear Brutus, is not in our stars,
> But in ourselves, that we are underlings.

Our fault is that we have failed to choose purposes that could fulfil life. Even in the most dire circumstances and against all rational assessment we are what we freely choose to be. Of course there is much that we cannot choose, including our genes. Nevertheless we do not have to let the world squeeze us into its mould, ever.

Charles Darwin tells us that his father at one time was discouraged about him and thought that he would amount to nothing: 'My father once said to me, "you care for nothing but shooting, dogs and rat-catching, and you will be a disgrace to yourself and all your family".' Who could have guessed what would happen when enthusiasm for a purpose in life dawned on that mind, marshalling its latent talents for a lifetime's work?

Thomas Bridges was an unwanted babe found by a riverside. They picked him up at a bridge; that is why they called him Bridges. They discovered him on St Thomas day; that is why they called him Thomas. He didn't have a chance. But for all that he picked out the hardest thing that could be found to do—working with the aborigines of Tierra del Fuego, at the desolate southern end of South America. Even Charles Darwin payed tribute to his work. For Darwin turned up at that forlorn place on his famous scientific voyage in the steamship *Beagle*. When he returned home, Darwin sent a financial contribution for the work amongst the Tierra del Fuegians saying that, having learned of the transformation wrought amongst them, he was glad to have a hand in it. Don't pity Bridges in Tierra del Fuego. Spare your pity for those who need it; the well educated, the well-to-do uninterested people who have never found anything to take themselves out of themselves by commitment to a purpose greater than themselves.

We don't have to go to Tierra del Fuego for that. We can do it here and now, right where we are. For several years I led a discussion amongst a diverse group of young people at the Wayside

Chapel in Sydney's Kings Cross. Some of them were drop-outs from life, others were involved in drugs, prostitution or petty theft. Some were on leave from mental hospitals. Others had just walked in from the boisterous streets of this cosmopolitan, anything-goes part of Sydney in search of yet another happening. Our discussion tended to get out of hand unless we had a book, chapters of which we could read before we met. I tried many books. Only two were acceptable to my group: Victor Frankl's (1964) *Man's Search for Meaning* and Erich Fromm's (1962) *The Art of Loving.* Frankl is fond of quoting Nietzsche's 'He who has a why to live can bear with almost any how'. The how of life had its problems for everyone in the group. Each desperately wanted a why. They hadn't found one in the work-a-day world, nor in formal religion, though some were flirting with Eastern faiths. They related to Frankl's book. It was evident to us that his meaning for life had made it possible for him to live through those terrible years in Auschwitz concentration camp. 'The sort of person the prisoner became,' wrote Frankl, 'was the result of an inner decision, and not the result of camp influences alone' (p. 66). Frankl was convinced that prisoners who had lost their sense of any meaning in life were the first to fall ill and die. They let their environment conquer them. Those who survived the terrible ordeal were usually those who were not totally at the mercy of their environment. They didn't fall victim to the camp's degenerating influences.

Here is a dramatic demonstration that not one of us, even in the most awful circumstances, is simply caught up in a situation. We don't have to be victims of circumstance. Human beings are always free to take a stand. You can harm my physical body, but no-one can harm me emotionally and spiritually. It is I alone whose attitude makes harm to myself possible. I always have some choice of action. This spiritual freedom, which cannot be taken away, makes it possible for my life to have meaning and purpose. Most of my freedoms can be taken away. But I can still preserve some vestige of spiritual freedom and independence of mind, even in the most awful conditions of physical and psychic stress. It is what we bring to the crisis and not the crisis itself that determines the prospect. Our problems are not there for us to solve but for them to solve us! Such an attitude sustained Frankl and his colleagues in their terrible circumstance. He showed to me and my little group in the Antipodes that life depends as much upon our response to events around us as upon the events themselves.

To find meaning is a primary motivating force in life. It doesn't have to be a distant purpose, but a meaning for this day, this hour, this moment. Life is anticipation. When that goes life ebbs away. Someone has said how dull it would be to wake up each morning always the same person. But if we anticipate something each day and move in that direction, then we wake up a different person each day. Thoreau (1908) says

> little is to be expected of that day, if it is to be called a day, to which we are not awakened by our Genius ... to a higher life than we fell asleep from; and thus the darkness bear its fruit, and prove itself to be good, no less than the light. That man who does not believe that each day contains an earlier, more sacred, and auroral hour than he has yet profaned, has despaired of life, and is pursuing a descending and darkening way ... It matters not what the clocks say or the attitudes and labours of men. Morning is when I am awake and there is a dawn in me. To be awake is to be alive. I have never met a man who was quite awake. How could I have looked him in the face? (p. 77)

So Thoreau tells us: 'I went to the woods because I wished to live deliberately' (p. 78). I found something of this spirit in some youths on a street corner in a village in the heart of the Mato Grosso. I had come from the bustling city of Sao Paulo to this far-away village. 'What do you do here?' I asked the youths. 'Why we live here' came their reply. And their tone of voice really meant live.

Meaning brings motivation. Motivation leads to action. Action leads to transformation. Transformation is possible because human life can rise above present circumstance.

On being all there

Every moment of life presents us with the possibility of creative novelty. No-one has to think or act as he or she has been taught to think and act. To be all there is to be fully present for each moment. And that means imaginatively transcending the daily round and in so doing to be transformed. Imagined experience is the mainspring of motivation in life. To be human is to be passionately committed to something that grasps and transforms us. That's why Hegel said, 'Without interest and passion nothing great has ever happened in history.' Historians refer to the Stone Age, the Dark Age, the

Renaissance, the Enlightenment, the Industrial Age and the Post-Industrial Age. Each successive age gained something in rising above the past, and always at great cost. The cost was deemed to be a price worth paying. The human being is made for creative transformation as a bird is made for flight. To be sure, each of us is in a cage much of the time. We long for the door to be opened that we may be free to soar into the heavens.

In his *Voyage to the Beginning* Colin Wilson says that when he was very young he became more clearly aware than ever before that he was faced with a choice between meaninglessness and commitment. Martin Luther proclaims on the steps of the cathedral: 'I can do no other so help me God!' Paul Tillich (1955 p. 152) wrote about the innumerable concerns in our lives which demand attention, devotion and passion. They are important. We are concerned about our work, about our relationships to others and about ourselves as we grow and develop. Many of our concerns are a cause of worry and anxiety. Each concern tends to become tyrannical and wants our whole heart, our whole mind and our whole strength. Each concern tries to become our god. The concern about work becomes a god for some, as does the concern for pleasure for others. And as we become older concern about the infirmities of age can dominate life. We may then try to dismiss all concerns to maintain a cynical unconcern. Or we may attempt to practise the un-attachment of the Buddhist.

There is another way. It is, in Tillich's terminology, to be commited to 'ultimate concern', the one concern that matters ultimately. The only appropriate response to ultimate concern is 'with infinite passion' or, if you will, 'with all your heart and soul and mind and strength': no more emphatic utterance is to be found in all scripture. When I fail to give myself in full commitment to that which matters most I inhibit and frustrate myself.

But what can be so commanding as to elicit such a total response? Nothing less than that which fulfils human life in all its deepest possibilities. In the biblical story of Mary and Martha, Martha was so troubled and anxious about many things as she went about her household activities that she missed the one thing needful. Mary chose the one thing needful at the present moment, her total response to the visitor to her house. It happened to be Jesus. The one thing needful is to enjoy the visitor, whether the visitor be in the form of a friend, a stranger, a sunset, a tall tree or a bird singing by

its nest. Mary was committed to that which was of ultimate importance. That is always a value. And when values become realities in
human life we experience a richness of life that was not there before.

We know whether or not we are all there. Try, for example,
greeting people with the following question: 'On a ten-point scale,
where perfect health, maximum vitality, and ecstatic joyfulness are
represented by the number ten and suicidal depression by the
number one, how do you feel today?' You will no doubt find that,
although the question gives rise to amusement, an answer is given
readily, sometimes with instantaneous refinement of the scale as in:
'Oh, I would say, maybe six and a half'.

Besides Frankl's *Man's Search for Meaning*, my Wayside
Chapel group responded with enthusiasm to Fromm's *The Art of
Loving*. When Fromm (1962) says 'Love is the active concern for
life and the growth of that which we love' (p. 25), the link with
Frankl's thought becomes clear. Where active concern is lacking
there is no purpose and there is no love. Our purposes are determined by what we love which is what we set our hearts on. This is
the meaning of religion. For religion is the state of being grasped by
the infinite seriousness of the question of the meaning of our life and
our readiness to receive answers and to act according to them.

Following an interview on radio I had a telephone call from a
young listener who had been a member of our discussion group
some fifteen years past. His name is Greg. He said he wanted to talk
to me about purpose. He had been in and out of mental hospitals
and had been diagnosed as having schizophrenia. He had accepted
his condition. He knew the symptoms that indicated he should
present himself again to hospital, and in he would go for therapy.
When he got out again he would get what job he could to earn
something to live on. He knew some goals were denied him. But he
also knew that life was not denied him. Indeed, one of my strongest
recollections was when he would show me what he had written in
his extensive notebooks. There were poems and sketches and lots of
philosophising about his life. When he was not working in a flour
mill he must have been putting down his thoughts in vivid form in
his notebook. And more, he had discovered a sense of purpose and
fulfilment by becoming a counsellor at the Crisis Centre of the
Wayside Chapel. Many are the people who attempt to do this only
to find the crises of others too overwhelming. Not so Greg. He was
daily wading the Rubicon of life. He had touched bottom and found
it was sound. When he rang me he said he felt committed again to

restoring a definite purpose in his life. That very day he offered his services and time to the Way-Out centre of the Wayside Chapel in a back lane where people could get a cheap cup of coffee and paint and talk and do what they felt like doing. And that might include talking to Greg. When I saw him there, a few days after he rang me, he told me he could get odd jobs and help with the Way-Out centre. And although he was certainly eligible for support from the government he was going to stand on his own feet while he could.

Understanding of life comes to us from people like Greg. For me they include drop-outs who have dropped back into life, students who were almost total failures in their first years of study who, given another chance, made good. Others were students from Europe who became refugees after the Second World War. They had migrated to Australia on government-paid passages, in return for which they worked for three years in whatever work they were directed to do. A Ukrainian who was making cement pipes is now a senior research scientist. A Polish student who was scrubbing floors in hospitals is now a professor of neurosurgery in a leading American medical school. Some years ago I had a visit from a young man who said he was now a millionaire. Years before he had come to me for advice as a newly arrived Hungarian migrant. He said he took my advice which, he reminded me, was to learn English and earn some money before trying to become a student again. By working day and night he had managed both to learn English and to start the first factory to manufacture nylon in Australia. Why was he visiting me now? He wanted to know if I knew of any student in the predicament he had been in. If so he would like to pay his or her way through university. He had not forgotten others on his way to material success.

Such are our teachers on life's way, as well as the Paul Tillichs and A. N. Whiteheads. Having spent much of my life as a teacher I have come to realise that no-one really teaches anyone anything. We can teach others how to learn. We can lead them to the path of discovery for themselves. This indeed is the central principle of Plato's dialogue the Meno. Meno is a slave who, step by step, answers questions put to him by Socrates. Socrates tells him nothing. What he does is draw out from his pupil his latent capacities for discovery. He leads him to water to drink. Another great teacher, Jesus, did precisely this in conversation with a Samaritan woman by a well. He led her to a metaphorical well of living water, and invited her to drink.

The urge to live

The wonder is that life has surmounted the hazards of billions of years to bring us here. Imagine ourselves back some four billion years ago on this planet facing two scenarios: on one side, a vast turbulence, terrific volcanoes belching forth from the inexhaustible fires of the earth's core; on the other side the beginnings of living cells, microscopic, invisible along the water's edge of some shallow sea, quiet, vital. On which are we betting, as in imagination we stand there billions of years ago, volcanoes or life? Life has no credible chance to mean anything against the violent forces of volcano, earthquake, tidal wave and hurricane. Yet we see today what triumphed—life, spirit, art, music, prophets, martyrs, scientists and saints. The utterly unforeseeable, the unimaginable did happen. The vitality of life is mightier than all the forces of nature waged against it. For us today the perils are horrendous but the possibilities are momentous—all because of the urge that is implanted in life to lead to yet more life.

Whitehead (1929) affirmed that all living things are characterised by a threefold urge: '(i) to live, (ii) to live well, (iii) to live better. In fact the art of life is first to be alive, secondly to be alive in a satisfactory way, and thirdly, to acquire an increase in satisfaction' (p. 8). Life is bound up with an urge to live. It is not a mere fact. It is a value. Being alive is valuable in itself. If life were not prized by those who live, death would soon triumph. Indeed, the principle of the urge to live is far more basic to life than the principle of survival of the fittest. Apart from the urge to live there would be no survival, whether of the fit or the unfit, human or non-human. The urge to live is the appeal of life for life.

It is the urge to live that makes us subjects as distinct from objects. To be a subject is to have feelings. It is to be an experiencer. It is to be responsive inwardly. It is to be responsive to what is our past and what could be our future. 'The present,' said Whitehead, 'is the fringe of memory tinged with anticipation.' Descartes' 'Cogito ergo sum', as Whitehead (1966 p. 166) points out, is wrongly translated 'I think, therefore I am'. It is never bare thought or bare existence that we are convinced of. What we really know as subjects are enjoyments, hopes, regrets—in a word, feelings. The basic notion of a subject as distinct from an object is I feel therefore I am: I know I am a subject because I have feelings.

The worst we can do to a fellow human is to treat him or her as a mere object without feelings. An object is something to be manipulated, to be pushed around, to be in the service of another object such as a political party or state. The object has no value in itself. Its value is entirely its instrumental value. It is not recognised as having an urge to live. The Green Revolution in Asia broke up families because agribusiness took over their farms. Peasants were treated as objects whose value was non-existent for big farming. Many of them were driven off their small holdings and migrated to overcrowded cities such as Calcutta, where they added to the masses of unemployed.

To treat people as though they were mere objects is a desecration of life. Nazism was a doctrine that treated people as objects of the state and its leader. People were turned into numbers, in factories, in concentration camps where the rulers were deliberately deaf to suffering. In the BBC television program *The Ascent of Man* Jacob Bronowski is seen walking into a pond at Auschwitz concentration camp where the ashes of four million people were flushed. That was not done by gas. It was done by dogma; the dogma holds that certain people are mere objects. And as Bronowski bent down into the pond and lifted up a handful of mud in his hand he said: 'We have to close the distance between the push-button order and the human act. We have to touch people.' That means to take seriously every feeling and expression of another, entering into another's experience rather than turning away from it as irrelevant to us.

The concept 'economic man' treats human beings as objects, not as subjects. It is a substance view of humans. Their value is their value to the gross national product. Their value is their service. If that service can be rendered by a machine then their value disappears. The tendency of the technological society that puts a premium on efficiency is to treat people as objects for economic ends and not as subjects who have an urge to live. But what's the point of gaining top marks for GNP and losing your soul? The golden goose can lay rotten eggs. Traditional economists are slow to learn that society is more than 'the economy' (see Chapter 5).

By contrast we respect people as subjects when we value them, their urge to live and their aspirations, for their own sakes. Even in love between two people this element can be subjugated to an exploitation of one by the other. Respect implies the absence of exploitation. I want the other to grow for his or her own sake as he or she is, not as I need that person as an object for my use. We may think we really love another person when it is only ourselves we love. We want our way and not what the other wants. 'Selfishness,' said Oscar Wilde, 'is not living as one wishes to live. It is asking others to live as one wishes to live.' Respect is possible only if we have achieved such independence that we don't need to dominate or possess or exploit anyone. But this is indeed difficult. How do two people identify and feel related and not restrict each other? As a friend who was deeply in love said to me—maybe only saints are capable of that. 'Immature love,' writes Fromm (1962), 'says I love you because I need you. Mature love says I need you because I love you' (p. 3). Significantly, in both the Old and the New Testaments the central objects of man's love are the poor, the dispossessed, the stranger, the widow, the orphan and eventually the enemy. Only in the love of those who do not serve our purposes does love begin to enfold and enrich the lives of lover and that which is loved.

We are admonished to love our neighbour as we love ourself. If it is a virtue to love my neighbour as a human being, it must be a virtue to love myself, since I also am a human being. If it is a virtue to seek to enrich the life of another, it is a virtue to seek to enrich one's own life. The affirmation of one's own life and freedom is to enrich life, both of the self and of those with whom we associate. Some people affirm very little about themselves. It was said, at the funeral at the Wayside Chapel in Sydney, of a youth who had taken his life— 'Life was not too much for him, it was too little'. The selfish person does not love himself too much, but too little. He is narcissistically preoccupied with self, but he fails to love that which is lovable in himself. He sees the rest of the world in terms of what use it can be to him. And he remains empty and frustrated. He sees his life as though it were a sponge to soak up experiences instead of an outgoing urge to embrace the world. To love ourselves is to be open to influences that press in upon us from all sides, that could transform us as the energy of the sun transforms a plant. The selfish person blocks himself off from these influences by anxiously snatching from life instead of being open to life. We are to be like the birds of the air and the lilies of the field. They toil not neither do they spin. They are not anxious about their lives. Walt Whitman wrote in *Song of Myself:*

> I think I could turn and live with animals, they are so placid and self-contain'd,
> I stand and look at them long and long.
> They do not sweat and whine about their condition,
> They do not lie awake in the dark and weep for their sins . . .

Not one is dissatisfied, not one is demented with the mania of
owning things . . .
Not one is respectable or unhappy over the whole earth.

So they show their relations to me and I accept them,
They bring me tokens of myself, they evince them plainly in
their possession.
I wonder where they got those tokens,
Did I pass that way huge times ago and negligently drop them?

Be not anxious. Take no thought for the morrow. These are not
irresponsible injunctions. There are things we should care about
and others that don't need our care and concern. T. S. Eliot had a
prayer: 'Teach us to care and not to care'. It is akin to the prayer of
Reinhold Niebuhr (1976): 'Give us grace to accept with serenity the
things that cannot be changed, courage to change the things that
should be changed, and the wisdom to distinguish the one from the
other' (p. vii).

The selfish person becomes anxious because of a sense of
unfulfilment, a lack of meaning and the loss of an urge to live truly.
Anxiety has a Latin root, *angustia*, meaning shortness of breath,
lacking room to breathe freely. A person who suffers from angina
has coronary arteries that have narrowed so much that they no
longer feed the heart with sufficient oxygen for it to function properly. So the heart no longer beats freely. The Latin root of angina is
the same as the root of anxiety. Anxiety like angina narrows down
the gateway of experience so that we live in a bottleneck, no longer
fully and freely as do the birds of the air and the lilies of the field.

The anxious and selfish person (they are often the same) may
try to replace emptiness with fun. Fun consists in consuming com-
modities; food, drink, movies, drugs and so on. Fun of sorts one
may find. But it is not the creative kind of fun connected with play
and the urge to live creatively. It is a shallow greedy way of 'having
fun'. What eludes the selfish person is joy. The escape from one's
emptiness through fun makes joy impossible.

The joy of purpose

Friedrich Nietzsche, himself the son of a Protestant minister,
expressed his judgment about the followers of Jesus thus: 'His
disciples should look more redeemed'. In quoting these words
Tillich (1955 p. 143) said the experience of the suppression of joy

and guilt about joy in Christian groups almost drove him to break
with Christianity. But he asked the question—is that because these
groups were Christian or because they were not sufficiently
Christian? There is a pietistic moralism that is joyless and stunting.
'Puritanism,' said H. L. Mencken, 'is the haunting fear that someone somewhere must be having a good time.' On the other hand, joy
is an expression of a sense of fulfilment and enrichment of life. To
his followers Jesus said: 'These things I have spoken to you, that my
joy may be in you, and your joy may be full' (John 15:11). Joy
comes when we are driven towards things and persons because of
what they are and not because of what we can get out of them. The
lad who mows the lawn reluctantly at the command of his father has
no joy in the job. But the lad who mows the lawn because it is fun
and at the same time wants to please his father has joy. I knew a
young drug addict who was trying to break the habit by doing other
things. He got the job of mowing a large football field. He found a
certain pleasure in mowing anti-clockwise. He enjoyed what he was
doing. But the groundsman told him to stop and mow clockwise
because that was how it always had been done before. The young
man broke down as the one bit of joy he had found was taken from
him.

We are able to sacrifice all sorts of pleasures and even to take
pain upon ourselves for a purpose to which we commit ourselves.
No student worthy of the name hasn't given up many lesser purposes for the the sake of attaining the skills and understanding
needed for a chosen profession. We can disregard both pain and
pleasure because we are directed towards the things or persons we
love. In that pursuit we discover a new richness of experience which
brings joy. That joy is the expression of a central fulfilment of life. It
is the expression of a discovered meaningfulness that lifts us up. It
is the expression of being open to ever new depths of experience. It
is the expression of something unearned, of something given, despite oneself and something greater than oneself. There is great joy
in attempting to do something we thought we could not do, did not
have it in us to do, then finding we could do it. Our best friends see
in us possibilities we could never see in ourselves. They trusted us
when we had not learned to trust ourselves. They led us to the joy of
fulfilment that we could hardly have led ourselves to. We experience
a plenitude that seems far beyond anything we have earned, yet
freely given and abundantly. Whitehead (1942) speaks of 'The experience of Peace [which] is largely beyond the control of purpose.

It comes as a gift' (p. 327). It is the peace that passes understanding. Whitehead uses the word Peace to include the sense that one's personal adventure of life is included and at one with the adventure of the universe. We return to this idea in Chapter 3.

The ambiguity of purpose

People in the Western tradition have long recognised a tension in life between evil and good. They have understood themselves in terms of a duality of nature and spirit or of a duality between genetic endowment and culture. What makes us aggressive and selfish? Are these propensities bequeathed to us in our genes? Or has our culture moulded us this way? Biologists such as Konrad Lorenz and Robert Ardrey argue that human beings have aggressiveness and selfishness built into their biological inheritance. This attempt to locate evil in our genetic inheritance just does not stand up to deeper analysis as Barnett (1989) has so clearly shown. There is that which lifts us up and that which drags us down. Niebuhr (1941) recognised this incongruity as the fundamental human problem. He saw that although the Bible recognised the tension it refused to identify either side with evil. Neither nature nor culture is bad. That we participate in both is our glory. But this glory is at the same time the condition that leads us continually into sin. One main consequence of locating evil with either nature or culture is that it makes the human problem something outside the human will. It is not we who sin. We say we are simply placed in a situation that produces evil. We are simply victims ourselves or spectators of other victims. My genes made me this way says the rebellious youth. Another blames his home and upbringing. Niebuhr adresses us in terms of our personal responsibility. We are not simply caught up in a situation. It is not the situation in which we find ourselves, but what we freely do in it that is the basic evil. In short, we must reckon with sin and not primarily with fate, be fate identified with genes, environment or divine predestination.

Niebuhr (1972) recognised the urge to live as a 'will to live truly'. He also saw it transmuted in human lives into the 'will to power' or the desire for 'power and glory'. The same person who is ostensibly devoted to the 'common good' may have desires and ambitions, hopes and fears, which set him at variance with his neighbour and the world. The urge to live becomes transmuted by overweening self-interest into a will to power that is destructive.

Human beings are not just interested in physical survival but in prestige and social approval. They invariably seek to gain security against competing influences by enhancing their power. Possessing a darkly unconscious sense of insignificance in the total scheme of things, we seek to compensate for this insignificance by pretensions of pride. 'The conflicts between men are thus never simple conflicts between competing survival impulses. They are conflicts in which each man or group seeks to guard its power and prestige against the peril of competing expressions of power and pride' (Niebuhr 1972 p. 29). Niebuhr goes on to add that the fact that the will to power inevitably justifies itself in terms of the morally more acceptable will to realise our true nature means that the egoistic corruption of universal ideals is a much more persistent fact in human affairs than any moralistic creed is inclined to admit. The error of liberal humanism is its too great reliance upon the human capacity for transcendence over self-interest. There is this capacity, but the same person who displays this capacity also reveals varying degrees of the power of self-interest and the subservience of life to these interests. Is there a way which takes into account the ambiguity of our purposes? Niebuhr's answer is that alongside the urge to live we need a special sort of wisdom if we are to harness and restrain self-interest, both individual and collective, for the sake of humanity. It is realistic wisdom and eternal vigilance, not utopian dreams, that may guide us through these rapids.

'The self,' says Niebuhr (1972), 'can become its true self only by a continual transformation over self' (p. 43). The same person who has the capacity for transcending self-interest also reveals varying degrees of the power of self-interest and the subservience of the will to those interests. Sometimes this egoism stands in frank contradiction to the professed ideal and sense of obligation to wider values. Who else but we know the secret of our hearts?

> Milan (at Santa Maria della Grazie's):
> For the Last Supper in the refectory
> Leonardo sought a model for Him.
> The choir-boy from the cathedral, very
> Suggestive of grace, firm of face and limb,
> Clear of line and colour—yes, he would do.
> Lime, water, umber, ultramarine blue.
> Rome (another time, another painting):
> For the face of Judas, he scoured the belly

Of alleys and found one, vice-lined. Swore
His sitter: 'I'm Pietro Bandinelli—'
He strained his breath. 'I've sat for you before—'
As nervous as at his vocation, theft.
The artist smiled. 'Turn a bit to your left.'
R. P. Dickey, 'Leonardo da Vinci — A Legend'

The morally good act optimises the harmony and intensity of living for all those lives that can conceivably be influenced by the act. It is also one that is in harmony with the unity of nature and of the universe in the sense in which Whitehead's 'Peace' is an individual experience including within itself the harmony and integrity of the universe. By contrast, evil is always the assertion of some self-interest without regard to the whole, whether the whole is conceived as the immediate community, the total community of humankind, or the total order of the universe. In short—good unites, evil divides.

The purpose of this chapter has been to show that future possibilities are real causes in our lives. Subjective they may be. Nevertheless they are as real as the external causes in life, such as food and disease. The proposition is that a fundamental category for understanding human life is the urge to live, anticipation, purpose, realistic hope—call it what you will. It is not simply the imaginative entertainment of attractive possibilities. It is the efficacy of the future in the present. There is within life an eros toward the realisation of greater, rather than lesser, values. To be effective this must be resident in experience. It must be immanent in the present, yet given from beyond itself.

If, as a society, we are to make a creative response to the overwhelming challenges of war, injustice and environmental destruction of our time, there need be agreement about purposes that are stronger than the differences that divide us. We confront some of these social issues in Chapter 5.

CHAPTER 2

Purpose in Nature

Many a scientist has patiently designed experiments for the purpose of substantiating his belief that animal operations are motivated by no purposes. He has perhaps spent his spare time in writing articles to prove that human beings are as other animals so that purpose is a category irrelevant for the explanation of their bodily activities, his own activities included. Scientists animated by the purpose of proving that they are purposeless constitute an interesting subject for study.

A. N. Whitehead (1929 p. 16)

I cannot think that the world . . . is the result of chance; yet I cannot look at each separate thing as a result of Design. I am, and shall ever remain, in a hopeless muddle.

Charles Darwin (Darwin F. 1888 Vol. 2 pp. 353–4)

Neither pure chance nor the pure absence of chance can explain the world.

Charles Hartshorne (1984a p. 69)

The central question of this chapter concerns whether non-human creatures are purposive. If non-humans are not purposive, if they have no sentience, no freedom and no internal relations, then a huge gap exists between them and us. Our answer to this question has profound implications for the way we behave toward non-humans. Indeed, much of the terrible suffering of non-humans caused by destruction of their habitats and our treatment of animals in captivity can be attributed to lack of any real convictions that non-humans are in their deeper selves like us. This leads into discussions that are highly controversial amongst biologists and philosophers. Nevertheless we need to find a way through these dilemmas.

Two ecological worldviews, referred to in the Introduction, namely deep ecology and the postmodern ecological worldview, both forge strong links between non-human creatures and us. And both, though in quite different ways, extend the links well beyond the living to the inanimate world. The postmodern ecological worldview of this book finds intrinsic value in all those entities it calls individual entities, from protons to people. Deep ecology finds value, not so much in the individual as in the system, be it an ecosystem or the biosphere as a whole, each with its 'interests' in self-maintenance. The deep ecologist seeks an extension of the sense of self, as far as possible, with the rest of nature and that includes trees, ecosystems and the biosphere as a whole (Fox 1984, Naess 1989). Hence the alternative name of transpersonal ecology given by Fox (1989) to deep ecology.

There has always been a tendency in the Western world to make a dichotomy between humanity and the rest of nature. The book of Genesis refers to man as 'made in the image of God'. A widespread, yet superficial, interpretation is that no other creature is so made. But the book of Samuel contains the strong emphasis that 'We are bound in the bundle of the living'. We are a part of nature. Tillich (1967) affirms: 'We come from nature. If God had nothing to do with nature, he finally has nothing to do with our total being because we are nature' (p. 422). The strong affirmation of biology ever since Charles Darwin is that our roots are in nature. Yet our branches reach into the heavens. It is no denial of the uniqueness of humanity to also affirm our continuity with the rest of the living world. The theme of Chapter 1 is that human life makes no sense except in terms of purpose. Humans are purposive creatures. We are not just contrivances, even though aspects of our anatomy and physiology can be understood in those terms. We now ask if humans are unique in this respect. Or are other living organisms also more than contrivances? Are they purposive?

There are two senses in which this question might be asked. Living organisms serve purposes in the sense that they serve useful ends. Grass serves a purpose for the deer that depends upon it for food. Everyone agrees that organisms serve purposes in this sense. The question of this chapter is different. Do non-human organisms have purposes? Do they pursue goals in the sense in which humans do? Are we bound in the bundle of the living in this sense? If they do not have purposes, a sharp line would have to be drawn between humans and all other living organisms. To have purposes is to make choices. So we are asking if organisms besides humans choose. In other words, do they have some degree of self-determination? If they do, it inevitably follows that they are subjects and not just objects. Or again, in the language of Chapter 1, it would be saying that they have internal relations, as well as external relations. The meaning of internal relations as we humans experience them, is the influence of people and other things in our lives and the influence of the purposes we choose to serve. These relations are all internal relations. They make us what we are; that is, they are constitutive of our being. With other internal relations we would be different persons.

The urge to live

Those of us who have pets, such as cats and dogs, consider them to be more than machines. We really believe they suffer when they are ill and enjoy company when they are well. We do what we can to keep them happy. We create societies to protect cats and dogs and other domestic animals from cruelty. In other words, we regard them as subjects. We put them into a different category from our motor car. We value them on two grounds. One is the sort of value we give our motor car. Both have instrumental value to us. We enjoy the services they render to us. In the case of a dog it might be the pleasure of its company or its usefulness in rounding up sheep in a paddock or guarding our premises. We consciously or unconsciously attribute a second sort of value as well as an instrumental value to our pets. They have an intrinsic value. They have a value in themselves for themselves. They too want to remain alive. Like us their life is bound up with an urge to live.

The urge to live is more fundamental to life at all levels than Darwin's principle of survival of the fittest. As Bohn (1982) says:

> If you look at nature, you find that elaborate and complex forms appear that are not explained by the mere requirement of survival. If our notion of time postulates that each moment is creative, then at every moment the possibility arises for new structures, along with a continuation of some of the old structures. Therefore you could say nature is constantly and intentionally exploring new structures and when these new structures are able to survive (by the process of replication) they will build up and become stable. (p. 39)

Bohm correctly asserts that the urge to live is a *sine qua non* for survival. Whoever has the greatest chance to survive is another matter. When Bohm speaks of each moment as creative he refers to the notion of anticipation tied up with the urge to live. That living organisms have an urge to live means that life has value for them. And that value is presumably greatest when life is full and happy rather than when they are sick and miserable. An ethical principle follows. We should respect their experience of life and seek to enhance it. It is the animal's feelings of the world that give it intrinsic value. Without feeling there is no intrinsic value. In using the word feeling it is important to recognise that it pertains not simply to conscious experience but to much that merges into the unconscious.

There is as much reason to attribute to our pets awareness and consciousness as there is to attribute these characteristics to other humans besides ourselves. I cannot have the experience of another human being, nor that of my cats. But it is reasonable to suppose that they too have experiences. They are like us.

There are those who are willing to grant that non-human animals have feelings but they want to make a distinction between humans and non-humans by attributing to humans alone what they call self-awareness or self-consciousness. But what other kind of consciousness could there be? When I experience pain it is my own self that has the experience of pain. So it is redundant to speak of self-consciousness. What the term self-consciousness is evidently meant to convey is some degree of self-reflection. I might have a toothache without reflecting much at all on my misery. But I would probably reflect a lot about notice of dismissal from my job.

We reflect a lot about what we want to do and to become. The

human being can be self-conscious in this sense. Yet this quality
may be quite poorly developed. Indeed, in human history, we can
trace different levels of self-consciousness being achieved at different stages of cultural evolution. Palaeolithic peoples disciplined
their lives extensively for the sake of their distinctively human purposes. Life was not simply a matter of one experience following
another, without any sort of order or unification. The unified human
experience or human psyche came with developing purposes and
reflection as culture evolved. Pre-rational sources of meaning
became replaced more and more by rational ones with a conflict
between the two ever present. Perhaps we can speak of full self-
consciousness appearing for the first time only by the first millennium BC when quite independently in China, India, Persia, Greece
and Israel spiritual leaders arose who proposed new ways of ordering the whole of their experience. From then on we find people
devoting a great deal of their time to reflecting upon the meaning of
life and what they should do.

Self-consciousness is not an all or nothing matter. There are
degrees of self-consciousness. It probably evolved culturally this
way in ourselves. But even amongst people today there is a great
difference between a deeply reflective person and one who hardly
reflects at all. Likewise there is a great difference between a reflective person and any non-human animals we know. But who knows
if reflection is zero in the higher animals? For ten years David and
Ann Premack (1983) trained a chimpanzee, Sarah, for three to four
hours a day five days a week. For each type of problem Sarah was
first taught the answers for a training series and then tested for her
understanding of a new set of problems that were formally similar.
If she could give the correct answer on the first trial of such problems she must have had an intelligent understanding of the problem. For example, experiments showed she could understand that a
can-opener is to a can as a key is to a lock. Intelligent understanding
implies some sort of mental reflection. There are no good grounds
for drawing a hard and fast line between the higher animals and us.
The difference is one of degree. In 1871 Charles Darwin wrote:
'The difference in mind between man and the higher animals, great
as it is, certainly is one of degree and not of kind'. This statement is
as true now as it was then.

Purpose in the lives of animals

The evolution of human purposes is evident in what is called
cultural evolution. Culture is what is learned and transmitted from

one generation to the next. As has been already indicated, the evolution of culture from palaeolithic times to the scientific age is a consequence of the evolution of self-consciousness. All along the route humans made choices as they reflected upon them. This changed their world. Whilst humans developed culture *par excellence*, they are not alone in choosing purposes, learning from others and so transmitting culture from one generation to the next.

Exploratory behaviour and learning are known to be a feature of many non-human animals. We see it most clearly in the higher mammals. Books have been written about this (e.g., Thorpe 1956, Donald R. Griffin 1976, 1984). Amongst a troupe of macaque monkeys on Koshima island in Japan a young female was seen to wash sand from sweet potatoes in the sea. Her playmates were the first to imitate her, followed by their mothers. Subsequently the infants of these monkeys learned the custom from their mothers. Later, different styles of potato washing developed along kinship lines (Kawai 1965). In England some great tits, through their exploratory behaviour, invented ways of opening milk bottles to enable them to drink the milk. First they coped with cardboard tops and later metal tops. The invention was learned by subsequent generations and spread through the population, not just of England, but in continental Europe as well. A tit learned behaviour that achieved a goal it found rewarding. And so we can go down the animal kingdom finding examples of exploratory behaviour leading to new ways of life, amongst insects and lower forms (Birch & Cobb 1981 p. 57). The understanding of this is important for evolutionary theory. We tend to think of the animal as being at the mercy of its environment. Those individuals with genes that adapt them to the environment survive and reproduce. But animals also create their environments. They do this in at least four ways (see Lewontin, Rose & Kamin 1984 pp. 274–5). The way of interest in the context of this argument is by selecting the habitat in which they live. The tits selected doorsteps with milk bottles on them.

Much work has been done on non-human animals that strongly points to the conclusion that they make choices, have feelings andare therefore subjects. Donald R. Griffin (1976, 1984) argues it is high time students of behaviour relaxed their behaviourist stance and led the way to an experimental science dealing with the mental expression of animals, and not just of higher animals. For example, Donald R. Griffin (1976 p. 23) discusses the behaviour of the swarming of honey bees when they are about to establish a new colony. The bees exchange information about the location and suitability of potential locations for the new hive. They do this by means of complex dances which symbolically trace out on the vertical surface of the honeycomb the direction and distance of the new localities from the hive. Individual bees are swayed by this information to the extent that, after inspection of individual localities, worker bees change their preference and dance for the superior place rather than the one they first discovered or that was communicated to them by their mates. Only after many hours of such exchanges of information, and only when the dances of virtually all the scouts indicate the same site, does the swarm fly off to it: 'This consensus results from communicative interactions between individual bees which alternatively "speak" and "listen". But this impressive analogy to human linguistic exchanges is not even mentioned by most behaviour scientists' (p. 23). The bees do not appear to be acting as programmed robots. It is not a totally stereotyped behaviour. A bee does not always respond to the dance. If the 'language' were in words rather than in dances and bees were the size of people, we would be inclined to attribute to them similar 'experiences' to those we have when we communicate about whether to go to this place or that one.

Mind evolving

How far down the scale of nature can we suppose that living organisms are subjects that have some element of self-determination, that have internal relations and so in some sense have mind and feelings? The conventional wisdom is that at some point in the evolutionary sequence from atoms to human beings, mind and feeling appeared for the first time. Something that was an object only, without any aspect of mind, becomes a subject with mind. The conventional way of putting this is to say that mind emerged. But that simply restates the problem. It solves nothing. And as one of the most distinguished evolutionary biologists of this century has said: 'the emergence of even the simplest mind from no mind at all seems to me at least utterly incomprehensible' (Wright 1953 p. 14). Birch and Cobb (1981) argue that the only satisfactory alternative is to interpret the lower levels of organisation in terms of the higher as well as the other way around. What we see clearly as mind in ourselves we may find implicitly in all creatures. None are mere contrivances or machines. The poet Robert Frost saw this intuitively in 'A Considerable Speck':

A speck that would have been beneath my sight
On any but a paper sheet so white
Set off across what I had written there.
And I had idly poised my pen in air
To stop it with a period of ink,
When something strange about it made me think.
This was no dust speck by my breathing blown,
But unmistakably a living mite
With inclinations it could call its own.
It paused as with suspicion of my pen,
And then came racing wildly on again
To where my manuscript was not yet dry;
Then paused again and either drank or smelt—
With loathing, for again it turned to fly.
Plainly with an intelligence I dealt.
It seemed too tiny to have room for feet,
Yet must have had a set of them complete
To express how much it didn't want to die.
It ran with terror and with cunning crept.
It faltered: I could see it hesitate;
Then in the middle of the open sheet
Cower down in desperation to accept
Whatever I accorded it of fate.
I have none of the tenderer-than-thou
Collectivistic regimenting love
With which the modern world is being swept.
But this poor microscopic item now!
Since it was nothing I knew evil of
I let it lie there till I hope it slept.

I have a mind myself and recognize
Mind when I meet with it in any guise,
No one can know how glad I am to find
On any sheet the least display of mind.

Maybe this little speck of life could not be called intelligent. But the poet quite correctly waxes lyrical about its urge to live and the presence of mind wandering on his sheet of paper.

Do we then draw the line at mites or perhaps the amoeba in a pond. The proposition of the ecological model is that no line is to be drawn anywhere down the line of what we call living organisms, and thence down through molecules, atoms and electrons and protons. This is not to argue for consciousness as such all the way down the line, but for some form of awareness or attenuated feeling associated with some degree of freedom to choose. Human experience is seen as a high-level exemplification of reality in general, that is of all individual entities from protons to people. Hence Whitehead (1978 p. 29, 1933 p. 129) calls his model 'the philosophy of organism'. Birch and Cobb (1981) refer to this as an ecological model of life since ecology puts the emphasis on relations. The geneticist Wright (1964) wrote:

> The only satisfactory solution . . . would seem to be that mind is universal, present not only in all organisms and in their cells but in their molecules, atoms and elementary particles. This is more plausible for the entities of modern physics than for the concept of matter that held essentially from Democritus to the end of the last century. (p. 114)

Modern physics has indeed moved far away from Democritus' atoms. About the year 400 BC he declared: 'There is nothing but atoms and space, all else is an impression of the senses'. His was a universe of multi-shaped little billiard balls moving in empty space, colliding with one another, grouping together and separating from one another. His ideas became part of the background of physical thought in the renaissance of science in the sixteenth and seventeenth centuries through the works of Copernicus, Bruno, Galileo, and later, Newton. But modern physics has moved away from this mechanistic model of the ultimate particles to a much more ecological model (see Chapter 3).

What has modern biology to say to the proposition that all living individuals are subjects with a degree of self-determination and not just complex mechanical objects? Reasons have already been given for regarding animals as subjects. But what about cells and their parts? A cell, unlike a machine, behaves differently in different environments. All the cells of an early embryo appear to be the same. But in due course their daughter cells differentiate. Some become nerve cells. Others become muscle cells and so on. They all have the same genetic information. So how is it that they become so diversified? Whilst the full answer is as yet unknown, at least we know that what the cell becomes depends upon the environment in which it finds itself. That includes the other cells around it and its orientation to these cells. When undifferentiated cells are put in a dish of nutrients that enables them to grow and divide, they fail to differentiate as they would in the embryo. Cells in the body take account of their environment and become different as a result. The DNA in the nucleus of the fertilised egg contains all the instructions needed to make all the different proteins and all the different sorts of structures in all the different sorts of cells in the body. But not all the instructions are used by every cell. The cells in the liver use some, the cells in the brain use others.

We all know that birds have no teeth. But only recently have we known that the cells in a bird contain the potentiality to produce teeth, the teeth of a reptile. When tissue from the jaw region of a chick embryo is wrapped in tissue from a mouse embryo from the region where teeth are formed and then incubated in the eye of an adult mouse, the chick develops teeth. The presumption is that these derive from genes for teeth bequeathed to birds from their reptilian ancestors. What is potentially possible for the bird becomes a reality in this experiment (Gould 1984 p. 182). Biologists who study the development of living organisms are beginning to find out how the selection takes place as each different cell is made and carries out its functions. More is known about these processes in the bacterium *Escherichia coli* than in other cells. Normally these bacteria reside in our intestines. If a culture of them is presented with lactose instead of glucose, which they normally use, within a few minutes the bacteria begin to produce the enzyme beta-galactosidase which was not there before. This enzyme is necessary for the bacteria to get their energy from the lactose. In their normal life in our intestines these bacteria must be ready to change their enzymes quickly in response to the sort of sugar they find in their environment. They choose from several enzymes their DNA allows them to produce. The part of the DNA that is not used at any time is prevented from expressing itself. When a new sugar arrives it must first be detected by a receptor on the surface of the bacterium. Then a signal is passed through the cell, a process of de-repression is set in action, and the DNA is activated to spell out its message in the form of appropriate RNA (this is called transcription). The message in the RNA molecule is then 'translated' into a particular protein (enzyme). The chemical factory for this is in the part of the cell outside the nucleus. The cell does not set up its factory *de novo*. The factory has already been made for it in the course of its evolutionary history. The factory can make many different sorts of things but there is a choice as to what is made at any one time. The story is yet more complex than this. If the bacterium is confronted with glucose and lactose at the one time, the lactose pathway is re-pressed. There is a trigger mechanism in the cell for this. The advantage to the bacterium for this is that lactose has to be con-verted to glucose before it can be used, so its use involves the loss of energy compared with using glucose.

H. S. Jennings, a student of animal behaviour early this cen-tury, suggested that if a single-celled organism such as an amoeba were the size of our pet dog we would not hesitate to ascribe some form of mind to it. Lewis Thomas entitled one of his books *The Lives of a Cell* (1974). He might also have written a book on the lives of a DNA molecule. In describing the various chemical path-ways the DNA molecule sets in train, biologists speak of this path-way being chosen rather than that one. Most of them use the word choice in this context metaphorically. They fall accidentally into anthropocentric language. It is a happy accident. All we know about these fascinating activities of cells is quite consistent with the notion of choice being included rather than completely excluded from the action.

We don't have to suppose, with the complete mechanist, that everything the cell does is completely determined by its genes and its environment. What we do know is that the DNA molecule can express itself in a great variety of ways. Which ways depend upon the environment of the cell (and therefore of the molecule) at the time. The molecule and its chemical environment are in a state of perpetual dynamic equilibrium depending upon the magnitude of physical forces and the concentration of chemicals inside and out-side the cell. Which pathway is 'chosen' is a matter of probability rather than absolute determination. For example, in the presence of lactose alone the bacterium *Escherichia coli* may produce beta-galactosidase 99.99 per cent of the time. We might then say that the pathway is determined. But it is not completely determined. The difference between 100 per cent determination and 99.99 per cent determination is all the difference in the world. It is the difference between being completely determined by the environment and having a degree of self-determination. A thoroughgoing mechanist might argue that the difference between 100 per cent and 99.99 per cent may be due to defective functioning of a deterministic system. That is precisely the point. If accidents can happen in the system then determination is not complete. Choice becomes a possibility when determination is not 100 per cent. The billiard ball concept of matter is obviously no longer relevant in molecular genetics. The classical geneticist supposed that genes were pellets of matter that remained in all respects self-identical whatever environment they were in. This has to be abandoned in the light of modern knowledge.

To have self-determination is to exhibit mind. It is to have some degree of freedom, no doubt minute at the molecular level. I am not saying that having investigated the life of the cell and its molecules biologists have found mind. What they have found is more consistent with the proposition that the cell as an entity and the DNA molecule as an entity have internal relations.

The more we know about complex molecules the less they appear to resemble the strict mechanical models that textbooks tend to portray. In the ecological model of nature all molecules and cells are recognised as subjects. They take account of their environment in the deep sense of taking account. The individual entity, in this case the bacterium, is constituted by its relations. If a bacterium has never been introduced to lactose the DNA inside it is different from the DNA in the bacterium that has been introduced to lactose. Both have the potentiality of taking account of lactose. One has, the other hasn't taken account of that possibility. The analogy with the human is precise. Each of us is what we are by virtue of the DNA we did not choose and the environment in which we have lived, including our internal relations with other organisms. All our experiences have made us what we are. We are what we experience. So it also seems to be the case with the cell and its molecules.

The contrast of the mechanistic and the ecological model of life can now be restated at the level of molecules and beyond to entities such as electrons. The mechanistic model entails that the constitutive elements in the cell behave like the constitutive elements of a machine. Their behaviour is considered to be relatively independent of their environment except in so far as they are subject to the laws of mechanics. In the ecological model the elements in the cell relate to one another and to the cell as a whole, more like the way an animal as a whole relates to its environment. Most research on the inner functioning of the cell has been carried out by biologists chiefly influenced by the mechanical model, but what has been learned appears to fit the ecological model better. Some biologists who have recognised this are Wright (1953, 1964), Waddington (1969, 1975) Young (1978, 1987), Sheldrake (1981) and Sperry (1983a, 1983b). Whitehead (1966) before them recognised this when he wrote: 'neither physical nature nor life can be understood

unless we fuse them together as essential factors in the composition
of "really real" things whose interconnections and individual characters constitute the universe' (p. 150). This is the strong
affirmation that what is real in the physical world, be it electrons or
what have you, must have the germs of qualities we find more
accessibly expressed in the living world. This is the unity of nature.

Why did human consciousness evolve?

A central feature of the ecological model of life is that the universe is
made up of entities that act and 'feel' as one. Every individual entity
from protons to people has its degree of self-determination. We
arrive at this concept by working backwards from human self-
consciousness to inanimate objects. We find no breaks. At the
human level the most characteristic feature of life is that we serve
conscious purposes and reflect upon the world around us. But
consciousness has arisen in evolution from 'proto-consciousness'
(proto means primitive or first) which is some form of awareness
less than conscious awareness. Proto-consciousness is the aspect of
mind in all entities. But why did it ever become fully conscious
mind?

   This question has always been a problem for evolution. There
are two questions here. One is a question for the mechanist. How is
it that conscious mind arises from no mind? My answer has already
been given. It can't. The second question is for the evolutionist.
What is the survival value of consciousness? According to some
evolutionists all major features of living organisms must have some
survival value, else they would not have evolved. It is not difficult to
find uses for consciousness that enhance the chance to survive and
reproduce. It is one way of solving problems to be able to think
ahead and work out plans for the future. But that is not the issue.

   The real issue for the evolutionist is why aren't living organisms all unconscious mindless robots? A robot can have inbuilt into
it systems that make it respond appropriately to dangers such as a
red hot poker and to useful objects such as a fruit on a tree. A recent
attempt to find survival value in consciousness that exceeds anything that a robot could accomplish is Humphrey's (1983) proposal
that consciousness evolved in order to help the individual to deal
with other members of the species. The idea is that you need to
understand the behaviour of others and you can do this only by
reflecting consciously on your own and their activities. But, as

Sutherland (1984) has argued, a robot could be programmed to take account of the behaviour of other individuals in its environment. So presumably could the brain in the course of its evolution. Indeed we already know that the brain contains a representation of the position of parts of the body, but this representation does not appear in consciousness; it is easy to invent functions that consciousness might subserve. What is difficult, and has never been achieved, is to show which functions can be subserved only by consciousness. As far as we know there is, in principle, no behaviour, no matter how complex, that could not be exhibited by an organism or by a computer that lacked consciousness. Indeed, many of the unconscious calculations made in perception or in controlling activity of the limbs and other organs appear to be as complex as the thinking of an Einstein. Why then did human consciousness evolve?

This debate is an old one. As Gould (1983) pointed out it goes back, at least, to a bitter disagreement between Darwin and the co-discoverer of natural selection, Wallace. Wallace believed that natural selection should account directly for every trait in the evolution of all oganisms. But for him there was one exception—the conscious human brain. Wallace was a non-racist who believed in the equal mental capacities of all people. But he believed in the overwhelming superiority of Western European culture. Now, if natural selection constructs organs for immediate use and if brains of all people are equal, how could natural selection have built the original brain of the 'savage' (Wallace's terminology)? After all 'savages' have capacities equal to ours, but they do not use them in devising their cultures. Therefore, he argued, natural selection which constructs only for immediate utility cannot have fashioned the human brain. Darwin was flabbergasted. He wrote to Wallace: 'I hope you have not murdered too completely your own and my child'. Darwin's simple counter-argument held that the brain is a very complex machine that performs functions that have great survival value. This doubtless was responsible for its increase in size and complexity. And as Gould (1983) interprets Darwin:

> selection has probably built our large brain for a complex series of reasons, now imperfectly understood. But whatever the immediate reasons, the enlarged brain could perform (as a consequence of its improved structure) all manner of operations bearing no direct relation to the original impetus for its increase in size. (p. 10)

He went on to say that one might put a computer in a factory for the simple purposes of issuing paychecks and keeping accounts, but the device can complete (as a consequence of its structure) many complex calculations that go well beyond the simple requirements for which it was purchased. Historical origin and current function are different properties of biological traits. Features evolved for one reason can, by virtue of their structure, perform other functions as well. In the case of the brain these side-functions become of prime importance. Consciousness, argues Gould, could be one of them.

Dobzhansky (1967 p. 70) considered that the first evidence we have of self-consciousness in human beings is the ceremonial burying of the dead in Neanderthal man. This indicates death-awareness, and therefore probably self-consciousness. This is not to say that death-awareness and self-consciousness may not exist below human beings. Perhaps, as Gould suggests, nothing that our large brain has allowed us to learn has proved more frightening and weighty in importance than awareness of death. Did our large brains evolve in order to teach us this unpleasant fact? Yet consider the impact of this knowledge upon a diverse range of human institutions, from religion to kinship and divine right. The specific forms of religion need not be seen as direct adaptations for tribal cohesion. Religion with culture may arise as a direct consequence of a large complex brain and not as an adaptation for survival. The adaptive analysis of human cultural characteristics may be an inappropriate methodology. Gould and Lewontin (1979) wrote an article for the *Proceedings of the Royal Society of London* with the intriguing title 'The Spandrels of San Marco and the Panglossian Paradigm: A Critique of the Adaptationist Programme'. Spandrels are the spaces left over, above and between the great arches that support the huge dome of a cathedral. They are a consequence of having arches and, at least in some cases, have no structural function. The spandrels of San Marco in Venice have been filled with wonderful mosaics that enhance the whole scene. A structure that may have no structural value in itself is put to another use. So it is with evolution.

Hence the evolutionist who can find no convincing reason why consciousness evolved can argue that it is a corollary from the evolution of structures that did have survival value. We didn't have to have brains that could do pure mathematics and endow us with an artistic capacity that made a *Mona Lisa* possible. What survival value is there in being able to paint a *Mona Lisa*? Nor did we need to have brains that could reflect upon the world leading some to spend their lives contemplating the mysteries of the universe, others to beatific visions and yet others to found great religious movements. In many ways the logic of this argument is unassailable. I find it far more convincing than attempts to pin survival value on every single human characteristic. Evolution is more than survival of the fittest.

Yet this argument, important as it is, evades the central question of mind and consciousness arising from a mindless world that preceded it, which is the assumption that Gould, and with him, most biologists make. But if we see the mental as an aspect of all individual entities involved in the evolutionary process we have no such problem. Evolution is then inevitably the evolution of mind-matter. It is the evolution, not of substances, but of organisms. The mind aspect of the cell is different from the mind aspect of the human brain, yet there is a continuity the one with the other. The capacity to take account of the environment internally, that is to have internal as well as external relations, develops with evolution until we have the self-conscious human who invents the future and responds to an infinitely rich environment that includes aesthetic, moral and spiritual values.

In the ecological model the environment is not simply food, other material resources, predators and the like. Our environment is far richer than that. It includes values and purposes. We have the capacity for a richness of experience denied the frog or the amoeba. This is not to deny that these creatures have their own experiences (proto-consciousness) that may be rich for them. The ecological model makes sense only in so far as these qualitative elements of environment are given a reality as real as the material objects around us. This is a central insight of the great religious movements that helped to transform the human scene for better and for worse. The lives of people can be governed by long-distance purposes that include the idea of a better world for future generations whom they may never see. To the question—why did human consciousness evolve?—we can now reply: because what evolves is not a substance (mere matter) but mind-matter.

Recent years have seen the rise of an alternative model of mentality which is popular amongst those who investigate 'artificial intelligence' or 'cognitive science'. Machines are now made that do all sorts of jobs humans did in the past. Robots are part of the assembly lines of automobiles and other machines. Robots can be made to play chess. Programmed with the rules of the game, they make formidable adversaries. This raises the question—if a machine could be constructed that would act like a human, would it think and feel and have purposes of its own? This startling question is answered yes in much science fiction and by some students of artificial intelligence.

While there are some parallels between a complex computer and a human brain, it is widely agreed that if a brain is like a computer it is like a computer no-one has ever yet designed. And in terms of complexity perhaps no-one ever will. For the cortex (the thinking part of the brain) has over 10,000 million nerve cells with probably billions of different possible connections. Computers that operate robots obey instructions programmed into them by their makers. These are rules of arithmetic. Our brains perform functions of many sorts besides arithmetic ones. Nevertheless, one might argue that eventually a computer will be constructed that does perform other functions besides arithmetic ones. A major case against the claim that computers can think, or eventually will think, is given by Searle (1984) in his Reith Lectures. An example which he, with others, claims is irrefutable is the following. Put a man in an empty room and provide him with a set of rules for combining Chinese ideograms together in ways that make sense (to Chinese speakers). Then imagine that a number of Chinese-speaking people outside the room are able to present him with bundles of ideograms which the man must combine together according to the rules provided. To those outside the room he may well be performing like an intelligent machine. But to the man, the process will be devoid of meaning. This system, says Searle, is exactly equivalent to a digital computer. The difference between the man in the Chinese room and an intelligent human being is that the former has been provided merely with the formal syntax of language with which he is working, but human beings attach meanings to symbols. Thinking implies feeling and understanding. Hume said reason is the slave of the passions, and in a sense it must be so. If you do not care about the answer to a question, or do not enjoy thinking, you will not be thinking. If a machine solves problems for us, caring nothing as to which problems are put to it, and never enjoying or suffering any pleasure or pain, then what it does is not thinking. For thinking is basically feeling things and ideas as valuable and pursuing those regarded as of greatest value.

There is but one theory, known to me, that casts any positive light on the ability of brain cells to furnish us with feelings. It is that brain cells can feel! What gives brain cells feelings? It is by the same logic that we may say—their molecules. And so on down the line to those individuals we call electrons, protons and the like. The theory is that things that feel are made of things that feel. 'Thinking machines' are made of microchips, wires and the like, all of which are aggregates of molecules as contrasted with individual entities that constitute a brain—namely brain cells that are composite individuals. The basic parts of a machine, being aggregates, do not feel any more than do nuts and bolts. Maybe one day someone may construct an exact copy of the millions of cells in the brain with billions of connections with microchips and whatever, then set electronic currents flowing. That machine may perform more complex operations than any machine has ever performed before. I still see no reason for supposing that it would have feelings and think.

Chance and purpose in evolution

The proposition of the previous section is that non-human animals are like us in having feelings and purposes that are real causes in their lives. In this respect there is no sharp line between them and us. But you may ask—does not the Darwinian theory of evolution claim we have all come into existence by pure chance, that only those arrangements of atoms and molecules and cells that promoted survival persist? If the answer is yes, it would give support to the thesis that living organisms are machines and, moreover, made in a somewhat extraordinary way. For this reason Haught (1984) says: 'the central issue in science and religion today is whether nature in its entities has any purpose or ultimate meaning' (p. 7). It is as well to confront the issue head-on. The distinguished evolutionist Jacques Monod answers no to this proposition. 'Chance alone,' says Monod (1974 p. 110), 'is at the source of every innovation, of all creation in the biosphere' (p. 110). For Monod, chance is the one and only principle in nature. He contrasts his position with those who seek to find in every detail of nature evidence of deterministic design in which living organisms are compared with contrivances which a man designs. There is no room for chance in designing a space vehicle. It is thoroughly determined by its designer. The deists of the eighteenth and nineteenth centuries said the design of the universe was like that. The order of nature is the creation of an all-powerful deity who left nothing to chance nor, for that matter, to any entity the deity created. The world and all that is in it are thoroughly determined from outside. This is the concept of deism. But is the only alternative to an order of nature created by chance one created by complete determinism from outside? It is true, as Monod would claim, that the Darwinian theory of evolution overthrew the doctrine of deterministic design. But does it follow that chance alone rules supreme? To answer this question we need to be clear as to the role given to chance in the Darwinian theory of evolution.

Darwin began his epic voyage on the *Beagle* a convinced determinist and, moreover, a deist. He had read Paley's *Natural Theology* as a student at Cambridge University and was impressed by its arguments for the existence of God from the design of nature (Darwin F. 1888 Vol. 1 p. 309). The 'doctrine of divine carpentry', as it has been called, was promulgated by bishops from their pulpits. Students at the great universities were expected to believe it. Scientists were expected to provide more and more evidence for it. In that respect Darwin was a traitor, for the voyage of the *Beagle* around the world changed completely his view of the source of the order in nature. The author of *The Origin of Species* had failed to perform what the public expected of its biologists. It was as if the Archbishop of Canterbury had announced his conversion to Buddhism. Darwin had discovered that nature was not made complete and perfect once and for all time. Nature was still in the process of being made. Moreover, the process involved a 'struggle for existence'. And, even more devastating for the design thesis, the process involved chance! The element of chance in Darwin's theory was the genetic variation on which natural selection acted. Instead of the tiger being designed with its stripes for camouflage, once and for all, Darwin invoked the notion that originally tigers had all sorts of patterns of coats. This was a consequence of chance genetic variation. But only that pattern persisted that gave the animal an advantage in its struggle for existence. This is the principle of 'chance and necessity' which Jacques Monod considers to be the one and only principle in nature; chance at the level of genetic variation, necessity in the working of natural selection.

Darwinism came as a shattering blow to the notion that the order of nature was completely determined in all its details by a deity outside nature. This does not mean that Darwin showed there was no purpose in nature. What he did show was that existing views of design by an external agent were invalid. And as Passmore

(1959) points out, Darwin's theory did nothing to prove that God did not exist. But it did destroy the only argument by which many people thought the existence of God could possibly be established. Darwin put the emphasis on chance variations at the heart of the order of nature. But as we shall see, that does not mean that design is replaced by chaos.

Neo-Darwinism, which is the dominant view of biologists today, is an interpretation of Darwinism in terms of a modern understanding of genetics. The basic source of genetic variation in the living world is chance variation of the DNA molecule. It can come in a variety of forms; which form is a matter of chance. At the beginning of life on earth there may have been just one DNA molecule, maybe associated with another sort of molecule, namely protein. The DNA molecule had the peculiar capacity of being able to replicate in the appropriate environment. Had it replicated for ever with deterministic perfection, that is without any change at all in its constitution, there could have been no evolution. Evolution was, and is, utterly dependent upon occasional change in the molecule when it replicates. That is what mutation is in its most basic form.

Mutation involves rearrangement of the base-pairs in the steps of the ladder-like DNA molecule. This basic event in evolution is a random change, a chance change, an accident, if you will, during replication. Thomas (1979) asked whether molecular biologists would have thought of this had they flown in from another planet to create life on earth.

> We would have made one fatal mistake: our molecule would have been perfect. Given enough time, we would have figured out how to do this, nucleotides, enzymes, and all to make flawless, exact copies, but it would never have occurred to us, thinking as we do, that the thing had to be able to make errors. The capacity to blunder slightly is the real marvel of DNA. Without this special attribute, we would still be anaerobic bacteria. (pp. 28–9)

And if our imaginary molecular biologist had the wisdom to create flaws, would he also have the wisdom to keep some flaws and repair others, which is what the cell does? So important is the capacity to change that there are some genes whose job it is to speed up the process of change, that is the rate at which accidents in replication occur. An intriguing example is the gene or genes that control the rate of formation of antibodies used in the body's defence against disease. When the body is invaded by a foreign agent such as a virus, antibodies are formed to neutralise the virus. Genes exist that increase the variety of antibodies that can be produced on such occasions. The advantage of this to the organism is obvious when the invading virus may itself mutate to a variety of forms, as often happens.

One might well expect that accidental changes in DNA during their replication would be deleterious to the organism that harbours the changed DNA. That indeed is the case. Most mutations are deleterious to the organism in which they occur. Some few are not. By chance they confer some advantage upon the organism that harbours them. So we talk about chance mutations as being the basis of all genetic variation in the living world.

The meaning of chance in this context is quite specific, but it is often misunderstood. It does not imply that mutation has not a cause. We know many of the causes of mutation such as radiation and certain chemicals. Whether or not a particular mutation will increase the chance of its possessor to survive and reproduce is dependent upon a second chain of events which is quite independent of the event of mutation itself. This second chain of events has to do with the environment in which the organism finds itself. The DNA of a fly mutates to confer upon its offspring resistance to DDT in its environment. This chain of events is quite unrelated to whether or not the environment contains DDT. If the environment doesn't contain DDT the mutation confers no advantage upon the organism. It is important to understand that the DDT itself doesn't cause the mutation. All it does is act as the selecting agent eliminating those insects that lack the gene for resistance and letting those that have it survive and reproduce. The mutant fly is at an advantage in an environment with DDT compared to the fly that doesn't have that mutant DNA. The significant point is that the two causal chains are entirely independent—that is, the particular mutation and the environment at that moment.

So we say that mutation is random in relation to the needs of the organism at the time the mutation occurs. That the two chains of events intersect with advantage to the organism is a matter of chance or accident. The word chance does not imply without a cause, rather it means that the intersection of two causal pathways 'is not decided by any agent and is not fully determined by the past' (Hartshorne 1984a p. 16). Darwinism introduces an indeterminacy into the concept of the evolutionary process. Nothing determines that the appropriate mutation will occur just when it is needed. There is a chance that it will because of the enormous capacity of the DNA molecule to vary. The number of its possible forms is infinitely large. We know that insects must have been producing genes that conferred resistance upon the possessor even before DDT existed on the face of the earth, that is to say before it was invented by man. But the fullness of time for this gene came only when DDT became part of the environment of insects. Likewise today insects are doubtless producing DNAs that could confer upon them resistance to chemicals not yet invented by man. Such is the fantastic profligacy of nature! What I have described is a thorough-going neo-Darwinian interpretation of the evolution of resistance to an insecticide by insects.

An alternative theory of the mechanism of evolution to neo-Darwinism is Lamarck's doctrine of the inheritance of acquired characters. According to this doctrine the giraffe which stretched its neck to feed on higher branches acquired a slightly longer neck by so doing. Its offspring were supposed to have longer necks, the character being inherited from the parents. This transformation was supposed to occur because the animal wanted more food. Its need instigated an adaptive response that was inherited. Since plants were not regarded as having feelings of need Lamarck did not apply his theory to them. So it is ironical that the only sure demonstration of this type of change, for over a century, has come from experiments on plants. When flax plants were fed with fertiliser they increased in size, as might be expected. What was not expected was that subsequent generations of flax plants would be large like their parents, even in the absence of the fertiliser. It seems that the fertiliser increased the number of ribosomes (tiny organelles in the non-nuclear part of the cell). This additional dose of ribosomes was passed on in the cells of pollen and ovules to subsequent generations through the non-nuclear part of the cell. Having more ribosomes made the plants grow bigger. This sort of inheritance seems to be very rare, otherwise it would have turned up more often in experiments.

Lamarckian inheritance has had a certain appeal since it does not include any role for chance in evolution. But the fact of the matter is that neo-Darwinism with its role for chance variation better accounts for how evolution operates for the most part. It would be incorrect to conclude from the account I have given of the way neo-Darwinism works that the two chains of causes, one to do with mutation and the other to do with the environment, are completely determined. A determinist might want to say that there is an omnipotent observer who sees that the appropriate mutation occurs at the appropriate time so that the two chains of events interact with benefit to the organism. That this is not the case is a scientific fact known from careful experiments. There are no two ways about it. All sorts of mutations occur all the time. Most are deleterious. By chance, some are not. The result of the interaction between the causal chain involving mutation and the causal chain involving the environment is not predictable from either chain of events taken separately. But we can go further than that. The two chains of causes can, and in the ecological model do, involve creativity, choice and decision. The presence or absence of DDT in the environment involves human choice. And the changes in DDT from one form to another are not completely determined by the past history of DNA. There is an indeterminacy here in the sense that we can speak of a 'choice' being made to become this sort of DNA rather than that sort. The sense in which the word choice is used in this context is similar to the way it is used earlier in this chapter in accounting for the different enzymes produced by the bacterium *Escherichia coli*. The schematisation of the interaction of the two pathways tends to exaggerate the separation of purpose and chance. In the ecological model every event involves intersections that introduce elements of chance, but every causal pathway has elements of purpose, expressing itself in choice, or decision, or self-creativity. The acceptance of a role of chance in nature does not exclude a role for purpose. Indeed, as we shall now see, it makes a role for purpose possible.

The world of Paley's *Natural Theology* was a completely determined one. The world for Jacques Monod, a modern interpreter of Darwinism, was one of chance and chance alone. But there is a third possibility. Neither pure determinism nor pure chance alone, but chance and purpose together. As Hartshorne (1984a) has said: 'Neither pure chance nor the pure absence of chance can explain the world' (p. 69). The recognition of chance and accident in the natural order is critically important in the ecological model of nature. Without chance there could be no freedom. If the universe and all happenings in it were fully determined by some omnipotent power, attributed by some to God, there would be no freedom. As Hartshorne (1984a) says:

Agent X decides to perform act A, agent Y independently decides to perform act B. So far as both succeed, what happens is the combination AB. Did X decide that AB should happen? No. Did Y decide the combination? No. Did any agent decide it? No. Did God, as supreme agent, decide it? No, unless 'decide' stands for sheer illusion in at least one of its applications to God and the creatures. The word chance . . . is the implication of the genuine idea of free or creative decision making— 'creative' meaning, adding to the definiteness of the world, settling something previously unsettled, partly undefined or indeterminate. (p. 16)

To take chance seriously is the first step in moving away from the concept of deterministic design, whether by an omnipotent designer or as some inbuilt principle of nature. It is also the first step in moving toward a realistic concept of purpose. Monod, who took chance seriously, failed to see the implications for freedom. For him, chance alone was the one and only principle of nature. Darwin never came to this conclusion. It seems that he could not admit the reality of chance, despite the role he attributed to it. In this respect he was like Einstein when he said he could not believe that God plays dice (Pagels 1984 p. 148). Darwin probably greatly admired the deterministic universe of Newton and the sort of thinking that led Newton to that concept. At least we know he had studied and admired the life of Newton (Darwin F. 1902 p. 229). Perhaps he saw himself as the Newton of biology. The key to Darwin's thinking on chance and determinism is not to be found in *On the Origin of Species* but in Darwin's correspondence, especially with the Harvard botanist Asa Gray in 1860 and 1861. The first person, so far as I know, to appreciate the significance of this correspondence is Hartshorne (1962 Chapter 7, 1984a Chapter 3). The critical passage in Darwin's letter to Asa Gray is the following: 'I cannot think that the world . . . is the result of chance; and yet I cannot look at each separate thing as the result of Design . . . I am, and shall ever remain, in a hopeless muddle' (Darwin F. 1888 Vol. 2 pp. 353–4). And 'But I know that I am in the same sort of muddle . . . as all the world seems to be in with respect to free will, yet with everything supposed to have been foreseen or pre-ordained' (p. 378). Darwin repeatedly declared in his letters to Asa Gray, as well as to others, that chance cannot explain the world as an ordered whole. To a Mr Graham, for example, he wrote: 'you have expressed my inward conviction far more vividly and clearly than I

could have done, that the Universe is not the result of chance'
(Darwin F. 1888 Vol. 1 p. 316).

Again and again Darwin's letters reiterate this refrain—is it all
ordained, or is it all a result of chance? Because of his dilemma
Darwin gave up theism. At the same time he could see there must
be pervasive limitations upon chance since unlimited chance is
chaos. In the following quotation Darwin actually suggests that
perhaps the solution is 'designed laws' of nature, with all details,
good and bad, depending upon 'what we call chance':

> I cannot persuade myself that a beneficent and omnipotent God
> would have designedly created the Ichneumonidae with the
> express intention of their feeding within the living bodies of
> Caterpillars, or that a cat should play with mice. Not believing
> this, I see no necessity in the belief that the eye was expressly
> designed. On the other hand, I cannot anyhow be contented to
> view this wonderful universe, and especially the nature of man,
> and to conclude that everything is the result of brute force. I am
> inclined to look at everything as resulting from designed laws,
> with the details, whether good or bad, left to the working out of
> what we may call chance. Not that this notion at all satisfies me
> ... But the more I think the more bewildered I become.
> (Darwin F. 1888 Vol. 2 p. 312)

Why?

Hartshorne (1962 p. 207) makes two suggestions. Darwin
tended, like many others, to think of science as committed to determinism; what we call chance may not be chance at all. Secondly, it
was not apparent to Darwin why cosmic purpose should leave
anything to chance. God was identified with absolute law and non-
chance. The dominant theology of Darwin's day was of no help to
him in this respect. It had no clearly conceived creationist philosophy. God must do everything or nothing. And if God is responsible for everything, then why all the evil in the world? To Asa Gray
Darwin wrote (Darwin F. 1888 Vol. 2) about his dilemma thus:
'You say that you are in a haze; I am in thick mud; the orthodox
would say in a foetid, abominable mud; yet I cannot keep out of the
question' (p. 382).

The 'mud' in which Darwin found himself immersed was, as
Hartshorne (1962) says, 'the opacity which always characterises a
deterministic world-view' (p. 208). Darwin argued correctly that the
facts of evil are in conflict with a belief in deterministic design by a

benevolent designer (Darwin F. 1888 Vol. 1 p. 315, vol. 2 p. 312). But only one of his correspondents suggested to him that God was other than an omnipotent determiner of all the details of nature. That was the English vicar and novelist Charles Kingsley. He wrote to Darwin: 'I have gradually learnt to see that it is just as noble a conception of the Deity, to believe that He created primal forms capable of self development into all forms needful . . . as to believe that He required a fresh act of intervention to supply the lacunas which He himself made' (Darwin F. 1888 Vol 2 p. 288). And elsewhere Kingsley wrote about Darwin's contribution thus: 'now they have got rid of an interfering God—a master magician as I call it—they have to choose between the absolute empire of accident and a living, immanent, ever-working God' (quoted by Raven 1953a p. 177). In the evolutionary epic *The Water Babies*, which Kingsley wrote for children just four years after the publication of *The Origin of Species*, he tells of how God 'makes things make themselves' (1930 p. 248). At the time Kingsley's lonely voice must have been drowned out by that of the majority of his fellow clerics who could see no saving grace in Darwinism at all. Nor is there evidence that Darwin appreciated Kingsley's alternative to the omnipotent deterministic God of the deists.

Darwin needed a Jacques Monod to convince him that chance and accident were essential to the order of nature. He needed also a Charles Hartshorne to persuade him that there was a credible alternative to the deism of Paley and other nineteenth-century divines. But in fact he never did resolve his dilemma of chance and determinism.

The great and positive contribution that Darwinism makes to our thinking about nature is the role of chance. It closes the door on absolute determinism and opens the door to freedom and choice. But many have never gone beyond the closed door of determinism. Hartshorne (1962) hit the nail on the head when he said: 'There must be something positive limiting chance and something more than mere matter in matter, or Darwinism fails to explain life' (p. 210). What is 'the something positive' that limits chance and what is the 'something more than mere matter' in matter? Darwinism rules out the notion of an all-determining orderer. It opens the door to another concept of ordering.

There are in fact only two ways of ordering. One is dictatorial. The other is persuasive. The something more than matter in mere matter I have already referred to as responsiveness or sentience.

The individual entities that constitute matter are subjects, be they protons or people. They are sentient to the possibilities of their future, within the limitations imposed by their past. What they respond to—'the positive something that limits chance'—are the persuasive possibilities relevant to their future. Creation is not by fiat but by persuasion. Order by persuasion is the factor limiting chance. Hartshorne (1984a) has said 'the only positive explanation of order is the existence of an orderer' (p. 71). This is a very different concept of ordering from the operations of the *deus ex machina* of the deists, which Darwin rightly rejected. Kingsley hinted at this notion when he said that things tend to make themselves. Creativity exists within the entities of the creation. That is the first step in our argument for order. Many people find this difficult to grasp. For as Hartshorne (1962) says:

> Since teleology has been thought of as unilateral creativity on the part of deity, unshared in any appreciable degree with the creatures, indications that the world had far reaching potentialities for self-creation were naturally startling. But only because creativity had not been grasped in its proper universality, as the principle of existence itself. (p. 209)

Today that should be a less startling concept. Science is leading more and more in that direction as witness, for example, the recognition of self-organisation as a principle in nature by Prigogine and Stengers (1984).

The combination of sentience in individual entities, together with the lure beyond themselves for their possible futures, is the source of their creativity. Nuts and bolts can't evolve. They are aggregates which consequently have no intrinsic creativity. Only individual entities that have some degree of creativity can evolve. Creativity is not simply the rearrangement of bits and pieces of stuff from simple to more complex arrangements. It is the anticipation and the move forward toward possibilities not yet realised. Possibilities or purposes are causes of the present, as are also influences (akin to memories) of the past. We recognise these as potent causes in human life. This recognition should be a guide to thinking about such causes in non-human individual entities.

A multiplicity of creative agents implies the need for the rule of one. Too many cooks spoil the broth. There must be something that sets limits to the confusion and anarchy possible with a multiplicity of creative agents. Individual purposing agents need to be coordinated. The key here is not manipulation of the individuals of creation, but persuasion. In the ecological model the persuasive ordering principle that coordinates the creativity of a multitude of creative agents is the divine Eros. An orchestra consists of many players. Each player interprets the music in his or her own way. All are coordinated by the conductor. A brilliant documentary film was made in 1984 of Leonard Bernstein conducting an orchestra during rehearsals of his own composition *West Side Story*. Those who saw that documentary were struck by the way in which musicians, composer and conductor became one. Bernstein originated the music. Each player was making an interpretation from what Bernstein had written and from the grimaces on his face as he conducted. Sometimes, indeed, the orchestra seemed to exceed the conductor's expectations and he responded with intense delight and participation. The individual entities in nature, like the musicians in the orchestra, have their own degree of freedom to respond or not to respond. This may be tiny at the level of the proton. It is highly significant at the level of the human person. Instead of being the all-powerful manipulator of the creation, the divine Eros is conceived as its great persuader, providing each individual with specific goals or purposes and coordinating the activity of all. 'What happens,' says Hartshorne (1967),

> is in no case the product of [God's] creative acts alone. Countless choices, including the universally influential choices, intersect to make a world, and how concretely they intersect is not chosen by anyone, nor could it be ... Purpose, in multiple form, and chance are not mutually exclusive but complementary; neither makes sense alone. (p. 58)

This argument has carried the principle of cultural evolution (as accepted for human evolution) all down the line of natural entities through the non-human, the non-living to the simplest individuals of creation. In cultural evolution we accept the role of choice as well as chance and the role of purposes that make choice possible. There is no reason to draw a line anywhere and say that below that line choice no longer operates at all in any sense. Of course the degree of choice or the degree of freedom of the entity must be minute at the level of the proton compared to what we know in the case of humans. The principle in the ecological model is that there is a continuum all down the line.

The individual and the ensemble

The creative evolution of individuals is inconceivable if they are thought to maintain their identity throughout all evolution. As one moves up levels of organisation—electrons, atoms, molecules, cells, etc.—the properties of each larger whole are given not merely by the units of which it is composed but by the new relations between these units. It is not that the whole is more than the sum of its parts, but that its parts themselves are redefined and recreated in the process of evolution from one level to another. An electron in a lump of lead is not the same as an electron in a cell in a human brain. This means that the properties of matter relevant at, say, the atomic level do not begin to predict the properties of matter at the cellular level, let alone at the level of complex organisms.

In the ecological model a contrast is drawn between an organism or individual and a machine. The parts of a machine are subject only to the laws of mechanics with its external forces acting upon these parts. In some modern machines nuts and bolts are replaced by transistors and microchips. The development of new and better computers involves rearrangements of the parts and the invention of better parts. There is no evolution of computers in any real sense of the word. There is change in design brought about by the designer outside the machine. There is also natural selection in the market-place! Likewise, in the mechanical model of life there is no real evolution. There are only rearrangements of parts and natural selection between the different arrangements.

Evolution involves change within the parts and in the organism as a whole. It is not simply a rearrangement of parts. Something of the difference between a machine and its parts and living organisms is captured by the English poet Henry Reed in his poem 'Naming of parts'. The poem contrasts the naming of the parts of a rifle and a recruit's perception of the almond blossom in the garden with the bees going backwards and forward. There is a difference between the gun in its bits and nature:

> To-day we have naming of parts. Yesterday,
> We had daily cleaning. And tomorrow morning,
> We shall have what to do after firing. But today,
> To-day, we have naming of parts. Japonica
> Glistens like coral in all of the neighbouring gardens,
> And to-day we have naming of parts.

. . .

And this you can see is the bolt. The purpose of this
Is to open the breech, as you see. We can slide it
Rapidly backwards and forwards: we call this
Easing the spring. And rapidly backwards and forwards
The early bees are assaulting and fumbling the flowers:
    They call it easing the Spring.

That machines can't evolve, that they can only have rearranged parts, means that a completely mechanistic account of evolution is a gross abstraction from nature. Whitehead (1933) perceived this distinction when he wrote:

A thoroughgoing evolutionary philosophy is inconsistent with materialism. The aboriginal stuff, or material from which a materialistic philosophy starts, is incapable of evolution. This material is in itself the ultimate substance. Evolution, on the materialistic theory, is reduced to the role of being another word for the description of the changes of the external relations between portions of matter. There is nothing to evolve, because one set of external relations is as good as any other set of external relations. There can be merely change, purposeless and unprogressive . . . The doctrine thus cries aloud for a conception of organism as fundamental to nature. (p. 134)

Whitehead understood and enunciated more clearly than anyone how the creative evolution of living organisms could not be understood if the elements composing them were conceived as individual entities that maintained exactly their identity throughout all the changes and interactions. He sought to identify both permanence and change in the entities. With some notable exceptions (see the next section and p. 153), evolutionary biologists have yet to catch up with Whitehead.

Whitehead's philosophy of organism is what I call the ecological model of nature. According to this image evolution is not just the rearrangement of building blocks into ever more complex structures from atoms to humans. That can account for the diversity of buildings one might find in a city. But it cannot account for the diversity of lives in the living world. Here we are dealing not with building blocks but with subjects. Evolution is the evolution of subjects. The critical thing that happens in evolution is the change in internal relations of the subjects. As environment changes so do the subjects, be they electrons or cells or whole organisms.

Most evolutionists ignore this aspect of entities in evolution. Whilst they in no way endorse a Whiteheadian concept of organism, Lewontin, Rose and Kamin (1984) have a similar appreciation of the relation of parts and whole:

> A living organism—a human, say—is an assemblage of subatomic particles, an assemblage of atoms, an assemblage of molecules, an assemblage of tissues and organs. But it is not first a set of atoms, then molecules, then cells; it is all of these at the same time. This is what is meant by saying that the atoms, etc., are not ontologically prior to the larger wholes that they compose.
>
> Conventional scientific languages are quite successful when they are confined to descriptions and theories entirely within levels. It is relatively easy to describe the properties of atoms in the language of physics, of molecules in the language of chemistry, of cells in the language of biology. What is not so easy is to provide the translation rules for moving from one language to another. This is because as one moves up a level the properties of each larger whole are given not merely by the units of which it is composed but of the organizing relations between them. To state the molecular composition of a cell does not even begin to define or predict the properties of the cell unless the spatiotemporal distribution of those molecules, and the intramolecular forces that are generated between them, can also be specified. But these organizing relationships mean that properties of matter relevant at one level are just inapplicable at other levels. Genes cannot be selfish or angry or spiteful or homosexual, as these are attributes of wholes more complex than genes: human organisms. (p. 278)

Lewontin (1983) makes the distinction between a biology that he calls constitutional and one that is relational, a distinction which I have called mechanistic versus ecological.

The profound question evolution raises is why did atoms evolve to cells and to plants and to animals? Why didn't creativity stop with the first DNA molecule? Materialism (which itself is a metaphysic) provides no real answer to this question. The ecological model opens up a way to understanding this in terms of lure and response.

A new dialogue with nature

It is one thing, says Lewontin (1983 p. 36), to call for a biology that is relational rather than compositional; it is quite another to put it into practice. There are already some pointers in the movement away from exclusive mechanism to a more ecological model of nature. There are, of course, aspects of the living organism that are to be understood in terms of machinery, such as the movement of the chambers and valves of the heart as a pump and the movement of limbs as levers. The triumphs of molecular biology in describing and manipulating genes are triumphs of the mechanistic approach. The ecological model is inclusive of much that is worthwhile in the mechanical analysis. But it calls for a more complete analysis. It is not a return to vitalism. Vitalism sought to solve the problem by arguing that in addition to the physical components of the living organism there is an additional principle or force. It was variously called life-force, *élan vital* and entelechy which is completely absent from non-living entities. Reasons why this can no longer be regarded seriously are given by Birch and Cobb (1981 pp. 75-7). Likewise the model of emergent evolution which is a half-way house between mechanism and vitalism has to be rejected. Emergent evolutionists argued for the miraculous emergence of life and of mind in a previously lifeless and mindless universe. The problem is still left as a mystery (Birch & Cobb 1981 pp. 77-9). I was present at a discussion between two of the greatest evolutionists of our times on this very topic. Professor Sewall Wright claimed that to believe in the emergence of mind from no mind was to believe in sheer magic. Whereupon Professor Theodosius Dobzhansky, a proponent of emergent evolution, retorted 'Then I believe in magic'.

A mechanistic physiologist analyses my sitting at my word processor in terms of light waves hitting my retina from the keyboard and the screen which then set in train chemical and electrical processes in my nerves and brain. Messages from the brain to my muscles cause them to contract in ways that result in the very complex movements of my fingers and arms as I sit as the machine. But this interpretation, which is fine as far as it goes, leaves out of its account the fact that I have some thoughts in my mind which I intend to put into writing. It is thoughts that initiate the complex sequence of events which the physiologist studies. The distinction between these two sorts of causes was clearly made by Socrates as reported in Plato's dialogue the Phaedo (p. 144). There are some, he tells us, who argue that the causes of his actions are the mechanical forces on his bones and muscles and sinews. Without these activities he would not be able to do as he pleased. But the real cause of his sitting in prison was that he had made a choice to bow to the sentence of the Athenians. The two sorts of causes so clearly set before us by Socrates became the famous distinction between mechanical causes and final causes, or as has been put in this book, mechanical causation and causation through purposes. The one involves external relations, the other involves internal relations.

A mechanistic brain physiologist thinks of the brain in terms of the circuits in a complex computer. If the brain is like a computer then it is like one that no-one has ever designed. Memory is not like electronic memory. Human memory can create new circuits. There are some activities such as the movement of the fingers that appear to be represented in particular areas of the brain. But there are others which cannot be so represented. According to Pribram (1977) and Pribram, Newer and Baron (1974), visual memory is of this latter sort. Large parts of the brain can be removed through injury, yet visual memory is retained. It looks as though, in this case, the brain does not store information locally but widely. Pribram and his colleagues have produced a model of the brain which they call the holographic model. As in a holograph (p. 82), the image is not represented in the brain as a point-to-point image from an object to a photographic plate. Rather, it is represented such that if some cells in the brain are removed this does not destroy just a part of the image but reduces the clarity of the image as a whole. It is not possible to dissect the visual image down to particular cells in the brain. The image is the consequence of the interrelation of many cells as a whole.

The mechanistic view of the relation of brain to mind has either claimed that the brain produces mind or has denied existence of the mental altogether. The ecological model sees mind and brain as two aspects of the same reality. Whereas the mechanistic brain physiologist does not regard purposes as causes, the non-mechanistic brain physiologist such as Sperry (1983a, 1983b) considers that a thought itself can initiate chemical and electrical impulses in cells in the brain. Brain physiologists can tell us a lot, but there is an enormous gap between what they describe, be it in terms of a computer or some other model, and what the human being experiences.

A mechanistic student of animal behaviour seeks to interpret all behaviour in terms of stimulus and response, analogously to the way in which a photoelectric cell receives a message from our approach to a door and responds with a message to a motor to open the door. These relationships can be made quite complex by adding negative feedback (cybernetic) mechanisms and so on. Much of this thinking goes back to Jacques Loeb who invented a mechanical 'insect' that followed the beam of a torch light held by the inventor who moved around a dark room. Today we have quite sophisticated robots that can perform very complex activities. Such models may add something to our understanding of animal behaviour. But we should appreciate that the environments of these robots are extremely simple as compared with the environment of an animal in the wild.

The non-mechanistic student of animal behaviour tries to study animals in their complex relations with a complex world, as Goodall (1971, 1986) has done with chimpanzees in Gombe Reserve and as Donald R. Griffin (1976, 1984) has proposed. These two ethologists attempt to understand the mind of the animals they study in a way analogous to the way in which you and I struggle intuitively to enter each other's lives. If I want to communicate with a culture radically different from my own, there are two basic options open to me: either they learn my language or I learn theirs. When the representatives of a different culture are also members of a different species, exactly the same options arise. Saint Francis, Lorenz and Tinbergen chose the first route. Goodall and Griffin chose the second. Goodall sought a rapport with her chimpanzees and they seemed to return the compliment. By contrast the attempts to teach chimpanzees, albeit by special symbols, have been fraught with difficulty, despite the early claims of success. Bedevilled by persistent ambiguity of their results, researchers deserted the field, leaving their primate proteges to survive in settings far from the humans' homes in which they were trained. Lucy now lives on an island in a river in West Africa. Her vocabulary of about seventy-eight signs is now a bizarre handicap. Others have suffered a similar fate (Linden 1986, Savage-Rumbaugh 1986).

A mechanistic sociobiologist argues that individual human limitations imposed by genes place constraints on society. The non-mechanistic student of societies argues that social organisations are able to negate individual limitations. Lewontin (1983 p. 37) makes the analogy of human beings and flight. No human beings can fly by flapping their arms and legs. Yet we do fly because of the existence of aircraft, pilots, fuel production, radios—all the products of social organisation. Moreover, it is not society that flies, but individuals who have acquired a property as a consequence of socialisation. The individual can only be understood in terms of the total environment. In different environments we have different properties.

The naive mechanistic geneticist says that genes are particles located on chromosomes, that the genes make proteins and proteins make us and that the genes replicate themselves. The non-mechanistic geneticist says genes are not like particles at all. What a gene is depends upon neighbouring genes on the same and on different chromosomes and on other aspects of its environment in the cell. DNA makes nothing by itself, not even more DNA. It depends on enzymes in the cell to do all these things. Geneticists no longer teach 'particulate genetics'. So molecular genetics is properly called molecular ecology. Molecular genetics was the last into mechanistic biology. Maybe it will be the first out.

The mechanistic developmental biologist thought an organism developed in complexity from a single fertilised egg to a complex living organism in the way a motor car is built up from individual bits and pieces. But we now know that if you cut out the limb bud of a developing frog embryo at a very early stage, shake the cells loose and put them back at random in a lump, a normal leg develops. It is not as though each cell in its particular place was initially destined to become a particular part. Each cell could become any part of the leg (but not of the eye), depending upon its total environment. Unlike a machine that can be pulled to pieces and reassembled, the bits and pieces of the embryo seem to come into existence as a consequence of their spatial relationships at critical moments in the development of the embryo.

A mechanistic microbiologist says that the cause of acquired immune deficiency syndrome (AIDS) is a virus. Yet many people apparently have the virus in their cells without, as yet, developing symptoms of the disease. Whether or not the symptoms develop depends upon the environment in which the virus finds itself. And this varies from person to person in ways we don't fully understand. The virus seems to be harmless until some change in its environment renders it lethal in its effects.

Many infectious diseases, once rampant in the Western world, began to decline in their incidence well before antibiotics came into being. Their decline paralleled a change in the human environment. People became better fed and practised simple hygiene. Many of us have the tuberculosis bacterium in our bodies but we have not had, and probably never will have, the disease. The death rate from tuberculosis dropped by 90 per cent between 1850 and 1945. The effect of streptomycin in 1947, the first effective medical treatment, only effected a further 3 per cent drop in death rates. Likewise malaria had largely disappeared from Europe and yellow fever had vanished from the United States before the causative agents were even discovered (Ornstein & Ehrlich 1989). Sir Macfarlane Burnet pointed out half a century ago (Burnet 1940) that the proper study of disease is the ecology of disease organisms.

A mechanistic ecologist would seem to be a contradiction in terms. Yet they exist. They come in two forms. One is the mathematical wizard who represents organisms as symbols in complex mathematical equations. The organisms are treated as billiard balls whose movements are subject only to mathematical rules of the game. No matter what the stage of the game, the billiard ball remains the same billiard ball. The second sort of mechanistic ecologist says the units in the game are not individual organisms at all but communities or ecosystems. But communities and ecosystems are abstractions from nature. The ecological study of nature involves, instead, the study of the relations between individual organisms within their natural environments. We want to know why a particular species of cactus which is relatively rare in Central America became so common after its introduction into Australia that an area the size of England became a dense forest of cactus. The relevant question to ask is what are the new relations the cactus had to its new environment and how can these be reversed.

The good ecologist goes further by taking into account the fact that organisms (including cells and molecules) are not simply at the mercy of the environment they happen to be in. They create their environment to some extent. One way they do this is to choose the environment in which to live. Animals are always doing this but sometimes they make a choice which is a radical break with the past, as for example when they choose a new host on which to feed. The environment is not something simply imposed on the living organism but to some extent it is the creation of the organism. In addition to choosing where they live, organisms make their own climate (bees), increase their food supply by grazing and fertilising the soil and so on (Levins & Lewontin 1985).

A thoughtful ecologist will try imaginatively to live the life of the creature being studied. An ecologist in charge of the eradication of

the mosquito responsible for the transmission of yellow fever in the
coastal cities of Brazil was asked for the secret of the success of his
campaign. He replied: 'I try to think like a mosquito'. He put
himself imaginatively in the place of the mosquito and asked—
where shall I go to get a blood meal? where shall I find shade in
which to mature my eggs? where shall I go to lay my eggs? and so
on.

Mechanistic biologists tend to resist incursions of another
model into their domain. This is understandable. After all, the
mechanistic method has been highly successful. But its great success, as Levins and Lewontin (1985 p. 2) point out, is in part the
result of an historical path of least resistance. Problems that yield to
the attack are pursued with vigour, precisely because the method
works there. Other problems are left behind, 'walled off from understanding by commitment to Cartesianism' (p. 3). No doubt the
ready road to success is to follow well-trodden paths that have
worked in the past. It has also brought forth the remark that the
eminence of a scientist is measured by the length of time that he
holds up progress in his field! The new dialogue with nature involves some radical breaks with the past which will be resisted by
the unimaginative. It is easy to fall into the prosaic fallacy (see
Chapter 5), which is to suppose the world is as tame as our sluggish
convention-ridden imaginations imply. The biologist J. B. S.
Haldane (1927) said: 'Now, my suspicion is that the universe is not
only queerer than we suppose, but queerer than we can suppose'
(p. 268).

Why is it, one might ask, as does Needleman (1988 p. 64), that
the science of biology has been so mute when we ask it about the
meaning of human existence. The answer lies in the sorts of causes
biologists tend to recognise and investigate. For the most part they
regard mind and purpose as epiphenomena, which means they are
recognised as effects only and not as causes and so are not studied
as causes. This disenchantment of nature by traditional science is
the denial of subjectivity, feeling and experience. Sir Fred Hoyle
(1989) goes so far as to comment: 'by eschewing issues that most
people feel deeply about, science has produced a situation in which
it has few friends outside itself' (p. 24).

The unity of life

In *The Expression of the Emotions in Man and Animals* Darwin
(1872) developed his conviction that the sentient quality of humans

has its origins in that of our forebears. The world of nature was for Darwin a world of intense feeling which gave him a sense of unity with the whole creation. In recognising this Hartshorne (1984b) wrote:

> One of Darwin's deepest convictions, overlooked by many, was that all life is somehow one and that human attributes, such as sentience, are not to be supposed (as Descartes taught) abrupt supernatural additions to a merely mechanical nature. Darwin was troubled by his inability to see how there could be feeling in plants, thinking that this weakened his evolutionary argument. Somehow he did not realize the importance of the idea of cells, invisibly small individuals making up a vegetable organism and far better integrated than the entire [plant] . . . Darwin would have liked Whitehead . . . so far as this problem is concerned. (p. 129)

In the ecological model we recognise in all those entities we call individuals some measure of responsiveness and freedom which we share. In addition to individuals there are aggregates of individuals such as rocks and stars. Plants seem to come into a category between. They are not simply aggregates of individuals (their cells) because there is a high degree of coordination between the parts. This is achieved through hormones and other means. But the plant lacks a nervous system which is the basis of the unitary feeling of the animal. A plant is not an individual in the sense we have defined this term. Nor is it simply an aggregate of individuals. Whitehead preferred to refer to a plant as a democracy of individuals. The distinction between individuals, aggregates of individuals and democracies of individuals, which of course includes human societies, is important. It avoids the pitfall of the 'pathetic fallacy' which is the attribution of feelings to things like rocks that don't feel.

Because of the unity of life, human love is something that can be extended to the whole creation. The humanist loves his fellow humans and appreciates nature. The ecological model of life implies that human love is to be extended to the rest of nature in the sense of sympathetic identification with the life of other sentient organisms. The greatest scientists were not simply curious about nature. They too loved nature. Darwin loved animals as fellow creatures. We too can make the attempt to identify with them, though this can never be complete. I cannot know what it is to be a tiger. I would have to be a tiger. But I may begin to understand something about what it is to be a tiger. The physicist J. J. Thomson said he couldn't really know what an atom was unless he could be one. He regretted his inability to identify with the world of atoms to that extent.

To really know is to be at one with that which is known. Perfect knowledge is perfect at-one-ment. Maybe God has that knowledge of tigers and atoms. The ethical consequences of extended love are enormous. Some of them are explored in Chapter 5.

CHAPTER 3

Purpose in the Universe

'Tis all in pieces, all coherence gone.

John Donne (1611), 'An Anatomy of the World'

To him who has only a hammer the whole world looks like a nail.

Abraham Maslow

In Chapters 1 and 2 the case has been put for the importance of purpose as causal in our lives and in the lives of other living creatures with whom we share this earth. But what about the universe as a whole, of which we and the rest of life are only a tiny part? Is it a vast contrivance devoid of purpose? The question is a critical one, for as physicist Bohm (1985a) says, 'If the universe means a vast machine to us, our whole being will unfold that meaning in the individual, in human relationships, and in society as a whole' (p. 124).

The astrophysicist Weinberg gives a brilliant account of the first three minutes of the universe in his book *The First Three Minutes* (1977). In his last chapter he contemplates the last minutes of planet earth as it faces an extinction of endless cold or intolerable heat and concludes: 'The more the universe seems comprehensible, the more it seems pointless' (p. 154).

The biologist Monod is no less pessimistic than Weinberg when he concluded *Chance and Necessity* (1974) with these words:

> If he [man] accepts this message—accepts all it contains—then man must at last wake out of his millenary dream; and in doing so, wake to his total solitude, his fundamental isolation. Now does he at last realize that, like a gypsy, he lives on the boundary of an alien world. A world that is deaf to his music, just as indifferent to his hopes as it is to his suffering or his crimes. (p. 172)

Why is it that a brilliant account of the origin of the universe and a brilliant account of the evolution of life each end upon a tragic note?

Neither Weinberg nor Monod find any meaning to purpose in the universe. They rightly reject the idea of a divine mechanic manipulating a mindless world machine. But both fail to find any other meaning to purpose. Haught (1984 p. 17) correctly puts the issue this way:

> If the world of nature is radically purposeful it is not sufficient that its purpose be extrinsic to it. Instead any teleological influence must be felt intimately by all aspects of the world. This means that the fundamental constituents of nature must have built into them a quality ... The name I shall give to this hypothesized quality of receptivity to meaning is 'mentality' ... Unless the universe is pervasively "mental" there would be no possibility of any global meaning taking up residence within it. (p. 17)

But first we must see how it is that the worldview of the universe as a mindless machine has become the dominant modern one.

The mechanistic worldview

The dominant model of nature for both astronomer Weinberg and biologist Monod is the machine. The universe is a gigantic machine made up of countless smaller machines, be they living organisms or atoms. The image goes back to the Greeks, but it was given its most complete expression in the sixteenth, seventeenth and eighteenth centuries with the rise of classical physics. The mechanistic model is properly called atomistic (from the Greek *atomos*, meaning indivisible). Its method consists in subdividing the world into its smallest parts, which at one time were thought to be atoms. The essence of atomism is that these parts remain unchanged no matter what particular whole they constitute, be it a star or a brain. Having divided the universe into its smallest bits you then try to build it up again, and of course when you do that you get a machine. The reductionist principle of atomism leads to the doctrine of mechanism—that the universe and all entities in the universe are machines. Newton's system of the universe, as it has been handed down to us, is atomistic and mechanistic. The earth and the sun are compared to atoms. Both the smallest and the largest objects obey identical laws. The universe is thus seen to be composed of bits of inert matter moving through space according to deterministic laws. In the Newtonian universe, once the initial conditions and the laws of force are given, everything is interpreted in terms of the mechanical movements of atoms and molecules and all is calculable for ever before and after. Laplace claimed that, given enough facts, he could not merely predict the future but retell the past. The prediction of the existence of the planet Neptune, which led to its later discovery was, for many, the vindication of the so-called Newtonian universe.

Whilst the elements of this view come from Newton, he himself was not a Newtonian. His views of matter were much more complex and in many ways more organic than mechanical. However, the simpler mechanistic picture held the day, together with his name. As a basis for a methodology of science it has been enormously fruitful for physics, astronomy and engineering and certain aspects of biology. The formation and development of the laws of motion and the law of gravitation occupied two generations. It commenced with Galileo and ended with Newton, who was born the day Galileo died.

The concept of a mechanistic universe became the dominant worldview soon after the rebirth of science in the sixteenth and seventeenth centuries. However, it is a mistake to suppose, as many historical accounts do, that the midwives of science were all mechanists. If any one year marks the beginning of modern science it is the year 1543. In that year modern astronomy was born with the publication of Nicholas Copernicus' *De Revolutionibus Orbium Coelestium*. The birth of modern physics comes nearly one hundred years later with Galileo's 1638 discourse on motion and force. In that same year that modern astronomy was born modern biology was born with the publication of *De Fabrica Corporis Humani* by the anatomist Andreas Vesalius in 1543. Neither Copernicus nor Vesalius were mechanists. The critical experience in the early life of Copernicus was ten years away from his native Poland in Renaissance Italy in Padua and Bologna, where he came under the influence of organic concepts in Neoplatonism and the writings of Hermes Trismegistus (Kearney 1971 pp. 96–104). Vesalius, a Belgian who became professor of anatomy in Padua, drew his inspiration from some of the biological writings of Aristotle and the anatomy and physiology of Galen (second century AD). Both Aristotle and Galen were keen observers of nature. Galen was one of the first experimenters we know of in biology; Vesalius developed the tradition of accurate observation and experimentation from Galen. He was not beholden at all to the mechanistic tradition of early Greek writers such as Democritus. Nor was William Harvey, the Englishman who came to the anatomy school in Padua where he discovered the circulation of the blood in the human body in 1628. 'It seems fair to say,' comments Kearney (1971), 'that Harvey developed his ideas on circulation of the blood within the general framework of the old philosophy' (p. 86). It was Descartes who later transformed the notion of circulation into a mechanical system of pumps and pipes and used it as a cornerstone for his mechanistic philosophy.

The importance of all this is that the origin of modern science was not dependent upon a mechanistic view of the world. It was later workers such as the Dutch astronomer Huygens and Descartes, who was an engineer, physiologist and philosopher, who developed the mechanistic model of the universe. Mechanism has been fruitful as a methodology. But it is not the only tradition that led to hypothesis formation and experimentation, which we regard as the hallmarks of modern science.

The work of the mechanists Descartes and Huygens falls within the lifetimes of Galileo and Newton. The lives of all four fall between 1564, when Galileo was born, and Newton's death in 1727. Whitehead (1933) judged that 'The issue of the combined labours of these four men [Galileo, Newton, Descartes and Huygens] has some right to be considered as the greatest single intellectual success which mankind has achieved' (p. 58). Yet for all its pragmatic value and its intellectual triumphs, the famous mechanistic image of the universe, of which they were largely the creators, lets us down in one major respect. 'Nature is a dull affair, soundless, scentless, colourless; merely the hurrying of material, endlessly, meaninglessly' (Whitehead 1933 p. 69). The point, and I make it a number of times in this book, is that there is an enormous gap between what natural science describes and what we know as living, sensing, experiencing human beings. Investigating the universe as if it were a machine has revealed much of its workings. This is methodological mechanism. To say that the universe is a machine is metaphysical mechanism. The Newtonian universe and elaborations which followed were a brilliant abstraction from nature. Its failure was to identify the abstraction with reality. This is Whitehead's (1933) 'Fallacy of Misplaced Concreteness' (p. 64), to mistake abstractions for concrete realities.

What is the universe made of? The abstraction, if the Newtonian worldview were to answer it, was bits of stuff, subject only to external forces that push and pull them. It was a billiard ball universe. The creed justified itself in that it worked. It explained much of the order of nature, both the fall of the apple and the movement of the planets.

For some, the picture of the universe as a machine reinforced belief in God. The metaphor of the universe as clockwork and God as the clockmaker goes back to a French bishop Nicole Oresme in the fourteenth century (White 1975). The churches then began to put clocks in church towers and inside churches to instruct the faithful in the ways of the creator. They were far more than timekeepers. They were homiletic devices. But Hume had written that the God whom you will find in a mechanical universe will be the sort of God who makes that mechanism. A mechanism can, at most, presuppose a mechanic. This was the belief of the deists—a mechanical universe presided over by a divine engineer, who having made it left it to run itself.

The French priest Marin Mersenne was Descartes' chief correspondent and his forerunner in advocating a mechanistic view of nature. It was his hope and intention to replace *The Imitation of Jesus Christ* by *The Imitation of the Divine Engineer* (Merchant 1980 p 226). In his *Principles of Philosophy* (1644) Descartes claimed that logical thinking led to the notion that the universe was a vast machine, wound up by God to tick for ever, and that it consisted of two basic entities: matter and motion. 'Give me matter and motion,' he said, 'and I shall construct a universe.' Spirit in the form of God hovers on the outside of this billiard-ball universe, but plays no direct part in it. Already in 1630 he had written to Mersenne: 'God sets up mathematical laws in nature, as a king sets up laws in his kingdom' (Berman 1981 p. 111).

Robert Boyle was aware of the problematic character of the clock as an autonomous machine and the image of God as the clockmaker. For when the clock is set in motion it will continue forever and God the clockmaker will have no cause to intervene in its operation. By the eighteenth century this argument was to come to a head in debates between Leibnitz and Newton. For Leibnitz, the universal clock was autonomous. It needed no external input once it was set in motion. For Newton, God had to intervene from time to time to prevent the clock from getting out of time or running down. In the eighteenth century an archdeacon, William Paley, takes over the arguments for a divine clockmaker. In his *Natural Theology* he tells us that mechanism presupposes an author of the mechanism. This was the so-called cosmological argument for the existence of God from design in nature. God is depicted as intervening in the nothing to initiate something—*creatio ex nihilo*—and thereafter intervening occasionally in the form of miracles. The latter had to be strictly limited, otherwise there would be no order of nature for science to investigate! The deists—there are plenty of them around still—held to the lawyer's definition of the acts of God as things that cannot be otherwise explained.

The God of mechanism inevitably retreats with the advance of science. This is not only because the gaps, where God could be thought to act, became narrower and narrower with the advance of science. It was also because the basic understanding of the world had altered. As Cobb (1983a) has said:

When nature was understood unhistorically as essentially changeless in its structure, occasional intervention to bring about new structures made some, though questionable, sense. But when nature is seen as a dynamic process, supernatural interventions are not required to account for the emergence of novel forms. (p. 45).

This is the main argument of the physicist Davies (1983) in *God and the New Physics*. He makes a convincing case for the demise of the interventionist God because of the new sort of world revealed by modern physics. But Davies fails to appreciate that the demise of interventionist thinking has opened the way to the development of an alternative theology of nature (see Chapter 4).

Whilst the picture of a mechanical universe provided some consolation for the deists, it provided none for others. In the chapter, 'The Romantic Reaction', in Whitehead's (1933) *Science and the Modern World* he points to the English poets who reacted against the mechanical universe. Wordsworth felt something had been left out. What had been left out comprised everything that was important for him. Tennyson's *In Memoriam* goes to the heart of the difficulty: 'The stars, she whispers, blindly run'. Each molecule blindly runs. The human body is a collection of molecules. The human body therefore blindly runs. All is set by mechanical laws. Where then is human responsibility? There is none. Wordsworth's characteristic thought about science is summed up in one line—'We murder to dissect'—from 'The Tables Turned':

> Sweet is the lore which Nature brings;
> Our meddling intellect
> Misshapes the beauteous form of things:—
> We murder to dissect.

Wordsworth was for grasping the wholeness of nature, to laugh with the daffodils and to find in the primrose thoughts too deep for words. For the poets, any philosophy of nature must include these three—aesthetic value, feeling and a sense of wholeness.

Challenge to the mechanistic worldview

While the poets were expressing their dissatisfaction with mechanism there was an alternative worldview which was strongly developed in the fifteenth and sixteenth centuries during the very rise of modern science. This tradition has been variously labelled Hermetic, Magical, Spiritualist, Organic, Alchemical and Neoplatonic. It had a long history, even prior to the rise of modern science.

This was a vigorous tradition in which scientific and religious concerns were inextricably combined. The movement played an important, some would say major, role in turning the world away from Aristotelian authoritarianism towards scientific enquiry. Evidence for this is provided by the following statement of the historian Trevor-Roper (1956):

> The scientific revolution of the sixteenth and seventeenth centuries, it is now generally agreed, owed more to the new Platonism of the Renaissance, and to the Hermetic mysticism which grew out of it, than to any mere 'rationalism' in the modern sense of the word. Ficino, with his 'natural magic', Paracelsus for all his bombast, Giordano Bruno in spite of his 'Egyptian' fantasies, did more to advance the concept of the investigation of a regular 'Nature' than many a rational, sensible, Aristotelian scholar who laughed at their absurdities or shrank from their shocking conclusions. (p. 132)

Copernicus, Vesalius and Harvey each owe much to this tradition of thought.

The Neoplatonic renaissance in organic thinking in the latter part of the fifteenth century was under the patronage of the Medici family in Italy. One of its founders, Marsilio Ficino (1433–99), made prominent the writings attributed to Hermes Trismegistus, supposedly an ancient Egyptian author. These Hermetic writings became the central authority for the 'magical' aspect of the movement. Also influential were the Jewish mystical writings referred to as Cabala which were brought into the movement by the towering figure of Giovanni Pico della Mirandola (1463–94). The alchemical side of Hermeticism was revived by Paracelsus (1490–1541). In his view matter and spirit were unified in a single active living substance. As a healer he sought to perfect the natural processes. That, he said, should be the aim of good medicine (Yates 1972).

Despite their identification in later times with the mechanistic model of the universe, both Robert Boyle and Isaac Newton were indebted to the organic movement. They met secretly with its representatives, even while disavowing them. Earlier work in the history of science played down this side of Newton's thought. Yet his interest in alchemy, for example, is attested by the fact that his library contained 175 books on it, that he left 650,000 words of notes on it and that he performed many alchemical experiments (Kearney 1971, Manuel 1968).

Classical mechanistic science said the world was made of bits of matter organised into bigger bits. What was the world made of in the eyes of the tradition opposing mechanism? There was an enormous diversity within this tradition but its central thinking stressed the necessity of experiment rather than reliance upon authority for understanding the world. Nature is replete with aims and sympathies and subjective qualities. God is present in the world and the world is present in God. There is an interconnectedness of all things, the unity of the universe is organic rather than mechanical, all fundamental entities from atoms to humans contain life. One of its noted exponents, Thomasco Campanella (1568–1639), said that God was immanent in nature and all matter was alive. Whitehead could hardly have improved on the following statement of Campanella:

> Now if animals have, as we all agree, what is called sense or feeling, and if it is true that sense and feeling do not come from nothing, then it seems to me that we must admit that sense and feeling belong to all elements which function as their cause since it can be shown that what belongs to the effect belongs to the cause. Consider, then, the sky and earth and the whole world as containing animals in the way in which worms are sometimes contained in the human intestines—worms or men, if you please, who ignore sense and feeling in other things because they consider it irrelevant with respect to their so called knowledge of entities. (from *De Sensu Rerum et Magia*, 1591, quoted in Merchant 1980 p. 104)

The same concept is implied by the modern physicist Wheeler when he asks rhetorically 'Here is a man, so what must the universe be?' (quoted by Davies 1982 p. 112).

In the middle of the seventeenth century a powerful movement for the organic view of nature existed in the writings of the Cambridge Platonists Henry More and Ralph Cudworth. The arguments are considered in detail in Cudworth's *The True Intellectual System of the Universe*, of which Raven (1953a) says:

> Cudworth, more clearly than any of his contemporaries, realised that if nature was in some sense a coherent and intelligible system, then it could not be explained in terms either of

the random movements of matter in space such as Hobbes supposed or of arbitrary and incalculable acts of God and other supernatural and demonic agents. It must be an orderly whole, manifesting not only a reign of law but a continuous and rational meaning. (p. 112)

However, the dominant mood of science became mechanistic. Science reified nature. Or, as Merchant (1980) puts it: 'As the sixteenth-century organic cosmos was transformed into the seventeenth century mechanistic universe, its life and vitality were sacrificed for a world filled with dead and passive matter' (p. 105). The removal of organic assumptions about the cosmos constituted what Merchant calls 'the death of nature'. This view, she claims, legitimated the manipulation of nature: 'the resultant corpse was a mechanical system of dead corpuscles, set in motion by the Creator, so that each obeyed the laws of inertia and moved only by external contact with another moving body' (1980 p. 195).

The church and the mechanistic worldview

The reasons for the virtual subjugation of the organic for a completely mechanical view in the subsequent history of science are complex. One was elements in the organic view that had to do with magic and mystery, many of which were fanciful. But the central core of understanding did not depend upon magic and mystery. What is really surprising in retrospect is the way in which the Christian church lined itself almost exclusively with the mechanistic view of the universe. In the seventeenth century there were three major traditions competing for dominance: the Aristotelian, the mechanistic and the organic, of which the last went by the various names already indicated. The church opted for the mechanistic model of the universe, though in many respects the organic view would have been much more supportive of Christian faith.

Up to the seventeenth century there was no single tradition of thought about the nature of nature within the history of the church. This is hardly surprising since there is no single view of nature within the Bible (Baker 1979, Koch 1979). In some parts of the Bible man is put in quite a different category from the rest of the creation, as in the later creation narrative in Genesis 1:1–2.4a. In the older creation narrative of Genesis 2:4b–25 this is not so; the animals stand alongside Adam. The *Adama*, ground, from which man and animals are formed is itself alive and active, though not in the same sense as Adam is alive. There remains therefore in these ancient texts an ambiguity (Pannenberg 1982 p. 152).

The earliest post-biblical writers are the so-called Apostolic fathers of the church. Their writings are very relevant for our times. As Moltmann (1985) says: 'It is the earliest traditions of Christian theology which frequently offer the most pregnant ideas for the revolution of our attitude to nature which is so vitally necessary today' (p. xiii). The first great theological system was that of Origen (AD 185–255) who was deeply influenced by Neoplatonism. He taught in what was up to then the greatest teaching seminary in Christendom in Alexandria. He was a student of its first great teacher, Clement of Alexandria. For Origen, all things that exist come within the divine influence or Logos:

> Although the world is composed of a diversity of functions, the constitution of the whole is not to be thought of as discordant and incoherent. As a body is an organism made up of many members, and it is held together by one soul, so, in my opinion, the whole world is a kind of huge and immense living creature which is united by one soul, namely the power and reason of God. (from *De Principiis*, quoted by Bettenson 1956 p. 260)

Origen went on to argue that divine omnipotence had no meaning for him unless everything that existed subsisted in some way in the divine. All are subjects! He introduces into his scheme the interesting idea that there probably have been many worlds before ours and there will be other worlds after this one. So God is never without a world of some sort. It is not difficult to see why interpreters of Origen such as Raven (1953a pp. 45–50) and Tillich (1967 pp. 55–63) see Origen's God as very much involved in the whole of the natural world. Origen was a prolific writer and his ideas developed in the course of his writings (Trigg 1983). So it is not surprising that Origen's interpreters don't all agree. For example, in contrast to the interpretation of Raven and Tillich, Santimire (1985 p. 50) concludes somewhat surprisingly that the world for Origen had no value in itself and is there simply for man. Origen was condemned as a heretic at Alexandria and later at Rome, but despite this his prolific writings remained influential in the early church.

Gregory of Nyssa (AD 331–89) was the only profound philosophical church father of the as yet undivided church who was accepted by the Orthodox tradition (Gregorios 1978, 1979, 1980). Gregory did not regard the universe as composed of matter in motion. Matter was an abstraction which we never encounter. What we encounter is matter with qualities. Nor was it stuff. It was process, dynamic and changing. As with Origen, the universe subsists in the divine nature. From our side we see a gap between the universe and God, but from God's side there is none. Gregory of Nyssa abandoned the notion that God and the world are two realities. But that was not to identify God with the world. To identify God with the world is pantheism. To make a distinction between God and the world yet to find God as involved in the being of the world is panentheism.

Gregory of Nyssa's thought is still influential within the Eastern Orthodox tradition which has a more organic view of the universe than the Western church. This is attested by the iconography and the great mosaics in the Eastern churches as, for example, in the apse of the twelfth-century San Clemente in Rome which is one of the masterpieces of Christian art. The centrepiece of the great mosaic is the cross from which the Redeemer reigns, drawing 'all things' to himself. And the vine which springs from the base of the cross spreads throughout the world in graceful curves as the tree of life enclosing in its branches 'all things': shepherds, their flocks, hens, healers, the sick, families, trees with fruits, a dolphin, fish, and other objects of the earth.

In Christian iconography in general a sharp difference emerges between the Eastern Orthodox tradition and the Western church, that is to say between the Greek church and the Latin church. As White (1972) says:

> In the Greek manuscripts pertaining to Man's Dominion the pictures show Adam sitting in the garden of Eden quite passively with the animals scattered around him. Sometimes in these Greek paintings the hand of God appears from a cloud to bless the whole situation. The Western pictures are very different in mood. God is standing with Adam and he has seized Adam's arm in his left hand. With a very hortatory gesture God is telling Adam exactly what should be done now. There's an urgency about this which is totally lacking in the Greek pictures, and the poor animals are far from being relaxed. They are huddled off into a corner looking scared—and in view of the long-term impact of the attitude reflected in these pictures, I think they have a right to look scared. (p. 31)

The Eastern church had a much softer attitude to the non-human world than the church in the West. And whereas the Western church adorned its churches with mechanical clocks to remind the flock of the engineering feats of the divine artificer, they were never used this way in the East. According to White (1972 p. 33), in the seventeenth century an Englishman, on the Czar's order, built a clock over the Saviour's Gate of the Kremlin. The Kremlin in Russian thinking had become identified with the Heavenly Jerusalem. There was a terrible reaction. The faithful rose up and complained that this was the contamination of eternity by time. As it happened the clock stayed there because the Czar had ordered it. But there were profound, highly emotional objections, and even today you do not find clocks on or in Eastern churches. They are kept at a distance. There is no doubt that from early times the West found mechanism spiritually congenial, whereas Eastern Christendom was highly suspicious of mechanism.

In the history of mechanism versus an organic view of the universe, the period from the third to the sixteenth century is virtually an interlude. Confrontation came in full force with the rise of modern science in the sixteenth century. Ever since, organic views have remained as one stream within theological and philosophical thought, though not the main stream.

The interesting question for us is why it is that the church in the West in the sixteenth century and ever since opted with the majority for the mechanistic view of the universe, particularly in view of the fact that the organic view is in many ways more supportive of Christian faith than the victorious mechanistic view.

The reasons for the choice were many and various. They could make a thesis on their own. Griffin (1986, 1988 pp. 1–46) has discussed this extensively. He points out that the medieval voluntarist theologians Duns Scotus of the thirteenth century and William of Ockham of the fourteenth century, both Franciscans, had a strong following. The term voluntarist derives from *voluntas*, the Latin for will. Voluntarism emphasised what it conceived to be the complete freedom of God's will from all constraints. God was in no way tied to the creation. He does what he wills. He can will anything. If he wanted to he could make good bad and bad good. The concept fitted well the mechanistic universe. Having made the universe God becomes unattached. On the whole it runs according to its originally divinely imposed laws. But God could change the laws, at the drop of a hat, if he so willed. The worst error was to confuse God and the

world in any way. And that is precisely what they accused the
organic thinkers of doing.

Among the most vehement of those who attacked the organic
view of nature was the priest Marin Mersenne. He saw the uphold-
ers of this doctrine as false prophets. Part of his opposition
stemmed from his desire to protect belief in miracles. If God is
involved in nature all the time, how can God be involved in special
ways at special times? If everything is a miracle then nothing can be.
Oddly enough, Protestants attacked the organic view because it was
associated at the time with magic and that seemed to protect the
Catholic view that miracles were not just biblical phenomena but
were post-biblical too. The Protestant reformers, especially Luther
and Calvin, held a legalistic view of God's relationship to the world.
That fitted better with a mechanistic than an organic view of the
universe. God makes the laws of the universe, then makes the
universe and it runs forever after according to those original laws.
Both Luther and Calvin stood in the tradition of voluntarism which
had been on the increase in influence since the fourteenth century.
Every detail of our lives, as well as those of the universe, depends
upon arbitrary decisions of God. In Calvin's doctrine of providence,
chance plays no part in the universe. Not one drop of rain falls
without God's command. Calvin said that when a branch breaks off
and falls from a tree, then kills a passing traveller, that too is at
God's express command (David R. Griffin 1976 Chapters 9 and
10). There were many other reasons for the rapid dominance of
mechanistic thinking in the church. Of course the organic view in
the sixteenth and seventeenth centuries was filled with false and
fantastic ideas. But so were the seventeenth-century versions of the
mechanistic worldview.

What happened in the sixteenth and seventeenth centuries was
a division of the world into different realms, one material which
science dealt with and the other spiritual which was the domain of
theology. It was a tragic carving up of the universe with resultant
wounds made even deeper in the nineteenth century with the rise of
Darwinism and its clash with religion. It became pretty clear then
that the God who was supposed to have made the world and its
creatures and then left them was an irrelevant hypothesis.
Darwinism could have opened up the way for a deeper natural
theology. Instead, opponents of Darwinism were more interested in
fighting a rearguard action to try to hold on to their outmoded
deistic natural theology.

The point of pursuing what went wrong is to be in a better position to do something appropriate about it. Referring particularly to the rise of the mechanistic view in the sixteenth century, Griffin (1986) says

> Historical understanding of the role of theology in the rise of modern science, a movement which soon resulted in the irrelevance of theology in the construction of culture's worldview, may give theologians the perspective from which they can overcome their complicity in this irrelevance. Knowledge of the existence of a vital third (organic) tradition—the others being Aristotelianism and mechanism—in the seventeenth century, of its early success in promoting scientific discoveries, and of the dubious reasons for its defeat, may help embolden some theologians to revive this tradition, in purified form, in a way that would be beneficial both to the religious life of humanity and its 'scientific' understanding of the reality in which it finds itself (p. 41)

The accidental universe

The alternative to a universe that is completely designed in all its details is not a universe where chance and accident reign supreme. As was elaborated in Chapter 2, neither pure chance nor the pure absence of chance can explain the world. The modern discovery is that chance and purpose can live together. Indeed, one is not possible without the other. This was pursued in Chapter 2 in relation to the living world. The same principle can be applied to the universe as a whole. In this section some attention is given to the role of chance in the universe at large. Following that we take up the role of purpose.

There was a chance, possibly a very large chance, that life might not have arisen in the universe. According to Weinberg (1977 p. 5), a slightly different sequence of events in the first few microseconds of the 'big bang' would have resulted in a universe of all helium and no hydrogen. Without hydrogen there would subsequently have been no heavy elements, which were formed by the fusion of hydrogen nuclei. Heavy elements such as carbon and iron are essential for life as we know it. Had the chain of events in the big bang been one micro-second different, they could not have been formed. One chain of events led to hydrogen and subsequently to heavy elements. Another chain of events led from heavy elements to the origin of life. The second chain is dependent upon the first. There were indeed many more than two such chains of causes. Pagels (1984) points out that if the relative masses of protons and neutrons were different by a small fraction of 1 per cent, making the proton heavier than the neutron, hydrogen atoms would be unstable since the protons that constitute their nuclei would spontaneously decay into neutrons. Hydrogen, which constitutes 74 per cent of the material of the universe and on which the origin of life as we know it was dependent, could not then have existed.

If the force of gravity were adjusted upward just slightly the stars would consume their hydrogen fuel much more rapidly than they do now and the sun would burn itself out faster. If on the other hand gravity were nudged downward a notch, the sun would burn more slowly and become too chilly to sustain life on earth (Pagels 1984).

These and other examples (Barrow & Tipler 1986, Davies 1982) suggest that the universe is finely tuned for our existence. The coincidence of a series of chains of physical events that are necessary for life as we know it seems to some to put too great a burden on chance. Hence the formulation of what some physicists have called the anthropic principle. The 'strong' form of the principle asserts that there must exist a guiding principle which ensures the fine-tuning of the cosmos to enable life to evolve. The early states of the universe are to be explained by the fact that they have made subsequent states possible. But, as Eastman and Fales (1984) point out, it is fallacious to infer that because the present is sufficient for inferring the occurrence of a given past history, it explains that history. This is no better than supposing that the symptoms of syphilis explain syphilis. The physicists who promote the strong anthropic principle seem to think that this universe has exactly those properties that ensure the eventual production of physicists! This is the fallacy of *a posteriori* reasoning, or thinking backwards, which is discussed further on page 120 *et seq.*

Davies (1982 p. 121) points out the 'strong' anthropic principle is akin to the deistic explanation of the universe—that God designed it in all its details for humans to inhabit. Shades of it are to be found in Montefiore's (1985) advocacy of the anthropic principle in his argument for the existence of God. The strong anthropic principle wasn't invented by physicists. The biochemist Henderson (1913) wrote a book that was widely read in the first half of this century, called *The Fitness of the Environment*. He maintained that this world is 'the best of all possible environments for life', and argued that the environment of earth had exactly the properties that enabled living organisms to exist in it. If water did not decrease in density as the temperature approached freezing, the water in ponds and rivers would freeze from the bottom up instead of from the top down and lots of fish and other forms of life would perish in the winter. And if the ozone layer of the upper atmosphere were thinner it would be ineffective in shielding ultraviolet radiation and life would not be possible. The error of the argument is that organisms evolve to fit the environment and not vice versa. It is the organisms that are fit, not the environment. Their fitness is a consequence of natural selection.

In its 'weak' form the anthropic principle asserts little more than that the universe is such that we are able to exist and observe it. A further variant is that it exists because we observe it.

If we accept that the universe in all its details is not determined by some outside power, and if we accept a role for chance and accident, there is no need to invoke the 'strong' anthropic principle. The principle of natural selection at the cosmic level and secondly chance together with purpose, as organising principles, provide another way of looking at the order of the universe. Our universe may be but one of many possible universes that could exist, have existed or exist now. Ours happens to be the one in which the physical realities are such that life as we know it could evolve. From the foundations of the universe there was the possibility that life could evolve. But it had to wait for the appropriate coincidence of many chains of physical events. Maybe it had to wait trillions of trillions of years. There was no inevitability that the chain of events that led to stable hydrogen and then to heavy elements had to occur. There was always the possibility that they would.

The dinosaurs that had dominated the earth for 100 million years became extinct about 65 million years ago. The early mammals lived in the interstices of the dinosaurs' world. Had the dinosaurs continued the mammals would probably still be small creatures living in these interstices. A conceivable cause of the extinction of the dinosaurs is the impact of some large extraterrestrial body upon earth. Suppose that without it the dinosaurs might not have died out. We know of only one lineage of primates, a little animal called *Purgatorius*, that lived before this hypothetical asteroid hit. Suppose this lineage had become extinct? Many lineages of mammals did become extinct at that time. The primates would not have evolved again, for evolution does not repeat itself. In this scenario the impact of the large extra-terrestrial body, that greatest of all improbabilities, may have been the *sine qua non* of the development of the primates, hence of our existence. And as Gould (1983), who gives us this scenario, points out, hundreds of other historically contingent improbabilities were also essential parts of human evolution.

The different sorts of possible universes defy the imagination. There is no reason to suppose that life as we know it is the only sort of life that might exist in this universe or in some other universe. There could be other universes in which life as we know it is not possible but life as we do not know it is possible, based let's suppose on silica and not hydrogen. Writers of science fiction have field days imagining how universes with stronger and weaker forces of gravity or different ratios of weights of protons and neutrons could lead to forms of intelligent life.

The 'new' physics, especially quantum theory, strongly argues against absolute determinism. Instead it provides a role for chance and the notion of probability of events occurring. Inevitability is replaced with probability. That flies in the face, not only of the mechanistic 'Newtonian' universe but also of deterministic fundamentalism, be its origin in Islam or the Christian churches. Pagels (1984 p. 101) tells a story of a teacher in post-revolutionary Iran who began a lecture on probability theory by holding up a die which he was going to use in a demonstration. Before he got any further an Islamic fundamentalist student called out 'A satanic artifact'— referring to the die. The teacher lost his job and almost his life.

Davies (1984) says: 'The new physics and the new cosmology reveal that an ordered universe is more than a gigantic accident' (p. 9). His understanding of physics leads him to reject the notion of an outside designer of the details and to accept a role for chance. But it does not lead him to reject a role for purpose. His book concludes with this sentence: 'If physics is the product of design, the universe must have a purpose, and the evidence of modern physics suggests strongly to me that the purpose includes us' (p. 243). Davies keeps us guessing what this purpose might be.

I argued in Chapter 2 that unlimited chance produces chaos. There must be something that limits chance; otherwise there could be no order. That something has to do with purpose, which is the subject of the next section. We can anticipate the argument by asking a question. Is the universe like us? We are determined to some extent by the genes we were bequeathed at birth, which was partly a matter of chance, and to some extent by the environment in which we were brought up. We didn't always choose that. We are nevertheless free within limits. We are free to choose the next steps in our lives. We can ourselves be creative and responsive. We can do our own thing and take advantage of those chains of events that intersect creatively in our lives. We can accept with some degree of equanimity those chains of events that intersect to our disadvantage. One is not possible in our sort of world without the other.

Is the universe as a whole so different from us? At any moment it is what it is by virtue of its history. At any moment there are new possibilities for the future. It is shaped by chance events and accidents along the way. Some pathways are blind alleys. Other chains of events intersect creatively to make a universe. What happens is not completely determined at any stage. New possibilities open up in the fullness of time. It would be a universe of chance alone, 'a gigantic accident', if what happened simply depended upon the juggling of inert bits of stuff. But that does not seem to be its nature. Ours is a universe where purpose can operate if the entities that are created in its evolution are themselves responsive and creative toward each new possibility of cosmic evolution. The alternative to a 'gigantic accident' is not complete determination in every detail but chance and purpose together.

A postmodern ecological worldview

If the universe is a lock then the key to that lock is not a measure but a metaphor. The mechanistic model puts the emphasis on substances that obey mechanical laws which can all be measured. It is called modern because it is the dominant model of the universe since the rise of modern science in the sixteenth century. The ecological model puts the emphasis elsewhere—on relationships. But, as we shall see, the relationships are not those between substances but between events. The ecological model is thus a process or event way of looking at things. It is called postmodern because it is destined to supersede the dominant model of today.

In the mechanistic or substance model, the universe is reduced to building blocks which are the ultimate substances. We may compare this model with a building which is made from piles of bricks of different shapes. We can reduce the building to a pile of bricks again when we demolish it. The same piles of bricks could make a

factory or a cathedral. It is simply a matter of the arrangement of the
bricks. The bricks of the universe were, according to this model, at
one time in a chaotic arrangement. Then they formed different sorts
of clusters: molecules, stars, galaxies and eventually living creatures.
Each brick is subject only to the laws of mechanics which are
essentially Newton's laws. That is to say the relations they have to
the environment are external relations. They are pushed or pulled
by neighbouring bricks and piles of bricks. A motor car is pushed
by the force of explosions in the cylinders of its engine. The world is
substance through and through. It is mechanical through and
through because it obeys only mechanical laws.

Mind and consciousness have always been a problem for this
view of the universe. They have either been excluded as epiphenomena, like the rattling of the train, or they have been regarded as a
peculiar sort of substance like a ghost in the machine. The latter is
the dualist view of mind and matter. In some dualist schemes God
is a mind outside the universe. But, whatever the version of substance thinking, they all have in common the notion that the bricks
of the universe remain the same no matter what environment they
are in. The atom, the electron, the proton, the cell, whatever sort of
brick or combination of bricks, is the same be it located in the
centre of the sun or in the centre of a human brain. The brick
retains its exact identity throughout. All that changes is its external
environment and therefore its external relations.

If you say that the universe is made of nothing but substances,
call them what you will, you are not making a statement of fact but
a metaphysical statement—metaphysics meaning beyond physics.
This is not a criticism but a recognition that every explanation has
some philosophical aspect to it. The ecological model of the universe differs in two important respects from the substance or mechanical model. There are no substances. And there are two sorts of
relationships, not just external relations. The second sort of relations are internal relations which we have already discussed.
Descartes defined substance quite precisely: 'And when we conceive
of substance, we merely conceive an existent thing which requires
nothing but itself in order to exist' (quoted by Whitehead 1930 p.
92). And as Whitehead says: 'there is no entity, not even God,
which requires nothing but itself in order to exist' (p. 94). So in fact
there are no substances. This is now quite widely accepted in
modern physics. But it seems to be news to most people. To the
quantum physicist, no component of the universe has reality inde-

pendent of the entirety. The physicist H. P. Stapp has expressed the quantum concept of 'particles' in these words: 'An elementary particle is not an independently existing unanalysable entity. It is, in essence, a set of relationships that reach outwards to other things' (quoted by Davies 1984 p. 49).

Quantum physics shows that the laws of mechanics are not applicable to very small-scale phenomena nor to very large ones. Newtonian physics took for granted the separation of the world into matter and mind. Quantum physics forces us to view mind and matter as single aspects of one phenomenon. There is only one reality and it is not substance. It is mind-matter (Delbruck 1986).

So the concept of an individual, from protons to people, involves the notion that each is what it is by virtue of its relationships with its environment. There are, of course, objects that are aggregates of natural entities such as a wheel that is still the same wheel whether it is turning or stationary. That is because the unity of the wheel is a mechanical one built into it by the engineer. It is not a building block in the sense in which entities such as atoms and cells are. Nor is a brick in a factory different from the same brick in a cathedral. The brick is a relatively unorganised collection of entities quite different from an atom or a cell. When we say there are no substances we are not saying there are no bricks but that if we were to reduce a brick to its ultimate constituents we would not end up with a collection of substances. The brick is an aggregation of entities, atoms and molecules. But the atom or the cell are not adequately described as an aggregate. They have an organisation that goes beyond an aggregation. They are individuals or, if you will, composite individuals.

There are no substances because the organised entities called atoms, cells, human beings and the like do not remain unchanged, no matter what their environment. This is because in addition to their external relations they have internal relations. The idea of an internal relation is a relation which is constitutive of the character and even the existence of the individual.

In substance thinking the substance is independent of relations and then enters into relations which are always external ones. In the ecological model internal relations are constitutive of the entity. Conventional thinking in terms of substance is turned on its head in a second respect in the ecological model. Since it is obviously not substances that have internal relations, what is it that has internal relations? Here we come to what is probably the most difficult concept of the ecological model. Instead of thinking of entities such as atoms as bits of matter that relate to other bits of matter, we think of atoms and other entities as occasions of experience themselves. To be actual is to be an occasion of experience. It is not to be a substance that then experiences; it is to be an occasion of experience. This is what an entity is in itself, for itself. In contrast to substance-thinking, this is called event-thinking. It is the deep meaning of thinking ecologically.

An occasion of experience has a twofold aspect. It is the experience of being what it is at this instant; that is, being sustained as an entity now. It is also creative for its future. This is the purposive element postulated for every entity or its 'subjective aim'. It is a subject that has aims. In sustaining its being as an occasion of experience it takes account of other entities in its whole history. The central notion by which Whitehead understands this sharing of entities one by another is 'prehension'. Consider the way in which experience of one moment flows into the next. I am always aware of being continuous with what I have been just before. The emotions of the immediate past perpetuate themselves into the present. What I am now is largely constituted by the presence within me of what I was just before. This is 'prehension'. It is a term for the way in which present experience includes, and thereby takes account of, past experience. But, as I have said, in addition there is the possibility that the occasion will embody some quality not received from the past and one aiming toward the future. This latter element is the element of self-determination of each entity. It is not absolutely determined to this particular pathway or that. It has a degree of freedom which is its self-determination. The element of self-determination and novelty in an occasion of experience is the germ of life in every occasion. It may indeed be trivial for the hydrogen atom. It is less trivial for the DNA molecule and of profound importance for the living organism. That is why Whitehead (1978 p. 156) considered aliveness to be tied up with novelty. Aliveness is a response that introduces something new.

Internal relations are tied up with the idea of feelings. It is through our feelings that we know we have internal relations. This is the subjective element of our lives. Internal relations, wherever they exist, imply feelings of some sort, be it as memory in relation to the past or anticipation in relation to the future. All entities are subjects. This is not to say that a cell or an atom is conscious. Far from it. It is to say that these entities are related to their environment internally in a way analogous to the way we ourselves are. Feelings don't have to be conscious. Consciousness enters only at the highest levels of organisation of the living organism. We ourselves have both conscious and unconscious feelings, the latter sometimes being referred to as the subconscious. Nor is it to say that stones have feelings. They are aggregations of natural entities that themselves have feelings.

A subject, as indicated in other contexts already, is that which acts and 'feels' as one. This is likewise the definition of a natural entity such as an atom or a cell.

All this does not mean that the ecological model should totally displace the mechanistic or substance model. When the events at the molecular level attain the kind of stable structure they may have in a stone, the relevance of the ecological model to the stone as a whole becomes trivial. For most practical purposes the behaviour of the stone can be discussed adquately in the simpler terms provided by the science of mechanics. The mechanistic model works well there. It is the working model of engineers. The quarrel is not with the practical use of the mechanical model where it is adequate, but with its misuse as, for example, applied to human behaviour and the assumption of its final explanatory adequacy in any worldview.

But what is the evidence in favour of the ecological model, of entities as subjects and of entities as dependent in their constitution upon their environment?

To take the last point first, it seems that atoms do indeed exhibit different properties in different environments. Hydrogen and oxygen are toxic gases. Water which is a combination of the two is wet. According to substance thinking the atoms of hydrogen and oxygen are unaffected by their combination. Hence, in principle, all the properties of water should be discoverable in hydrogen and oxygen atoms investigated in isolation. But in fact this proves impossible. Many scientists speak of emergent properties. But as ordinarily used the doctrine of emergence explains nothing. It merely restates the problem. It assumes that atoms remain unchanged, they have only those characteristics they had in isolation, and that water is nothing but the combination of these two atoms. Yet it recognises in water properties not derivative from the constituent atoms. With the ecological model we can do better. The events that are occurring at the atomic level are internally related to one another. The events that make up the hydrogen and oxygen atoms are affected by their environments. And when these environments include each other in appropriate ratios, the atoms exhibit properties they do not exhibit in other environments. When certain arrangements of carbon, nitrogen and hydrogen atoms, together with a few others, exhibit properties that we recognise by the name enzyme, and other arrangements of the same atoms result in cells that conduct nerve impulses, we have discovered something new about the nature of these societies of events we call atoms with their remarkably stable structures. When they are organised in these particular ways, the resultant events have characteristics they do not have when this organisation is lacking. An analogous argument is quite applicable to other levels of organisation such as that of electrons and protons in atoms.

What then has physics to say to the proposition that entities such as electrons and atoms are subjects that have internal relations? The new quantum mechanics opens the door to that question. Quantum mechanics did not simply replace Newtonian mechanics. It subsumed it within a broader perspective; one that called into question certain metaphysical assumptions inherent in the Newtonian universe. The universe of quantum mechanics in the first place is not the deterministic universe of Newtonian physics. There are degrees of freedom of action that mean that accident and choice become appropriate terms to use in physics. Einstein insisted that God does not play dice. 'It seems hard to look in God's cards,' he said. 'But I cannot for a moment believe that he plays dice' (quoted by Pagels 1984 p. 148). Quantum mechanics insists that God does play dice. No way can be found when and where a quantum of energy will hit. Nor is there any way of predicting, as Laplace thought he could, the future of the universe from measuring matter and motion. Heisenberg's principle of indeterminism tells us that if we want to observe and measure an electron or some such, we can install a device to measure its position or a device to measure its momentum but we can't do both at the same time. Moreover, the act of measuring has an inescapable consequence for what we can say about the electron then and in the future. Submicroscopic events are conditioned by the instruments with which we observe them, and perhaps even by one's consciousness of them. As Wheeler (1977, 1982) indicates, the detached observer is an illusion. The real observer participates in what is observed.

There is a second option for dealing with the question of how possibilities at the submicroscopic level are decided. Stapp (1972, 1977, 1979) suggests there is a randomness inherent in nature itself. This means that submicroscopic events are themselves 'acts of decision' by which certain possibilities for behaviour are actualised and others are cut out. Whereas the indeterminacy principle of Heisenberg 'emphasises the role of decision at the human level, Stapp emphasises the role of decision at the quantum level. The natural world is in a certain sense "free" ' (quoted by McDaniel 1983 p. 300). As McDaniel goes on to explain, the freedom at the submicroscopic level is minimal. Compared to human freedom it is negligible. What is possible for a given atomic event is heavily conditioned by the entire history of the universe, and by the instruments with which the event is observed if an observation is being made. McDaniel (1983) develops the thesis that quantum mechanics leads to the notion that submicroscopic events have this degree of freedom and make decisions. They are, in other words, subjects that 'take account of the environment' internally and are so constituted. Bohr's principle of complementarity does not tell us that matter at the submicroscopic level is either particulate or wave-like. It tells us that it is neither particulate nor wave-like. The slate is clean to start again. The new proposal which Stapp develops is that submicroscopic matter is partly life-like. 'Sub-microscopic actualities, whatever they are, seem to be able to take into account external influences (the root meaning of sentience) and actualise possible responses (the root meaning of creativity)' (McDaniel 1983 p. 302). A similar interpretation has been developed by Cochran (1966, 1972), who introduces the idea that life and non-life are words like hot and cold. They are positions on a scale graduated from simple (non-life) to complex (life).

The internal aspect of the submicroscopic events has been given a new depth of meaning by Bohm (1973, 1977, 1980) in his interpretation of quantum physics. Elementary particles, so called, are an abstraction. There are no particles. 'What is needed,' says (Bohm 1980), '. . . is to give up altogether the notion that the world is constituted of basic objects or "building blocks". Rather, one has to view the world in terms of universal flux of events and processes' (p. 9). So physicists are now saying what Whitehead said long ago: nature consists in the last analysis of 'events not things'. And further, 'neither physical nature nor life can be understood unless we fuse them together as essential factors in the composition of "really real" things whose interconnections and individual characters constitute the universe' (Whitehead 1966 p. 150).

In the view of Bohm (1973, 1977, 1980, 1985a, 1985b), science as we know it describes the objective aspect of things—the external aspect or what he calls the explicate order of the world. What it at present fails to see is that the explicate order is dependent upon what he calls an implicate order which is an inner aspect of things. For example, in the picture we see on the television screen points that are near each other in the ordered visual image are not necessarily 'near' each other in the form they are carried in the radio wave from which the image is translated. The function of the receiver is to explicate the order, that is, to unfold the image implicate in the radio wave in the form of a visual or explicate image. When the picture appears on the television screen, almost all its energy comes from the power plug on the wall. But its form comes from the very weak electrical wave picked up by the TV antenna. A very subtle energy picked up by the antenna moulds a denser energy picked up from the wall socket.

Another illustration of what is meant by implicate and explicate order came to Bohm (1985a p. 117) when he watched a television program which showed a device in which an ink drop was spread through a cylinder of glycerine. It was subsequently brought together again, to be reassembled exactly as it was before. When the ink drop was spread out, it had a 'hidden' order that was revealed when it was reassembled. On the other hand it appeared to be in a state of disorder when diffused in the glycerine. The order was enfolded or implicated in the ink when diffused in the glycerine. The order only became explicit when it was reassembled as a drop surrounded by glycerine. Generally speaking the laws of physics refer mainly to the explicate order which can be described in precise detail. Bohm proposes that the primary emphasis in physics should now turn to the implicate order. The logic of this is that the explicate order is not fully understood except with reference to the implicate order. This twofold distinction was anticipated long ago by Whitehead (1966) when he wrote:

> Science can find no individual enjoyment in nature: Science can find no aim in nature: Science can find no creativity in nature; it finds mere rules of succession. . . They are inherent in its methodology. The reason for this blindness of physical science lies in the fact that such science only deals with half the evidence provided by human experience. It divides the seamless coat—or, to change the metaphor into a happier form, it examines the coat, which is superficial, and neglects the body which is fundamental. (p. 154)

Since Descartes, people have lost sight of the implicate order and have come to think of the explicate order as self-sufficient. The sort of understanding physics has given us of electrons and atoms is of their explicate order. It leaves hidden the implicate order, of which the explicate order is an expression. It is clear from Bohm's writings that an aspect of the implicate order of the electron and the atom is the subjective aspect of these entities; what they are in themselves to themselves.

This new physics restores a sense of oneness to the universe. It recognises that 'we murder to dissect' (Wordsworth). Whereas in the old physics there was a seemingly unbridgeable gulf between the animate and the inanimate, in the new physics that gulf no longer exists. One reason for this is that the new physics leads to a new understanding of cosmological evolution. It deals with entities that truly evolve and are not simply rearranged in cosmic evolution. It is the view that Whitehead (1933 p. 134) saw was logically required by any serious doctrine of evolution.

The unity of the universe

Physics gives a conception of the unity of the universe that is little appreciated by non-physicists. The nature of nature seems to be remarkably constant from one 'end' of the universe to the other. Gravity is a universal principle. Nothing in the whole cosmos escapes its grip. I drop a stone in Sydney and it has some effect on a whale in the Antarctic ocean, small though that be. It even has some effect, though smaller, on a distant star. The poet is correct:

> All things by immortal power,
> Near or far,
> Hiddenly
> To each other linked are,
> Thou canst not stir a flower
> Without troubling of a star.
>
> Francis Thompson, 'The Mistress of Vision XXII'

Secondly there is the principle already discussed that individuals such as electrons and atoms are what they are by virtue of their relations to other individuals. So Davies (1984) tells us:

> We need the universe before we can give concrete reality to the very atoms that make up the universe! Which 'comes first', atoms or universe? The answer is 'neither'. The large and the

small, the global and the local, the cosmic and the atomic, are mutually supportive and inseparable aspects of reality. You can't have one without the other. The tidy old reductionist idea of a universe which is simply the sum of its parts is completely discredited by the new physics. There is a unity to the universe, and one which goes far deeper than a mere expression of uniformity. It is a unity which says that without everything you can have nothing. (p. 221)

In Galileo's universe there was a picture of unity in simplicity. Then as knowledge grew it looked more like a multiverse than a universe. Under the influence of Descartes it became a diverse of mind and matter. And now modern physics gives a picture of the unity of the universe such as we have never known before.

The new unity goes deep. It implies a continuity in origin of the subjective elements of individuals which we recognise so clearly in our human experience. Their origin is in the submicroscopic events of electrons and the like which first appeared billions of years ago. 'Cosmic evolution suggests that what we know most intimately, our own subjective experiences, are highly developed forms of what there was in the beginning, submicroscopic matter' (McDaniel 1983 p. 306). There is a continuity between matter and mind. 'Inasmuch as mind involves spatiotemporal properties, it is matter-like. And inasmuch as matter involves creativity and sentience, it is mind-like. "Matter" and "Mind" are simply names for different types of actual occasions of experience' (McDaniel 1983 p. 309).

So real is this unity, Bohm speaks of the 'undivided wholeness' of the universe and uses the hologram as an image (Bohm 1980 pp. 143–7). The hologram is to be contrasted with the picture from a camera with an ordinary lens. In this picture there is a one-to-one relationship between the object and the image. A particular point on the object becomes a particular point on the picture. If you cover half the lens you get half a picture. Half the points are lost. The hologram, as its name implies, pictures the whole, even if you do what corresponds to covering half the lens of an ordinary camera. But there is no lens. There is a mirror and the light is a beam from a laser. What we see when we illuminate only a small area of the photographic plate is not a partial image but a whole image some-what less sharply defined in detail. There is no one-to-one corre-spondence between object and image. In the past physics has tended to build up the object from its atomic bits. Bohm now suggests its task is to perceive the undivided whole. A consideration of the difference between a hologram and an image made from a lens camera can play a significant part in the perception of undivided wholeness, as contrasted with fragmentation.

As we penetrate matter we don't find isolated building blocks but a complex web of relationships between the parts of a unified whole. That world can to some extent be divided into parts, but the notion of independent parts breaks down. The parts are defined by their interrelations. To quote physicist Stapp again: 'An elementary particle is not an independently existing unanalysable entity. It is, in essence, a set of relationships that reach outward to other things' (quoted by Davies 1984 p. 49). Because the reaching out is continuous and because the other things are constantly changing as their relationships change, the universe is moment by moment in the process of transformation.

What may appear as static to our eyes is in fact a dynamic stability of continuous transformation. Think of a crowd in a huge stadium held in awe by the performance in the arena. The excitement of the performance changes the feelings of the crowd. But they are held together as a crowd as they themselves are transformed by shared emotion. Better still, think of the players themselves in the arena. They move with great speed. Each move is governed by past moves of each member of each team and possible moves in the future open to each player. In a sense there are no players. There is only the game. As Capra (1982) says:

> In modern physics, the image of the universe as a machine has been transcended by a view of it as one indivisible, dynamic whole whose parts are essentially interrelated and can be understood only as patterns of a cosmic process. At the subatomic level the interrelations and interactions between the parts of the whole are more fundamental than the parts themselves. There is motion but there are, ultimately, no moving objects; there is activity but there are no actors; there are no dancers, there is only the dance. (p. 92)

The ecological model of the universe and its entities shows the fundamental similarity of all individual entities from protons to people. In the words of William Blake's 'Auguries of Innocence':

> To see a World in a Grain of Sand,
> And a Heaven in a Wild Flower,
> Hold Infinity in the palm of your hand,
> And Eternity in an hour.

To really know a part would be to know the whole. But our knowledge of even the minutest part of the universe is incomplete and abstract. Tennyson saw this when he wrote 'Flower in the Crannied Wall':

> Flower in the crannied wall,
> I pluck you out of the crannies,
> I hold you here, root and all, in my hand,
> Little flower—but *if* I could understand
> What you are, root and all, and all in all,
> I should know what God and man is.

And that is really the point of the new physics. Indeed it is the point of the ecological model. You get to know the part as you get to know the whole.

The ecological model of the universe helps us to overcome the dichotomy between the individual and its relations to its environment, between the living and the non-living, between freedom and determinism and between nature and God. And it provides a basis for a non-anthropocentric ethic that includes nature as a whole. The doctrine of mere-matter, mere-mindless and feelingless stuff puts limits to things with which we can empathise. But if in physical nature also there is experience, then there is a universal community for mutual participation and sympathy. The degree to which a given entity requires ethical concern in its own right is relative to its capacity for experience.

The objective of this chapter has been to establish that the universe is the sort of existence in which purpose can operate. For that it was necessary to establish that the individual entities of existence are themselves of such a nature that they could be responsive to influences that can be called purposive. The nature of these influences is largely the subject of the next chapter. But this next chapter will make no sense at all unless we have grasped the distinction between the world as it appears on the one hand outwardly and as revealed by mechanistic science, and on the other hand the world that is hidden beneath appearances but is as real. The distinction is well made by Griffin (1985 p. 185) between what he calls the actual world of real causal efficacy and the world as it appears to our sensory perception, especially vision. This latter world is not the world as it actually is. It is the appearance of the actual world produced by our sensory and conscious experience. This appearance is not a total falsification of the actual world, but it involves gross simplification and distortion. 'In particular,' says Griffin (1985),

> it presents us with a world in which things appear to be passive rather than active, to be externally rather than internally related to other things, to have no experience, no aim, no self-value. And of course natural science has largely limited itself to this world of appearance—to the world as known to the senses and instruments designed to amplify them. Accordingly, if the world as it appears to scientific study is taken to be the actual world, we get a picture of the world as made of externally related, passive, aimless, valueless bits of stuff. And such a world can clearly provide no intelligible explanations as to why it behaves as it does. Explanation, as opposed to merely descriptive generalization (which is positivism), requires resort to something hidden beneath the appearances. (p. 185)

The dominant assumption among those seeking explanations in our time has been that the actual world is composed of entities whose reality is exhausted by their appearances. What they are in themselves is not thought to be essentially different from what they are in appearance. This has produced the materialistic mechanistic worldview.

In seeking an alternative model I have drawn clues for this chapter largely from two sources. One is the 'new' or quantum physics. For the uninitiated like myself, modern physicists have been generous in providing interpretations of the new physics. One of the best is Pagels' (1984) *The Cosmic Code*. My second main source is the thought of A. N. Whitehead and others in the tradition of 'process thought' who have come to the conclusion that individual entities in themselves are subjects, aiming at and realising value, and being internally related to other actual entities in their environments. In such a universe the God of the machine is totally irrelevant. Much the same conclusion has been reached from a rather different approach by scientist–theologian Arthur Peacocke (1984). He rejects mechanistic determinism and argues for a more ecological concept of nature and the continual involvement of God's creative activity in the universe. It is only within a universe where determinism no longer reigns and where entities have some degree of freedom that such a God can be involved.

CHAPTER 4

Cosmic Purpose

God is not before all creation, but with all creation.

A. N. Whitehead (1978 p. 343)

More than two thousand years ago, the wisest of men proclaimed that the divine persuasion is the foundation of the order of the world, but that it could only produce such measure of harmony as amid brute forces it was possible to accomplish

A. N. Whitehead (1942 p. 189)

I n previous chapters the case has been made for a crucial role for purpose as a causal agency in human life,
in the rest of the living world and in all individual
entities to the farthest reaches of the universe. The
proposition of those chapters is that materialism or
mechanism does not explain the world, but that individual
entities from protons to people are influenced, not only by their
external relations. They are influenced, moreover constituted, by
their internal relations with their environment. Internal relations
have nothing to do with the laws of mechanics. The laws of mechanics have all to do with external relations. The ecological model of
nature is put forward as a credible alternative to materialism and
mechanism.

The old notion of a divine being controlling the universe from
outside is no longer credible. The relevant question now is, in what
sense, if any, is there divine activity in the universe.

God is dead

Why bring God into the argument at all? Hasn't the notion of God
been disposed of by science and the Enlightenment and more recently by theologians themselves who have written about the death
of God? The critical question to ask is which God is dead? There
are many concepts of God and many of them should die. The
primary question is not, do you believe in God? but, what do you
think you would be believing in if you did believe in God? There is
the God who can do anything, who could prevent nuclear war, who
could have prevented the holocaust—but didn't. There is the God
who set the universe going in the first place and then left it except
for occasional interventions in the form of miracles which rarely
happen. There is the God of the gaps who is brought in to fill the
gaps left by science; that God grows smaller with every advance in
scientific understanding of the universe. There is the cosmic bellhop
who sits at the end of a cosmic telephone exchange dealing with
billions of calls every minute and whom the caller hopes will alter
the course of events to suit the caller. There is the God who requires
praise. There is the God who demands sacrifice. There is the God
who is on our side in wars who would have us kill for his sake.
There is the uncertain God of the soldier's prayer—please God, if
there be a God, save my soul if there be a soul! There is the God of
judgment who rules by fear and who dispenses post-mortem re-

wards and punishments. All these theologies of God make things pretty easy for atheists. I too am an atheist about those Gods.

A student of Columbia University came to see Harry Emerson Fosdick, who was pastor of Riverside Church in New York. He was agitated. Before he had time to sit down he announced to Dr Fosdick that he didn't believe in God. 'So you're an atheist,' said Fosdick. 'Describe for me the God you don't believe in.' The student did a good job of picturing God as a venerable bookkeeper taking notes of everyone's good and bad deeds. When the student had finished Fosdick surprised him by saying 'My boy, that makes two of us. I don't believe in that God either. But we've still got the universe on our hands, haven't we. What do you really think about it?'

The worldview that has been increasingly dominant since the seventeenth century, due to the work of Galileo, Descartes, Boyle, Newton and others is a mechanistic view of nature. In its first period this worldview was theistic and dualistic. It put both God and the human soul, as it was called, outside the mechanisms. God was the omnipotent external creator who had little to do with the world but something to do with human souls. In its second phase, following the Enlightenment, the mechanistic worldview became materialistic and atheistic. This led to reductionism and determinism. The student who came to Fosdick seemed to be recapitulating this bit of history, starting out as a theist and ending up an atheist. It was argued in Chapters 1 and 2 that both dualism (theistic or otherwise) and materialism are now in shambles. Instead, these chapters argued for a unitary view of creation and the sentience of all individual entities, not just humans. They stressed the role of freedom and of purpose throughout the creation. They found no place for the universe as a giant contrivance, nor for a God who manipulates the contrivance. Why then introduce God at all?

Three objections might be raised to introducing God into the picture. One is that the word stands for nothing that is credible or defensible in the modern world, so why carry this extra baggage of questionable belief? A second objection is that even if there is a defensible view, the word God is too tied to outmoded views and will always be identified with them, just as bad money drives out good. Blaise Pascal in the seventeenth century questioned if the God of the philosophers was the God of Isaac, Jacob and Abraham. A third objection is that ideologies tied up with a God are socially destructive, a cause of enmity and disastrous wars. We would be

better off without them. This objection has some force when each
day the newspapers report yet another internecine conflict between
religious parties. The world would be better off without religious
fanaticism. But it is not only religions that are a source of fanaticism; so are ideologies both of the right and the left. What has to be
opposed are fanaticisms of any sort, religious or otherwise.

An objective of this chapter is to suggest a faith in a cosmic
purpose that is credible in an age of science and that could lead to
harmony between human beings and between them and the rest of
nature. Another way of putting this is to ask—is there divine love at
the heart of the universe?

Three views of the relation of God to the cosmos

There are logically three views of the relation of God to the cosmos:

1. God is identified with the cosmos and in all aspects inseparable from it and all that exists. This is pantheism.

2. God is not identified with the cosmos and is in all aspects
independent of it. This is classical theism

3. God is involved in the cosmos but is not identified with it.
God is both within the system and independent of it. This is
panentheism.

A further breakdown of these views can obviously be made and
is given by Hartshorne and Reese (1953). The position developed
in this book is one of panentheism or what Hartshorne calls neo-
classical theism. It is known also as process theology because reality, including God, is conceived to be process (not substance).
God is involved in, but not identified with, the cosmos. It is also
called an 'ecological mode' of God (Birch & Cobb 1981) because of
the emphasis on relations, particularly internal relations.

The first modern thinker whose views were close to panentheism, according to Hartshorne and Reese (1953 pp. 225–7), was
the Italian Faustus Socinus (1539–1604) whose followers formed
the Socinian movement. Socinius broke away from the tradition of
classical theism by proposing that we contribute to the life of God.
But God in this view was not world-inclusive. Some more recent
supporters of panentheism, for whom God both contributes to and
receives from the world, are Shelling, Fechner, Peirce, Berdyaev,
Iqbal, Buber, Radhakrishnan, Whitehead, Hartshorne, Weiss,
Ogden, Cobb, Griffin, Haught, Suchocki, McDaniel and others. The
concept of panentheism is, of course, much older than these

modern representatives. Hartshorne and Reese (1953) include in what they call ancient or quasi-panentheism, Ikhnaton ('the first mono-theist'), Hindu scriptures (Vedic hymns and the Upanishads), Lao-tzu (the Tao Te Ching), Judaeo-Christian scriptures (for example, sections of Genesis 1, Psalm 103 and various parts of the New Testament), and Plato.

In panentheism or the ecological model of God, God is not introduced to save the collapse of the model of the universe and all that is in it. God is not introduced to fill the gaps left over from science. God is not supernatural. God is natural. What is, is natural. In the ecological model God is the most natural entity there is. 'God,' says Whitehead (1978), 'is not be be treated as an exception to all metaphysical principles invoked to save their collapse. He is their chief exemplification' (p. 343). It is true to say that the world is germane to God and God is germane to the world. The ecological model thus argues for the relevance of God to the being of and the understanding of the universe and all its entities. It is a view that attempts to combine the understanding of the best science with the best insights in religion. It seeks in Whitehead's (1933) words 'a deeper religion and a more subtle science' (p. 229). The previous chapters have been concerned particularly with the more subtle science. They have hinted at a deeper religion. This is made explicit in this chapter.

The divine Eros

Sallie McFague (1987 p. 38) makes the proposition that belief and behaviour are more influenced by images than by concepts. It follows that concepts without images tend to be sterile. Whitehead speaks of two aspects of God which he calls the primordial nature and the consequent nature of God. I refer to these in terms of the images of divine Eros and divine Passion respectively. McFague goes further with her images and speaks of God as mother, lover and friend, each of which includes divine Eros and divine Passion. She makes her images even more telling by referring to the world as God's body, as indeed did Hartshorne (1941 p. 185) long ago. This image suggests that God is to the world as self is to the body. It represents a thoroughly incarnational theology.

The meaning of divine Eros (eros means love) is that at the heart of the universe there is persuasive love sustaining all individual entities and enticing them to deeper experiences so far as their freedom allows. In the ecological model there is constant tension between chaos and order since order is neither the outcome of one all-powerful orderer nor of deterministic necessity. All individual entities have a degree of freedom which is their degree of self-determination. Their freedom is freedom to respond or not to respond to possibilities in their future. As has been emphasised, this must be tiny for protons but highly significant for persons.

What in particular do individual entities of creation respond to? The answer is—the possibilities for their being, including their future. At the heart of the universe, even before there were atoms or cells, there was the possibility of these entities coming into existence. The potentiality of the universe is conceived as cosmic mind. Such a reality is recognised, though not explicitly taken to be God, in Buddhism. In Hinduism it is thought of as Brahman. In Judaism and Christianity it is called God. The possibilities of the universe are realities that constitute a continuous lure to the creation. In the ecological model of God they are in the primordial mind. This is Whitehead's doctrine of the divine Eros or the primordial nature of God. In God's primordial nature God confronts what is actual in the world with what is possible for it. This is the aspect of the divine who is the same yesterday, today and forever. It is the immensely sensitive and outgoing nature within nature brooding over nature. It is the ordering principle at the heart of the universe, else there would be only chaos. Materialism, by contrast, refuses in principle to take order as a problem.

The principle, so often ignored by traditional religion uninformed by science, is that there are many orderers yet one supreme orderer. As Hartshorne (1967) has said: 'Order is in principle the rule of one' (p. 61). But

> it is not God alone who acts in the world, every individual acts. There is no single producer of the actual series of events; one producer to be sure, is uniquely universal, unsurpassably influential. Nevertheless, what happens is in no case the products of his creative acts alone. Countless choices intersect to make a world, and how, concretely, they intersect is not chosen by anyone, nor could it be . . . purpose in multiple form, and chance are not mutually exclusive but complementary; neither makes sense alone. (p. 58)

Apart from God there is no way to understand how there could be any limits to the anarchy implied by a multiplicity of creative agents —none universally influential.

God is thus the ground of order. But this is a changing and developing order. Order involves the many becoming one, else ours is a multiverse and not a universe. The creative activity of God involves the creation of novelty that itself adds to the existing unity. Nothing creatively novel is unattached. The whole is immanent in the part. The parts are members of one another. The novel becomes one with the many. This is the meaning of creative advance. Hence Whitehead's (1978) somewhat enigmatic phrase 'The many become one, and are increased by one' (p. 21).

To say that God is the ground of order is to say also that God is the ground of novelty. This is because, as Cobb and Griffin (1976) state, 'One aspect of God is a primordial envisagement of the pure possibilities. They are envisaged with appetition that they be actualised in the world' (p. 28). Hence Whitehead's name the Eros of the universe for the primordial nature of God. It is the active entertainment of all ideals and possibilities, with the urge to their concrete realisation, each in its due season. Where the divine Eros meets the human eros and is truly recognised the appropriate response is youthful zest with all of one's heart and soul and mind and strength, or in Tillich's phrase—with infinite passion. The response of the creature to the divine Eros is passionate and transforming. It is adventure involving continual creative transformation. In the last two chapters of *Adventures of Ideas* Whitehead speaks of adventure as belonging to the essence of civilisation, so the pure conservative is fighting against the essence of the universe.

The ordered universe contains within it much that is disordered and incomplete. Multiple creativity makes some disorder and conflict inevitable. It allows for the possibility of great disorder and evil. In the ecological model evils spring from chance and the freedom that allows—not from providence. The reason providence does not eliminate chance is because a world without chance is a world without freedom. Every natural entity, every atom must have an aspect of self-determination or spontaneity and the intersection of even two, let alone myriads, of acts of self-determination is precisely chance. For God to completely control the world would be the same as to annihilate it. It follows that it is nonsense to ask the question—why did God allow Vesuvius to pour its molten larva on populated Pompei, or why did God allow the Holocaust? People who ask such questions have not been liberated from the concept of

God as omnipotent dictator of the universe, responsible for everything that happens and who, if he willed, could change the course of
events by sheer fiat. This concept has infused tragedy into the
histories of Christianity and Mohammedanism. When catastrophe
strikes people ask—why did God do this to me? It is a non-question
because God does not manipulate things and people. God's is not
the power to do anything at all. God doesn't need that particular
false metaphysical compliment. Yet this notion of God has been,
and still is, a cause of much suffering and agony, as poignantly
portrayed by Kushner in *When Bad Things Happen to Good People*
(1982). The notion of an all-arranging, chance-excluding providence is cruel. It compels us to try and imagine that our worst
tortures are deliberately contrived. And it is dangerous because it
suggests we can do little to avert evil. Whitehead (1978) wrote that,
'When the Western world accepted Christianity, Caesar conquered.'
God became fashioned in the image of Egyptian, Persian and
Roman Imperial rulers:

> The Church gave unto God the attributes which belonged ex-
> clusively to Caesar . . . There is, however, in the Galilean origin
> of Christianity yet another suggestion which . . . does not em-
> phasise the ruling Caesar, or the ruthless moralist, or the un-
> moved mover. It dwells upon the tender elements in the world,
> which slowly and in quietness operate by love. (pp. 342–3).

There are things a God of love cannot do. The God of love could
not change the decision of the rich young ruler to whom Jesus
spoke. When persuasion failed, coercion did not take over. Let us
give up the destructive notion of divine omnipotence that plagues so
much of Christian theology. Hartshorne (1984a) argues that omnipotence, as usually conceived, denies God any world worth talking
about. It denies that in the world of the living there are any significant decision-making agents. All is determined by God. 'No worse
falsehood was ever perpetuated than the traditional concept of omnipotence. It is a piece of unconscious blasphemy, condemning God
to a dead world, probably not distinguishable from no world at all'
(p. 18).

The biblical image is of one who stands at the door and
knocks, who never forces entry. The valid analogy is the lure of
loving parents to creative response in the child. God is never coercive, ever persuasive. This image of God's creative activity includes the notion 'in the fullness of time'. At each step in the

evolutionary process of the universe, or of a life, there is an appropriate response. There are no short cuts. A billion years ago there was no possibility then and there of humans becoming a reality on earth. A million years ago human values began to be realised, but there was no immediate possibility of a mature society then and there. A Jesus or a Buddha would have been an anachronism a million years ago. But not now. In the fullness of time they appeared out of their own societies and some were ready to respond to the call. The future of the universe at any stage of its history is conditioned by the past and awaits the spontaneity of the novel occasions as in their season they come into being.

Russell (1935) said that if he were God he would have skipped the millions of years of the dinosaurs and gone straight to man:

> Why the Creator should have preferred to reach His goal by a process, instead of going straight to it, these modern theologians do not tell us. Nor do they say much to allay our doubts as to the gloriousness of the consummation. It is difficult not to feel, as the boy did after being taught the alphabet, that it was not worth going through so much to get so little. (p. 80)

God is not a magician, though Russell seemed to think this was the main quality endowed upon God by theologians, even those who in his time had accepted the concept of evolution. But Russell's warped view of theism can be understood when so many theists want God to be a magician.

The ecological worldview of the divine as conceived as a persuasive agency and not a manipulative one should be looked upon, says Whitehead (1942 p. 196), as one of the greatest intellectual discoveries in the history of religion. It was plainly enunciated by Plato in his view that ideals are effective in the world and forms of order evolve. 'Can there be any doubt,' says Whitehead, 'that the power of Christianity lies in its revelation in act of that which Plato divined in theory?' (p. 197).

The essence of Christianity is the appeal to the life of Jesus as a revelation of the nature of God's activity in the world. Jesus rejected the notion of God as coercive power. Did that mean that God was powerless? The paradox is that there is a power in persuasive love. In commenting on this paradox Whitehead (1930) remarks:

> The life of Christ is not an exhibition of over-ruling power. Its glory is for those who can discern it, and not for the world. Its

power lies in its absence of force. It has the decisiveness of a
supreme ideal, and that is why the history of the world divides
at this point of time. (p. 47)

The world is still divided on this issue. Most people seem to
discern no way out of the rivalry between nations other than a
power struggle. Those who think differently seem but a small voice
in the shouting and the tumult. Their call must still be made. At the
time of the peace negotiations between the Americans and the
Russians during Carter's presidency, the pastor of Riverside Church
in New York, William Sloane Coffin, said to his fellow Americans:
'We must be meek otherwise there will be no-one to inherit the
earth'. The way of the world is by might. The way of the gospel is
not by might nor by power—but by persuasive love. In the end that
is the only power that counts. Divine creativity is a consequence of
divine Eros finding a response in the world.

We tend to worry about the cares of the world and the problems of the morrow. Jesus spoke of the caring God whose resources
are sufficient for every moment, yet so often blocked by us. He is the
one in whom 'we live and move and have our being' (Acts 17:28).
So too the lilies of the field don't toil to be what they are. They too
are what they are by their participation in the divine Eros. All life is
responsive to the divine love. The gospel proclaims a love in the
universe which meets human life and other life as sustainer and lure
to a fuller experience.

Speak to Him thou for He hears, and Spirit with Spirit can
meet—
Closer is He than breathing, and nearer than hands and feet.
            Alfred Lord Tennyson, 'The Higher Pantheism'

The power of the Christian gospel is the experience of divine love
that transforms life. We experience God first and then spend the rest
of our lives trying to understand that experience and its relevance to
the whole world. The God of the universe touches us as we experience life in its fullness. But God is vaster than our experience of
him. When I go down to the ocean and swim on its shores I get to
know one part of the ocean; its near end. But there is a vast extent
of ocean way beyond my ken that is nevertheless continuous with
that bit of the ocean I know. So it is with God. We touch God at the
near end, yet that same God extends into the farthest reaches of the
universe and there too is pervasive love. This is the full meaning of

incarnation. The universe exists by its incarnation of God in itself. It is the sort of universe in which God can be incarnate. God could not be incarnate in a machine! The divine Eros works in the universe through influence (literally meaning inflowing) as its universal mode of causation.

To see the universe as a whole in this way, with the same God working in the universe at large, and in the life of Jesus, and in the lives of all of us, was put in highly symbolic language by the apostle Paul in his letter about the 'Cosmic Christ' in Colossians 1. In verse 4 is the phrase 'In him all things hang together'. This affirmation is repeated no less than five times in this chapter. It was Paul's conviction that the same spirit which was in Jesus animated the whole universe. The universal principle of reality is the free act of experiencing. For many people in his time the world was a dualism. Not so for Paul. God is the God of 'all things'. Nature as well as human history is the theatre of grace.

This cosmic panorama is caught up in the prologue to Saint John's gospel and becomes particularly pointed in Bishop John Robinson's (1967) paraphrase:

The clue to the universe as personal was present from the beginning. It was to be found at the level of reality which we call God. Indeed, it was no other than God nor God than it. At that depth of reality the element of the personal was there from the start. Everything was drawn into existence through it, and there is nothing in the process that has come into being without it. Life owes its emergence to it, and life lights the path to man. It is that light which illumines the darkness of the sub-personal creation, and the darkness never succeeded in quenching it. That light was the clue to reality—the light which comes to clarity in man. Even before that it was making its way in the universe. It was already in the universe, and the whole process depended upon it, although it was not conscious of it. It came to its own in the evolution of the personal; yet persons failed to grasp it. But to those who did, who believed what it represented, it gave the potential of a fully personal relationship to God . . . And this divine personal principle found embodiment in a man and took habitation in our midst. We saw its full glory, in all its utterly gracious reality—the wonderful sight of a person living in uniquely normal relationship to God, as son to father. (p. 98)

Here is a picture of everything being alive with Life from the very beginning. Such is this particular biblical interpretation of the creative process. It was personal from the beginning, but that only becomes fully evident in the light of its manifestation in human persons. Always it was transcendent to the world. Always it was involved with the world, drawing the world to itself, brooding over the face of the earth.

This light flickered uncertainly within the church as it wavered from commitment to a view of the total involvement of God in the world to one restricted to humans alone. In the process both humanity and nature lost out, for neither nature, humanity nor God can be understood alone.

The divine Passion

The divine Eros draws the world to greater richness of experience as each individual entity responds to possibilities for itself. The divine Passion is the response of the divine to the realisation of value in the world. With each successive evolutionary step the possibility for the concrete realisation of a greater richness of experience becomes the greater. It is tiny for the electron and for whatever else existed soon after the big bang that brought the universe into existence. It reaches its heights in the human. All this is the activity of the creative love of God in the world. But we may ask —what value is achieved if, in the long run, our earth collapses into the sun and life on earth is no more and indeed if the universe collapses upon itself to where it was before the big bang? That there will come an end to our earth seems inevitable. What then of the purposes of God?

There are those who contend that they all fall to the ground. T. S. Eliot in 'The Hollow Men' puts it thus:

> This is the way the world ends
> Not with a bang but a whimper.

Russell (1961) puts it dramatically in his stoic faith:

> That man is the product of causes which had no prevision of the end they were achieving; that his origin, his growth, his hopes and fears, his loves and his beliefs, are but the outcome of accidental concatenations of atoms; that no force, no heroism, no intensity of thought or feeling, can presume an individual life beyond the grave; that all the labours of the age, all the

devotion, all the inspiration, all the noon-day brightness of human genius, are destined to extinction in the vast death of the solar system, and that the whole temple of Man's achievement must inevitably be buried beneath the debris of a universe in ruin ... all these things, if not quite beyond dispute, are yet so nearly certain, that no philosophy which rejects them can hope to stand. (p. 67)

Accepting all or most of this, Sartre contends that a man must give himself meaning in a universe that itself is devoid of meaning. But if we have no value for the cosmos then we have no value. To pretend we have is simply self-delusion. Hartshorne (1970b) aptly says: 'The idea that the universe is absurd or meaningless is itself absurd or meaningless. It expresses a living creature trying to deny its aliveness' (p. 317). The crux of the matter is precisely put by Cobb (1959):

What happens really matters only if it matters ultimately, and it matters ultimately only if it matters everlastingly. What happens can matter everlastingly only if it matters to him who is everlasting. Hence, seriousness about life implicitly involves faith in God. (p. 84)

We come face to face with the greatest adventure of the human spirit. It is the proposition, the faith and the conviction that God, in addition to being creative outgoing love, is also responsive love which is the divine Passion experiencing the world. This is Whitehead's doctrine of the consequent nature of God.

There are two sides to love. Love not only gives. Love also receives. 'I just want to be loved by you,' sang Marilyn Monroe. That's sick! To love is to be the recipient of love and to return love. Is the God of love an exception to this principle? On the contrary, God's love must be responsive or it is not love at all. Indeed, a God whose influence is divorced from responsiveness and sensitivity is irresponsible. Without that aspect of God's nature nothing is saved after the world comes to its end in a fiery furnace of the sun or in a frozen waste. All in the end is as futile as the pessimistic Ecclesiastes supposed: 'Oh what a weary task God has given mankind to labour at. I have seen everything that is done here under the sun, and what a vanity it is, what chasing of the wind ... Vanity of vanities. All is vanity. For all his toil under the sun, what does man gain by it?' (Ecclesiastes 1:13–17). A thoroughly depressing assessment of life and the world by a thoroughly depressing character. He was a kind of Old Testament Bertrand Russell, ruthlessly honest and rational, profoundly cynical and pessimistic. Frustrating and difficult, life and the world may be—futile, no!

The divine passion is God's feeling of the world as the world is created. As every entity 'feels' the lure of God and responds to that lure then God becomes concretely real in a way God was not concretely real before. And that new reality makes a difference to God. God is the one who cherishes all; 'unto whom all hearts are open', says the collect. With each creative advance, be it in cosmic evolution or in an individual life, God becomes different. Every individual experience has its consequence in the life of God.

In Whitehead's image God saves the world in his experience as a sort of memory. God saves all of value that has become concretely real. Whitehead described God's consequent nature as the adventure of God in the universe. Haught (1984) begins a chapter entitled 'The Cosmic Adventure' with the statement 'In God's feeling of the world it is saved from perishing' (p. 119). And Whitehead (1978) says:

> The image—and it is but an image—the image under which this operative growth of God's nature is best conceived, is that of a tender care that nothing is lost . . . He saves the world as it passes into the immediacy of his own life. It is the judgment of a tenderness which loses nothing that can be saved. (p. 346)

Something happens to the life of God as God saves the world in the divine experience. Whitehead speculates that at that moment God becomes conscious in a way God was not conscious before. God becomes conscious as the world is made and as he realises the actual world in the unity of his nature. In this sense, says Whitehead (1978), 'God is the great companion—the fellow sufferer who understands' (p. 351). A woman in New York had nursed for fourteen months with loving care an abandoned baby with AIDS. The baby eventually died in her arms. She told her friends afterwards that her urge to rage at a universe that could subject a fragile innocent child to such suffering was tempered only by the memory of some words of William Sloane Coffin: 'When tragedy occurs, God's heart is the first of all to break'. Our existence from moment to moment, all the joys and suffering, become one with the divine life. Is there any more ultimate meaning of existence than this?

Hartshorne (1948 p. 58) predicted that a new era in religion may come into being as soon as people grasp the idea that it is just

as true that God is the supreme beneficiary or recipient of achievement as he is the supreme benefactor or source of achievement. If
the divine life is indebted to no-one and can receive no value from
anyone, then to speak of serving God is to indulge in equivocation.
For the most part, the church, following Augustine, has preferred to
regard God as unchanged by the world. The world can add nothing
to God. How can you add anything to absolute perfection?

This is a peculiar concept of perfection—that if God is perfect
God cannot change. Yet if God is love and if that love is responsive,
God is not the unmoved mover of classical theism. God to be love
must be intimately affected by the plight and suffering of the world.
The proposition is that God's experience evolves as the world
evolves. Perfection is not static. It is dynamic. 'Be ye perfect' does
not mean, says Hartshorne (1967), 'be ye immutable' (p. 18). The
passage in scripture translated 'I am what I am' (Exodus 3:14) has
been used to support classical theism of an unchanging God, what
is sometimes called the doctrine of the impassability of God. But
two Japanese scholars Ariga (1959) and Tanaka (1984) discovered
that the text is better rendered 'I am what I am becoming', which
meaning was lost in the translation to the Greek and then to English. Their conclusion is that the biblical God does not stand aloof
and immutable from the historical processes of the world.

The impassability or 'apathy' of God is a principle of classical
theism and much Christian orthodoxy today. Yet according to the
Jewish biblical scholar Abraham J. Heschel, precisely the contrary
—'the pathos of God'—is the central idea of prophetic theology
(Merkle 1985 p. 494). Heschel tells a story of a diplomat from the
state of Israel who in the late 1940s went on an official mission to
Poland. It concerned the emigration of Jewish survivors of Nazi
concentration camps. After finishing his work in Warsaw, he left for
Paris and was given a compartment to himself on the overcrowded
train. Outside his compartment he noticed an emaciated, poorly
clad young Jew who could not find a seat on the train. The diplomat
invited the young man to join him in his compartment. It was
comfortable, clean, pleasant and the poor fellow came in with his
bundle, put it on the rack over the seat and sat down.

The diplomat tried to engage him in conversation, but he would
not talk. When evening came, the diplomat, an observing Jew, re-
cited the evening prayer. The other fellow did not say a word. The
following morning the diplomat took out his prayer shawl and said
his prayer. His companion who looked so wretched did not speak

or pray. Finally when the day was almost over, they started a conversation. The young man said, 'I am never going to pray any-more because of what happened to us in Auschwitz. How could I pray? That is why I did not pray all day.'

The following morning on this long train journey the diplomat was surprised when the young man suddenly opened his bundle, took out his prayer shawl, and started to pray. He asked him afterwards, 'What made you change your mind?' The young man replied: 'It suddenly dawned upon me to think how lonely God must be; look with whom he is left. I felt sorry for him' (recounted by Merkle 1985).

The story contains a profound and original insight which Abraham Heschel, who told it, makes explicit in this startling sen-tence: 'Faith is the beginning of compassion, of compassion for God'. Is God really lonely? If so, this implies God's need for others, It means God suffers.

The divine concern for the creation is expressed in various passages in the New Testament. Jesus says not a sparrow falls to the ground without God knowing. What could this mean but that God is involved in the life of the sparrow such that even the experiences of the sparrow are of value for God? The sparrow is but a representa-tive of all entities of the creation. Whitehead said the merest puff of existence has some significance for God. For there is no such thing as mere matter.

When the writer of Romans 8 speaks of the whole of the creation groaning and suffering in travail as in the agony of child-birth, he adds that God is not simply watching from afar as a theatrical producer might watch his play from the wings. God is in the drama, feeling every feeling in ways that words cannot express. God is no mere detached spectator of the ocean of feelings which is nature, but is the supreme synthesis of those feelings. So too, Hartshorne (1979) says that 'all life contributes to the living one who alone can appreciate life's every nuance. He experiences our experiences and those of all creatures. His feelings are feelings of all feelings' (p. 60). This is a feeling universe. Our own feelings are feelings of feelings. 'The chief novelty of the New Testament,' says Hartshorne (1967), 'is that divine love . . . is carried to the point of participation in creaturely suffering, symbolized by the Cross taken together with the doctrine of the Incarnation' (p. 104). He goes on to point out that concrete awareness of another's suffering can only consist in participation in that suffering. There is no other way. So

God is the great fellow sufferer who bears all the burdens of a creation in continuous travail. Has there been any deeper symbol of the nature of persuasive love and a love that feels all joys and all suffering than the Cross? The two doctrines, the incarnation of God in all things and the responsiveness of God to the experiences of the world, are at the heart of the Christian religion. God's experience of the world is Whitehead's doctrine of the consequent nature of God —the divine Passion. There is no more speculative aspect of Whitehead's thought than this concept. Metaphysical views such as this are not provable as a mathematical theorem might be. They are visions of the world and are to be judged by their comprehensiveness, consistency, logic and by their adequacy to illumine our actual experience.

The inside story of cosmic evolution

The proposition of this chapter is that as the cosmos evolves God as divine Eros, transcendent to the universe, becomes immanent within the new creation. This is God's presence in the world. In addition the world is present in God as the divine Passion responds to each new creation and each existing one. This is not the image of the world as a contrivance and God as the artificer working from a pre-planned blueprint of the future. It is an image of the world as organically related to God who provides the purposes and values of creation moment by moment, yet leaves the creation with its degree of freedom and self-determination. In this sense the future is not determined. It is open-ended. The possibilities of creativity are immense, but not all possibilities are relevant at any particular stage of the evolving cosmos. Indeed, the realisation of some possibilities necessarily excludes others. Our universe took the path of hydrogen and life as we know it. Maybe there are other universes which have taken another path and have life as we don't know it. But that is not our universe, nor could our universe break with its past and hove into one detached from its past. We are caught in the web of history. Yet our future is still open-ended within the realm of possibilities relevant to that history.

Whitehead (1930) said 'whatever suggests a cosmology suggests a religion' (p. 141). The cosmology of ancient biblical times suggested the religion of the early chapters of the Bible. The cosmology of Hinduism suggested the religion of the sacred writings of Hinduism. This is not to say that religion starts with a cosmology. It starts with experience that leads to a cosmology. The scientific world has produced a cosmology. It is now relevant to think of religion within the context of that cosmology. And in doing so we are not building a religion out of a cosmology but suggesting a religion relevant to that cosmology.

In the ecological model the evolution of the cosmos is the evolution of order at successive levels from chaos through atoms to complex living organisms. But according to the second law of thermodynamics the universe as a whole is moving from a stage of greater order to one of lesser order. There is said to be an increase in entropy. Entropy literally means transformation of energy. According to the second law, all the energy of the universe will eventually be converted into heat which will be evenly distributed throughout the universe. This means that no more work can be done, such as happens when simple arrangements of matter become more complexly ordered. Maximum entropy is the hypothetical state when everything will be at the same temperature and all processes will therefore have ceased and order is minimal. So the immediate question that arises is this—does the evolution of life from non-life run counter to the second law of thermodynamics, resulting, as it does, in local decreases in entropy? No it doesn't, because the earth is not a closed system. Energy reaches the earth from the sun. Increase in order of living matter on earth is gained at the expense of the sun, whose order decreases correspondingly ever so slightly. If the universe were not running down life would have no source of energy on which to draw. Perhaps we should be thankful then for the heat death of the universe. Without it we might not be here at all. But in the universe as a whole, entropy increases. There can still be local decreases in entropy, as happens with all living organisms while they are still alive and in some other situations as, for example, when complex organic molecules are made from their constituent atoms in outer space, as now seems to be the case.

The existence of the second law of thermodynamics and the existence of local enclaves of decreasing entropy, as is the case with life, means that less ordered systems within the whole system of the universe have become more ordered. But our religion has also to take into account the cosmological prediction that our world and its universe will not go on for ever. What then is the point of the evolution of complex order and all the novelty and richness of experience that is a consequence? In the ecological model what has been achieved of value in cosmic history is saved. It is saved in the consequent nature of God. The universe in its evolution is temporal. God who evolves with the universe is eternal. Without that our religion would, in the end, be empty. All purposes would be for naught. All value achieved would be as ephemeral as the flower that fades.

A modern cosmology suggests a religion that involves a God who evolves with the cosmos and who, whilst involved, is yet not finally dependent for his being upon it. Whitehead (1978) said: 'It is as true to say that God creates the world, as that the world creates God' (p. 384). God is created (in his consequent nature) by the world, but our world will eventually cease to be a source of creativity for God. Who knows, there may then be—indeed there may be now—other avenues for the infinite creativity of God. God in his consequent nature is dependent upon a world as the world is dependent upon God. But the world is fluent while God is permanent.

Wieman (1929 p. 213 *et seq.*) had an image far ahead of his time when he conceived the evolving cosmos in terms of a struggle for order with stability achieved at successive levels. There was a time, perhaps 20 billion years ago, when the association of elementary particles into atoms had achieved no stability. That epoch is now passed. The association of elementary particles into atoms has achieved marvellous stability with an adequacy of organisation such as to sustain their integrity through the shocks and strains of cosmic change. The frontier of the organisation of elementary particles into atoms has now passed.

The more complex and subtle association of atoms and molecules into cells in living organisms is not so firmly established. Here misfits occur. Nevertheless, there is an order and stability in living cells that has enabled them to endure the many shocks of change and circumstance since their first appearance, probably in some shallow tropical sea, three to four billion years ago. The frontier of life at the level of the cell is now passed. The organisation of cells into complex living organisms may have taken millions of years to achieve. Early on there were relatively simple aggregations of cells, such as we find in sponges today. Then came more complex assemblages in which the organism has greater unity and coordination, as in jellyfish and so on through the hierarchy of the animal kingdom from invertebrates through vertebrates—fish, amphibia, reptiles, birds and eventually mammals and ourselves. There is a stability at all these levels, yet not as secure as the association of atoms in molecules and elementary particles in atoms. But each

step is yet a basis for further advance to further levels of organisation. It is not a straight-line advance but one that has many
meanderings. Eventually, as a great river meanders to the sea, so
the river of life reaches higher levels of order.

In all these successions there is an outward evolution which
science can study and there is an inner evolution of experience
which only the individual entity, be it a proton or a person, itself
knows, together with God. Living cells certainly behave as though
aliveness is an experience for them. Sense organs first appeared
without much, if any, central coordination. The development of the
central nervous system and coordination of the sense organs must
have brought a new level of experience. The animal experience may
be partly conscious. This seems to be associated with the development of the central nervous system. It is the crossing of a great new
threshold of 'feeling' or 'experience'. At each stage we surmise that
the evolved entity is a subject, that is—an experiencing entity,
though not necessarily a conscious one in the way we are conscious.

In plants the assemblage and mutual coordination of cells may
enrich the feelings of an individual cell, but there is no indication of
any centralised feeling in the plant. The life of the plant is the life of
its individual cells and no more.

To some extent all animal experience functions for the sake of
purely bodily needs. In fulfilling the requirements of survival the
animal experiences the world. It also may enjoy that experience, as
when it is satisfying hunger. But as the brain becomes more complex we may surmise that the animal has experiences that go beyond
the mere service of the body. It may take risks for the sake of
enjoyment. In the case of humans a great deal of bodily activity is
performed without regard to its benefit to the body. We discipline
our bodies for the sake of distinctively human purposes. We may lay
down our lives for another. Indeed the whole of culture, in the sense
of acquired information that is handed from generation to generation by learning, is that sort of experience. We don't know when
such cultural activities became a dominant part of human life. Perhaps they became significant a hundred thousand years ago. When
that happened the human being had arrived. The unified human
experience with its consciousness through the life of the individual
and its dominance over strictly bodily needs is the human psyche.

There is a certain undisturbed harmony in the experience of the
cow in the fields or the well fed cat that enjoys a cared-for life in a
good home. The body is restricted from its spontaneous expression

only by external forces. But the human psyche introduced a certain disharmony into the human experience. Now the body could be inhibited from within and actions are deliberately taken which might be dangerous or uncomfortable. This is an example of what could be interpreted as 'the fall' (Birch & Cobb 1981 pp. 117, 136). Yet the 'fall' made possible far richer experience. With the appearance of the human psyche religion also appeared as life found time for reflection on the meaning of things. The human psyche crosses another threshold with the agricultural revolution some ten thousand years ago and the subsequent rise of cities. The new threshold was the emergence of rationality as an important factor in psychic life. The flow of water had to be controlled. Land had to be surveyed. All this required social organisation and planning. This was not an advance in intelligence. The Stone Age hunter was as intelligent as the Egyptian architect. Agriculture was a new use of intelligence. It paved the way for science and philosophy. The brain which had evolved largely as an organ of survival becomes used in ways that serve far more than bodily needs.

During the first millennium BC another threshold was crossed, another 'fall'. Apparently quite independently, spiritual leaders arose across the world in the sixth century BC. There lived then in China, Confucius and Lao-tzu, in India Gautama Buddha, in Persia Zoroaster. Thales and Pythagoras were founding Greek philosophy and the prophetic movement in Israel had reached a climax in second Isaiah (Cobb 1967 pp. 50–2). These leaders expressed and called for a quite new psychic development. Full self-consciousness appeared. Thus emerged rational religion as opposed to archaic systems of meaning. A new disharmony and conflict was thus introduced into human life. Furthermore the new ways differed among themselves and when they met, yet further conflict occurred. The upreach of the human spirit therefore was not without great cost. Every move forward seems to open up new possibilities of disharmony and evil. That is why each move forward is appropriately called a 'fall'. Much of the unity and harmony of life up to then was destroyed. But in its place there arose the possibilities of experiences that were quite beyond those that existed before. For more than two thousand years the teachings of these religions provided for most of the civilised world the norms in relation to which people took their bearings. New purposes became dominant in societies all over the world.

In the past two centuries this situation has changed. More and more of the world's leaders have given up seeking guidance from these ways. They have turned to science, philosophy, psychology and even drugs. Or they have denied the need for any direction at all. The ancient ways are far from dead, but they are in turmoil. That too may be a move forward if it leads to a reassessment of what is worth saving and how that can be brought to bear on modern understanding.

In the perspective of cosmic evolution it is here that the fighting frontier of progressive integration is now being waged. The life force, which is the divine Eros, is calling humanity to a new organisation of human societies. Here is where integration is most urgently needed. Here is where achieved integration is most incomplete and inadequate. So far as we know, human society is the utmost cosmic adventure toward creation of richer integrations with the possibility of richer human experience. Here is the great upreach toward values higher than any which have ever visited the realm of existence. Here the existing universe is groping out into the vast realm of the possibilities of God as yet unrealised on earth. Here the cosmic venture is under way. Here is where heaven and hell shimmer in a mirage of possibility. It follows that here is where the sufferings and joys of God and the creation must surely be most intense. This would appear to be the present frontier of cosmic evolution.

There was a time when the integration of electrons into atoms was the fighting frontier of progressive integration in the universe. There was a time later when the integration of atoms into cells and still later of cells into complex organisms was the outpost of organisation and increasing value in the universe. Those frontiers are now long passed. The storm now rages about the kind of association called human society. 'Religion of the noblest kind,' says Wieman (1929), 'is man's recognition of this creative cosmic struggle and his personal allegiance to the process of progressive integration' (p. 216). Therefore the religious person needs to be disciplined and equipped in body and mind for the task, with more calmness and mastery in the midst of peril and turmoil, more sensitivity and deeper insight into the bonds of interdependence that hold people together in rich community, a more passionate and richly integrated life purpose which can transmute the common things of daily experience.

All this we should have if we are to be the shock troops of the integrating process of the universe. All this we can have. For the divine Eros is the source of these gifts. And that is the only reason we have cause for hope. The future is not closed. It is open. The resources of God have not been exhausted. Faith is the conviction that there are values that have not yet visited this planet that are waiting to be appropriated. We do not need to go on as we are now. No man or woman need stay the way he or she is. No society need live for ever with the *status quo*. That God is involved and that we are involved in God does not mean that God will look after it all and all will be well. There could be a nuclear holocaust. God won't stop that. There is a real sense in which the future is in our hands. In the words of the Jewish scholar Abraham J. Heschel, 'God is waiting for us to redeem the world' (Merkle 1985 p. 495). For us to fail to respond to the forward call of life is not just a personal failure. It is a cosmic tragedy.

We need in a very special way to have hope, to have faith and to have love. Reinhold Niebuhr (1976) put it this way:

> Nothing that is worth doing is completed in a lifetime; therefore we must be saved by hope. Nothing which is true or beautiful or good makes complete sense in any immediate context of history; therefore we must be saved by faith. Nothing we do, however virtuous, can be accomplished alone. Therefore we are saved by love. (p. vii)

This chapter has been about purpose in cosmic perspective. It ends with our place in that cosmic scene. For all the creatures, for the human species, for each of us, life is to be enjoyed as it is lived, 'but,' says Hartshorne (1970b), 'its eventual worth will consist in the contribution it has made to something more enduring than any animal, or than any species of animal. The final beauty is the "beauty of holiness" ' (p. 321)—which beauty I take to mean the enrichment of the life of God.

CHAPTER 5

Purpose and Progress

Where there is no vision the people get out of hand.

Proverbs 29:18 (Jerusalem Bible)

Man cannot live without ideal aims which relate his endeavour and his suffering and his joy to something more lasting and more unitary than the sum of individual activities . . . Without such an aim he falls into cynicism or despair, by which the will to live is indefinitely nullified.

Charles Hartshorne (1948 p. 148)

I set before you life or death, blessing or curse. Choose life, then, so that you and your descendants may live.

Deuteronomy 30:19 (Jerusalem Bible)

O ur philosophy and our religion will be judged by their fruits. So we now ask in what way the philosophy and religion of the previous chapters illumines the momentous practical problems of our time. Ours is a time of three momentous tensions: the tension between war and peace, between social injustice and social justice, and between industrialisation and ecological sustainability. These tensions are global. So destructive are they that many now wonder whether what we call progress will lead eventually to our demise and the demise of the planet.

The meaning of progress in the modern world

Despite differences in ideology and political system, every nation in the world wants one sort of progress. Every nation, rich or poor, is intent upon increasing its economic growth in material goods and services. A measure of progress in these terms is the size of the gross national product per person. This ranges from $160 in the poorest countries (Bangladesh and Ethiopia) to $18,000 in the U.S.A. and Switzerland, which are the richest countries in the world (1988 figures). The rich countries want to become richer and the poor want to become rich. The rich nations have become rich by their dedication to the use of science and technology to produce things. The poor want to do the same. The idea of progress in the modern world is closely tied up with a belief that science and technology will open up an infinite cornucopia of goods to replace the ones we use up. In the case of petroleum we shall have consumed in less than a century nature's endowment for all time. Some forty years hence, eight or more billion human beings will have to co-exist on this small planet and will have to find energy, food and other resources to maintain their societies. There are signs that resources, one of which is the pollution absorption capacity of the planet, may not suffice for the five billion human beings already on the earth. Yet we are told to have faith in science and technology. They will deliver new goods as yet undreamed of. When fossil fuels run out we shall have invented ways of using the energy of the sun to drive our industries. And when all the iron ore is gone we shall invent plastics to take its place. The technological optimist tells us that a breakthrough a day keeps the crisis at bay. Science and technology are our cargo cult.

So there was a sense of outrage when the Club of Rome produced its report entitled *Limits to Growth* (Meadows et al. 1972), which gave reasons for supposing that the goal of economic growth in material goods had limits, despite the possibilities of progress of science and technology in the future. This marked the beginning of serious concern of nations about the 'sustainability' of the earth if current ideas of progress were persisted with indefinitely. New ecological movements called for a redirecting of attitudes and the discovery of new values for the future, if there was to be a future (Birch 1976).

By the eighties it became clear that the greatest threat to the sustainability of the earth for future generations was the application of science and technology for war. The ecological movements became peace movements as well. Peace and ecological sustainability became closely linked. This was not only because of the enormous amount of resources that the military in all countries were using up but also the ultimate threat of a nuclear war that might, in one stroke, destroy the life-support systems of the earth. These are the biological systems that ensure that we have food and water and breathable air. Estimates were made that the deployment of even one-tenth of the nuclear arsenals of the 1980s could lead to a 'nuclear winter' over most, if not all, of the planet. Nuclear war would not only kill us directly by blast and radioactive fallout. It would also destroy the life-support systems of the earth (Ehrlich & Sagan 1984). By the late 1980s it became clear that global atmospheric pollution causing both the greenhouse effect and the hole in the ozone layer had become critical threats to life on earth (Henderson-Sellers & Blong 1989). The year 1989 marks the year in which, throughout the world, environmental issues moved from being politically peripheral to being central.

Modernity and its conception of progress had dead-ended in world wars, the Holocaust, genocide, the exploitation of Third World countries, the increasing pollution of the earth, the disappearance of resources and the terrible spectre of omnicide. Progress through technology began to sound like the empty clanging of a funeral bell.

It was clear to many of us that peace and ecological sustainability were to be forever closely related. Furthermore, both are tied to the issue of justice and injustice. In the 1970s there was much talk about a new international economic order that would redress the injustice of poverty-stricken nations alongside rich nations that were overdeveloped. In the 1980s this theme is sadly muted. There is no global consensus that the world is a community and should be made more tolerable for all its people. The rich are intent upon becoming richer because they see in wealth their source of power to maintain their prestige and position amongst nations.

So when the Club of Rome produced its second major report on the state of the world (Mesarovic & Pestel 1974) its central proposition went unheeded. Restated in 1984 it was as follows:

> It is a well-established fact that in the world's developed, industrialised regions material consumption has reached proportions of preposterous waste. In those regions there must now be a relative decline in the use of various materials. On the other hand in some less fully developed regions, there must be substantial growth in the use of some essential commodities, either for food production or for industrial production. (p. 235)

The critical problem, as Mesarovic and Pestel (1984) and Pestel (1989) saw it, was how to make a global transition from undifferentiated growth all round to organic growth in which some nations ceased to grow in the use of material resources while others grew faster.

Not only do the powerful nations resist the concept of organic growth of nations involving a curbing of their own growth, but traditional economists refuse to take seriously the need for an economics of sustainability. Traditional economics in both capitalist and socialist countries is based on the notion that economic growth was a good that could be continued indefinitely. It gave little, if any, attention to the idea of an economics that took into account limits to material growth. A few economists—they are outstanding exceptions—have worked on an economics for a sustainable society. These include Boulding (1971), Daly and Cobb (1989), Daly (1977), and Leontief, Carter and Petri (1977).

What confronts the modern world is not a series of separate crises but a single basic defect, a fault that lies deep in the design of modern society. Too many people want too many things too quickly, with little concern for the sustainability of the earth on which all depend. Justice for all, peace and sustainability are interconnected. One cannot be achieved without the others. 'Peace,' said Allan Boesak, the human rights campaigner in South Africa, 'is more than the absence of war, it is the pursuit of active justice.' There can be no justice without sustainability and no sustainability without justice. Science and technology won't save us. But together a new science and technology and a new economics and politics informed by an ideal other than unlimited growth and power might.

The world of modernity, which Alvin Toffler dubs 'the second wave', has dominated Western consciousness since the Enlightenment. 'That wave is receding now and leaving on the beach the debris of abstract thinking, compartmentalised knowledge, warring specialisms, fragmented facts, and a general sense of alienation between human consciousness and wider reality' (Peters 1985 p. 193). A third wave about to break upon us is the wave of postmodernity.

The meaning of progress in the postmodern world

The word progress derives from the Latin *gressus*, which means step. Progress means stepping from a less satisfactory state to a more satisfactory one. The Judaeo-Christian tradition is steeped in the idea of a movement from an unfulfilled state to a more fulfilled one. In classical theism, destiny is in the hands of God. Renaissance man and Enlightenment man refurbished this concept of progress, putting man at the rudder to direct the course of the future. Out of this presupposition of the concept of progress arose the Renaissance utopian writings, the anticipation of *outopos* or no place in history, yet nevertheless expected. In utopias man creates the world anew and improves it through his own exertions. He begins as a tenant or lodger in the world and ends up as its landlord. And as his environment improves so, it alleges, will he. Men look forward, never backward and seldom upward.

Two world wars and the threat of nuclear war led to the demise of crusading utopias. Instead there appeared what Tillich (1966 p. 70) calls negative utopias such as Aldous Huxley's *Brave New World* and George Orwell's *1984*. Here the future is painted in terms not of fulfilment but of dehumanisation.

Today we need a new assessment of the concept of progress in the light of the dashing of utopian hopes and liberal optimism. We see only through a glass darkly. No-one in our age was more perceptive about this than Reinhold Niebuhr. In *Discerning the Signs of the Times* he expounded on the passage from 2 Kings 19:3: 'This is a day of trouble, and of rebuke, and blasphemy: for the children are come to the birth, and there is not strength to go forth'. Niebuhr (1946) wrote:

> We are living in an age between the ages in which children are coming to birth, but there is not strength to bring forth. We can

see clearly what ought to be done to bring order and peace into the lives of the nations; but we do not have the strength to do what we ought. A few hardy optimists imagine that the end of the Second World War represents the end of our troubles; and that the world is now firmly set upon a path of peace. Yet it does not require a very profound survey of the available historical resources to realise that our day of trouble is not over; in fact this generation of mankind is destined to live in a tragic era between two ages. It is an era when 'one age is dead and the other is powerless to be born'. The age of absolute national sovereignty is over; but the age of international order under political instruments, powerful enough to regulate the relations of nations and to compose their competing desires, is not yet born. The age of 'free enterprise', when the new vitalities of a technical civilisation were expected to regulate themselves, is also over. But the age in which justice is to be achieved, and yet freedom maintained, by wise regulation of the complex economic interdependence of modern man, is powerless to be born. (pp. 39–40)

Niebuhr went on to attribute modern man's lack of strength to bring forth the historical new birth to lower and narrower loyalties which stand over against newer and wider ones. The powerful nations, for example, are not single-minded in their desire to maintain the peace of the world. They undoubtedly desire peace but each also desires to preserve or enhance its own power and influence. They speak glibly of their passion for peace and justice, yet so obviously betray interests which contradict peace and justice. They are as yet unprepared to create the kind of moral and political order which a technical civilisation requires. The self-righteousness of the great powers will resist efforts at greater justice. This is the conflict between the urge to live and the urge to power (see pp. 13–15).

There are plenty of reasons for giving up hope in a better future. What then are the reasons for being hopeful at all? How can I hope when the cards seem stacked against the future? The initial reaction of some people to the world's problems is refusal of serious belief. I can deny that the situation is really that bad. Surely the authorities with power and knowledge at their disposal will take care of the situation. For me it will be business as usual. The future I suppose will really be much like the past. So I try to put out of my mind the apocalyptic threats under which I live. For others the recognition of the awfulness of the situation breaks down their defences. Their reaction is then one of despair. Isn't history, they ask, just a succession of opening of doors in Bluebeard's castle? What use is it for me to attempt the impossible task of altering the course of history, especially when my influence is so slight? It is important to recognise the similarity of these two responses— complacency and despair. Their results are the same. They let me off the hook. I am left free to eat, drink and be merry. If I am booked to travel on the *Titanic* I may as well travel first-class!

Saint Paul declared 'We are perplexed, but not unto despair'. One might divide the world, commented Niebuhr (1946 p. 169) into those who are not perplexed, those who are perplexed unto despair, and those who are perplexed but not unto despair. Those who are not perplexed have dissolved all the perplexities of life by some simple and cheap scheme of meaning. The scheme is always too simple to do justice to the depth of man's problems. When life reveals itself in its full terror these little schemes of meaning break down. Optimism or complacency gives way to despair.

Against complacency and despair there is the attitude of perplexed but not unto despair. This is the attitude of realistic hope. There is a light that shines in the darkness. Reason does not light that light. Hope never did rest on proven facts and rational assessments. The facts may be on the side of the pessimists. What then gives hope its light to penetrate the darkness? It is the conviction that the future is not yet determined. It is open-ended. Why believe the future is open-ended? For me it is the conviction that there are values of existence that I but dimly see, that have not as yet visited this planet, yet they are waiting as it were to become concretely real. Human values waited for millennia after the origin of life before the fullness of time for their concrete expression on this earth. The concept of the fullness of time is a critical one in our reassessment of the meaning of progress. The fullness of time means that conditions are appropriate for something that was potentially possible to become concretely real. So far as human relations are concerned, that has to do with two sets of relations, those we have with our neighbours and those we have with the rest of the creation.

We live in two orders. One is the order of the world as it is now. The other is the possibilities of the future as it might be. Possibilities are creative influences in society. They are not made by us. They are appropriated by us. We have an eros toward them. They have a persuasive lure toward us. The point is that to have hope is to feel the call of the possibilities of the future pressing in upon us, blocked only by us. What gives hope its power is not demonstrated facts. It comes from something that empowers us.

Hope is the refusal of despair. Despite oppression, suffering, grief and death, hope need never die. The one who hopes seeks openings, endures failure, and still seeks new openings for fresh efforts. In the depths of the Depression, Franklin Delano Roosevelt said the only thing we had to fear was fear itself. Today, facing the many things that would hurl us into the abyss, we might say analogously, our only hope is hope itself. If we act with complacency and despair there is no hope. If instead we hope, the future lies before us full of uncertainties and risks, yet containing the creative power of hope. What holds men back is not the pressure of reality but the absence of hope. To hope is to stay open to possibilities.

In place of utopianism which sees the new world just around the corner, and in place of progressivism which sees progress as inevitable, we can think of progress in terms of possibilities that are realistically appropriate for this present moment. We keep ourselves open to these possibilities. The Greek term *kairos* refers to the right time, the time in which something decisive happens, the fulfilled moment. There is a 'power in history', says Whitehead (1966), '. . . belonging to each historic epoch, the character of a drive toward some ideal, to be realised within that period. This ideal is never realised, it is beyond realisation, and yet it moulds the form of what is realised' (p. 120). Can we discern the signs of the times and let ourselves be instruments of new values that could transform just this small slice of history of which we are a part? Maybe the slice of history relevant for me is the present moment when I can react creatively instead of negatively to the tasks in hand.

We can't short-circuit history with gigantic jumps from the present into a new future. One step at a time at the right time is what we are called to take. The step may seem small and our numbers few. But there is such a thing as the leaven in the loaf. This is the small component that makes the whole loaf rise. The great reforms of the past were minority movements that worked by degrees until some sort of critical threshold was passed and reform became inevitable. The Quakers organised the first anti-slavery society in Philadelphia in 1775. It was a citizens' movement based on moral and ethical principles which eventually swept the world. Slavery was a long-accepted institution. It was abolished. Our hideous preoccupation with death in the form of war is an accepted institution at present. That calls for a similar effort of abolition. And so with all institutions of injustice in the world. The goal may seem unrealistic. But the abolition of slavery was also at one time regarded as impossible.

The vanguard of reformers for peace, justice and ecological sustainability are not the political leaders. They are the grassroots movements fighting poverty, political oppression and environmental destruction across the world. In the late 1980s there were, for example, in Bangladesh 1200 indigent grassroots movements, in Brazil 100,000 Christian communities with three million members committed to land reform and the elimination of poverty, and in Indonesia 600 independent groups working on environmental protection (Durning 1989).

Eight fallacies of the modern world

In this section we draw together fallacies inbuilt in the modern worldview, some of which have been alluded to in the previous chapters. And suggestions are made of some axioms for a postmodern worldview. The last two sections drew a contrast between the concept of progress in the modern worldview and progress in the postmodern worldview. The modern worldview has come to mean the view that has become increasingly dominant since the seventeenth century with the rise of science. It incorporates a strong legacy from the Enlightenment which shaped an understanding of science in conflict with dogma, superstition and an authoritarian church. It is a worldview based on a science that understands the world in terms of a mechanistic philosophy. Science has made the difference between a pre-scientific world of superstition and the modern world with all the products of its technology. The benefits of the scientific–technological world have been immense (Brown 1986). But it has had its costs. This is largely because it has been tied to a mechanistic philosophy with an ultimate faith in the capacity of science and technology to solve our problems. The world becomes a factory for churning out products. Secondly, it is deficient as a total worldview and has left us in a dilemma about ethics, values and purposes. We are seeing now the exhaustion of modernity.

In a postmodern worldview the world is not primarily seen as a factory existing for the purpose of making goods. Nor does it view the world in mechanistic or materialistic terms. It is not a 'substance' view of reality. It views progress as a step-by-step process in fulfilment of spiritual possibilities. What matters is not growth in power and possessions but in richness of experience of all that lives. In other words its objective is healthy people in a healthy environment with healthy relations between people and their environment. What then are some of the fallacies inbuilt in the modern worldview?

1. The fallacy of misplaced concreteness
This is a fallacy enunciated by Whitehead (1933 pp. 64, 72) of identifying an abstraction with the concrete or real. To say that the human has some machine-like properties is correct. To say the human is a machine is to commit the fallacy of misplaced concreteness. Besides having bones that operate like levers and a heart that has pump-like properties, a human being experiences and feels and wonders. The fallacy has terrible consequences when we proceed to treat human beings and animals as machines and manipulate them as such. They key word, says Habgood (1968), is respect. We respect the person who made the machine. The machine itself doesn't warrant respect.

The fallacy of misplaced concreteness is sometimes called the fallacy of reification. To reify is to 'thingify'. It is the idea that a particular sort of behaviour (being aggressive) or an institution is subject to the laws of mechanics. It is the cardinal fallacy of some forms of sociobiology that would reduce all behaviour to genes.

Another variant of the fallacy of misplaced concreteness is the so-called 'naturalistic fallacy'. It is classically the fallacy of trying to derive human 'ought' from what 'is' in the non-human world. It is a fact that in nature there is a 'struggle for existence'. As Darwin showed, of all the individual plants and animals that are born into the world, very few survive to maturity. Most die soon after they come into the world. Some argue that since the 'struggle for existence' is a 'law of the jungle' it must be a law for humans too. This is 'social Darwinism'. The argument was used by Mussolini to justify his invasion of Abyssinia. The mistake is to suppose that ideas of justice can be derived from the jungle. The history of humanity is, in part, a history of human victories over 'nature', of disease being eradicated and deserts made to bloom. Nature in some of its aspects may be 'red in tooth and claw', as Tennyson said, but that is no reason for humans to kill each other. To be civilised is the opposite. The 'naturalistic' fallacy consists in making false connections and in equating a mere aspect of nature with the whole of life.

The term 'naturalistic fallacy' is unfortunate. It gives the impression of a division between the natural and the human. The emphasis of this book is that the nature of the universe, the nature of nature, the nature of the human and the nature of God are one. It is not a case of non-human nature being natural, of human nature being non-natural nor of God as super-natural.

2. The genetic fallacy

Much of the opposition to the idea of evolution in the nineteenth century derived from a revulsion against the idea that humans were descended from ape-like creatures long ago. The opponents of evolution said that humans were not apes, not even transformed apes. Humans can't have such a lowly origin. I remember, as a school boy, hearing a sermon entitled 'Man—an ape or an angel?' I was offered no other choice. The genetic (genesis meaning origin) fallacy is the supposition that the origin of something (or an idea) settles the question of its falsehood or its truth. Not even the highest religions had an immaculate conception. The Judaeo-Christian tradition as found in the Bible reveals an evolution of ethics and an evolution of the idea of God. The genetic fallacy is not so much a fallacy common within the scientific community as it is of the community at large as it seeks to interpret science.

3. The prosaic fallacy

This is refusal to attribute feeling to things that do in fact feel (Hartshorne 1977 p. 95). The world is not as tame as our sluggish convention-ridden imaginations imply. The most important thing about us is that we have feelings. That is how I know that I am. What we feel is what gives value to our lives. To be alive is to feel. To be alive intensely is to feel intensely. The urge to live is fundamental to life. This we may accept about ourselves. But what of non-human nature? I have argued that experience or feeling in some sense, however attenuated, is characteristic of all individual entities, not simply people (see Chapters 2 and 3). The world is much more a feeling world than a superficial view tends to make of it. The postmodern ecological worldview does not propose that all things are or have minds, but that all concrete physical things are themselves feeling entities or are composed of feeling entities.

I once had a discussion with an astronomer who said there was only one obstacle to his becoming a panpsychist: he believed it would require him to suppose that the solar system was an organism (i.e., a feeling entity). The panpsychist or mentalist has the problem of explaining away the negative things—lack of feelings in rocks and solar systems. The physicalist has the problem of explaining away the positive things—our feelings.

There are at least four reasons for thinking that aggregates such as rocks, chairs, the solar system and computers are devoid of mind and feeling (Hartshorne 1977 p. 91):

First, their inertness. They don't seem to do anything. (Computers obey orders given them in mathematical form but they hardly get about doing things.)

Second, their lack of freedom in the sense of initiative and creative departure from mere routine. The predictability of the movement of the planets in the solar system is an example.

Third, their lack of individuality in the sense of unity and uniqueness. If a chair has parts such as pieces of wood and screws, why assign feeling to the whole chair rather than to each piece of wood or screw? The whole chair and the screw are in the same category of being aggregates. The same holds for the transistors and circuits in a computer.

Fourth, their lack of apparent intrinsic purpose. A chair and a computer have an instrumental purpose imposed on them by humans. They have no intrinsic value or purpose in themselves. The case is quite different for individual entities, as we have argued in earlier chapters.

It follows that feeling entities are identified by their activity, their freedom or initiative, their individuality of action and by their having intrinsic purpose and intrinsic value.

The opposite of the prosaic fallacy is the pathetic fallacy. This is to attribute feelings to things that don't feel, such as rocks and chairs (Hartshorne 1977 p. 95). By attributing feeling to natural entities we are not going back to a primitive animism that made no distinction between what feels and what does not feel, though some critics of panpsychism fail to appreciate the difference.

4. The fallacy of a posteriori reasoning

A geographer might be struck by just how fit the Amazon River is for its valley. It flows exactly in the right direction, with exactly the needed contours and tributaries, to ensure the draining of waters from the Andes and Mato Grosso in Brazil. In doing so it passes conveniently by every wharf and town on its route and its tributaries pass conveniently under every bridge. The geographer might attempt to replace the Amazon River in his imagination by the

Mississippi River. Superimposing the Mississippi River upon a map of Brazil he would notice that it flows from north to south. This would not work as it would flow into the interior of the country and over the mountains. Even when he turned it in the right direction he would notice many difficulties, the chief one being that it did not at all fit the drainage basin of Amazonia. He would conclude the Mississippi was unfit and the Amazon eminently fit for its purpose. This is *a posteriori* reasoning. It supposes that the Amazon River was designed especially to fit the Amazonian region. In fact the Amazonian topography is the cause of the particular course and shape of the river and its tributaries.

The so-called 'strong anthropic principle' (see p. 70) is another example of *a posteriori* reasoning. Physicists who invoke this principle tell us that the physical properties of matter and the universe at large are those that are conducive to life. Had they been just a tiny bit different, life as we know it would not have been possible. The strong anthropic principle asserts that the universe was made to fit life. The biological principle of evolution argues the opposite, that life evolved to fit the environment.

A posteriori reasoning leads to the notion of preordained design. This concept is strongly tied to the theistic version of the modern worldview. Classical theism is characterised by a mechanical universe with God outside it. The order of nature is more wonderful than that. The entities themselves are involved in their own design (see pp. 41–44) by virtue of their own degree of freedom to choose. They are not simply at the mercy of some external designer, not even their external environment. They too help to create their own environment. This is, of course, especially true of humans. The organism is not simply clay in the hands of a potter. It has itself its degree of self-determination in response to influences that impinge upon it. This is its freedom. There is no freedom in an *a posteriori* universe.

5. *The fallacy of objectivity*
The fallacy of objectivity is the notion that science is objective in the sense that subjectivity does not enter into the scientific analysis. Yet any issue in science that is at all complex can be interpreted in a number of ways. Which side of the explanation one comes down on is a matter of subjective judgment. When all the facts that can be garnered are in, subjective judgments have to be made because not all the facts are in or can ever be unearthed, and facts anyway have

to be interpreted (Andrewartha & Birch 1984 pp. 190–1). A good scientist, as compared with the average (mediocre) one, is more often correct in his assessments of which facts are relevant. Secondly, a good scientist sees connections between facts others don't see. A theory is valued primarily not for the extra facts it tells us but for the way it connects up the facts we already know. This connecting up is a way of seeing facts. It depends upon the observer. There are no mechanical rules for that.

What are facts? Often there is no agreement on what the facts are. This is irksome for politicians and for the public. They have difficulty in understanding why experts disagree, whether it be on the safety of particular procedures for disposing of radioactive wastes or on the chance of a herbicide producing deformities in new-born babies.

What we choose to call a fact is strongly conditioned by our interests and biases. Whoever said 'You can't argue with facts' cannot have been reading scientific journals or for that matter the daily newspapers. Let us assume that we could, for any particular problem, amass all the pertinent facts and work through these difficulties. What then? No mere accumulation of facts can tell us how to decide on the definition of clinical death, whether a human foetus is a human being, whether aversion therapy for homosexuals is good, or whether the risks of nuclear power outweigh the benefits. All such decisions involve more than facts. They involve assessment of uncertainties and values.

Western man has had his excessively empirical moments when he thought the truth somehow sprang miraculously from heaps of data. He has also had his excessively authoritarian moments when he thought that ethical and social decisions could be made by consulting a list of norms or axioms. Both approaches are defective.

Facts and values cannot be so neatly separated. It is rare to have a discussion on ethical issues in science without someone asking 'Is that a fact or a value judgment?', as though it cannot be a fact that Hitler was a bad man. Value-laden facts enter the domain of science as well as of ethics. This becomes patently clear when consultations are called to bring together scientists and ethicists on such issues as nuclear power or genetic engineering. It is never a matter of scientists putting their facts on the table and having them shuffled around by ethicists according to the rules of the game. Good decision making requires access to pertinent information, recognition that in practice facts are not value-free, a human sensitivity to values, uncommon sensibilities and common-sense. And all this needs to be done in the context of private evaluation and public discussion (Shinn 1982 Chapter 12).

The modern worldview, as we have defined it, depends largely upon a mechanistic and materialistic image of the world derived from a particular interpretation of science. Because of this, science fails to bestow values on the facts with which it deals. An increasing number of commentators say that the main problems we face in a world moulded by the modern worldview result from a scientific technology divorced from religious inspiration. Both the objectives of science and the spirit of investigation are very different when this divorce is not made and science is not simply investigation for the sake of investigation or for satisfying one's curiosity. But that would be a different science from the one we know today.

The failure of science and technology to bestow values on the facts with which they deal contributes to a world-wide malaise or sense of meaninglessness. Our technological rationality is letting us down. The loudest advocates for creationism as opposed to evolution in the U.S.A. are not from uneducated backgrounds. They are middle-class citizens who are technically trained. Fundamentalist religious beliefs tend to flourish in those parts of the U.S.A. that have recently become centres of high-tech industries such as southern California and Texas (Nelkin 1977). The people who work in these industries feel let down by the image of the world their technology gives them. And so they are.

Science and technology as such will not save the world. The problems of world hunger, poverty and war will not be overcome by the application of more of the same sort of science and technology. 'Science will solve it' is the cry of the technological optimist. It is pretty plain to see that this approach has failed to solve our problems. And the reason again is that our most difficult problems involve values and purposes. Different people have different values and purposes. We need to be more than experts. The ultimate issue in education is not the multiplication of more and more specialised skills, important though they be. It is how all the interests and vitality of life can be integrated into some sort of meaningful purpose and effort. The 'is' of life and the 'ought' of life are bound together. Indeed one wonders how much longer scientific investigation and technology can survive without a more fully developed conscience on the part of scientists. We need as well a fundamental change in the mind set of teachers of science at all levels (Gosling & Musschenga 1985). That subject is explored further in Chapter 6.

6. The dogmatic fallacy

To think is to tie one's thoughts together in some implicit system, however vague or simple that might be. Those who think profoundly may be more explicit about the system that holds their thoughts together. Progress in thinking is very largely a result of the discordance of competing systems of thought. Certainly in science a clash of ideas is not a disaster. It is an opportunity for further exploration. Whitehead (1942 p. 171) points out that the history of European thought to modern times has been tainted by a fatal misunderstanding. He calls this the dogmatic fallacy. The error consists in supposing that we can produce notions about complex issues that are adequately defined. Karl Popper (1971) would seem to agree. 'I have proclaimed the emptiness of definitions for thirty years,' he said, 'and I have refuted the superstition that if we want to be precise we have to define our terms' (p. 11). An exaggerated interest in words and definitions leads to empty verbalism.

During the medieval epoch in Europe theologians were the chief offenders in respect of the dogmatic fallacy. The Enlightenment was a reaction against theological dogmatism. During the last three centuries the bad pre-eminence in this habit of theologians has passed to scientists. This is surprising in view of the history of science which sees the successive collapse of dogmas. Newtonian science has given way in part to Einstein and relativity. Modern quantum theory challenges both. It is surprising for a second reason. The hallmark that differentiates a real scientist from a fraud is the moral quality of daring to be shown to be wrong. To insist that the universe is a machine or that the human being is a machine is dogmatism. Dogmas are dogmas whether they have to do with science or theology. Dogmas we don't need. Convictions we do need. The difference is that dogmatists are not willing to be challenged. Those who hold convictions without being dogmatic about them are willing to be challenged. Aristotle said his own philosophy was an attitude in the face of ignorance. 'There is,' said Whitehead (1933), 'a Nemesis which waits upon those who deliberately avoid avenues of knowledge. Oliver Cromwell's cry echoes down the ages, "My brethren, by the bowels of Christ I beseech you, bethink you that you may be mistaken" '(p. 20). The apathy of many people is a sort of dogmatic slumber from which they need to be awakened into an intellectual rebirth. In the words of William Blake, 'May God us keep from single vision and Newton's sleep'.

7. The fallacy of the perfect dictionary

'Seek simplicity but distrust it,' said Whitehead. The fallacy of the perfect dictionary holds that language in single words or phrases expresses accurately the fundamental ideas of science, philosophy, faith or politics (Whitehead 1966 p.173). There are fuzzy edges to an understanding of any complex issue. Sometimes our reach exceeds our grasp and words cannot yet express what we know.

There are two aspects to an understanding, and especially a scientific understanding, of the world. One is imagination. Without that there is no science. Imaginative ideas tie together what would otherwise be isolated facts. A theory is no more a heap of facts than a house is a pile of bricks. The second is criticism. Not all ideas are equally worthy of attention. The scholar is able to bring observation, imagination and criticism together in ideas that are expressed accurately, yet not too neatly tied up into final bundles. Catchphrases have their role in catching the attention of people. But they are not enough without the next step, which is to pursue the deeper meaning (when there is one) behind the words. Catchwords and phrases are not short cuts to proper understanding. There is more in the universe than meets the eye. In scientific circles one often hears reference to the principle of Ockham's razor. The Australian Broadcasting Corporation has a popular radio program in science called 'Ockham's razor'. William of Ockham (1270–1349) was a famous Franciscan opponent of the papacy. He was probably influenced by his Franciscan forbears, Grosseteste and Roger Bacon, sharing their strong interest in the way knowledge is gained by measurements and experiments. His famous 'razor'—'entities are not to be multiplied beyond necessity' (Raven 1953a p. 74)—is a principle of parsimony fundamental to logic. Unfortunately it is often misinterpreted to imply that the simple explanation is more likely to be true than the complex one. That, of course, is nonsense. The simple explanation may have a greater appeal than the complex, but there is no reason why it should be truer.

Scientists need to be on their guard in this respect as much as anyone. A great student of the nervous system was Ramon y Cajal, who was awarded the Nobel Prize in 1906 for his work. In his autobiography he reflected on an error made early in his career when he was seduced by a very simple concept about nerves:

I wish to warn young men against the invincible attraction of theories which simplify and unify seductively. We fall into the trap all the more readily when the simple schemes stimulate and appeal to tendencies deeply rooted in our minds, the congenital inclination to economy of mental effort and the almost irresistible propensity to regard as true what satisfies our aesthetic sensibility. (quoted by Witkowski 1986 p. 52)

Today countless sects and movements compete for our attention with their simplistic phrases purporting to provide a recipe to cure all our ills. This applies also to the mainline religions when contestants wage battles with competing biblical texts instead of engaging in any real thought. It is well to remember the statement of the American essayist H. L. Mencken: 'To every human problem there is a solution that is simple neat and wrong!'

8. The 'bricks to Babel' fallacy of knowledge

Arthur Koestler called his last collection of essays *Bricks to Babel* (1982). The reference, of course, is to the biblical tower of Babel in which brick was to be piled upon brick for the tower to reach the heavens. 'We seem to be compelled,' wrote Koestler, 'to shape facts and data, as we know them, into hard bricks, and stick them together with the slime of our theories and beliefs. And thus we continue to carry bricks to Babel' (p. 685). This is the view that knowledge grows by accumulation. There is another view: that knowledge grows by reorganisation. You don't add bricks to an old building. You tear down much of its structure and rebuild from the foundations, even to the extent of laying new foundations.

The modern worldview has put its faith in experts, each producing bricks of knowledge they hope will stick together with bricks from other disciplines. The general idea has been that if society has well-trained experts in all the disciplines the experts would guide us into truth and right action. It has not worked out that way. Instead we have a sea of information in which we are drowning. Since this fallacy goes deep into the educational systems of the modern world we pursue it further in Chapter 6.

In summary: fallacies of the modern worldview have to do with the conception of the world as substance or machinery, mistaking abstractions for reality, confusing origins and truth, failing to attribute feeling to things that feel, recognising ethics as exclusively anthropocentric, thinking backwards, objectifying facts as separated

from values, reducing the complex to the simple and dividing knowledge into distinct disciplines that produce experts who are often
wrong. In short, the errors of the modern worldview are that it is
mechanistic, dualistic, substantialist, anthropocentric, simplistic
and disciplinary. Quite a list of errors!

Five axioms for a postmodern worldview

The priorities of the modern worldview are reversed in the
postmodern worldview. In *The Death of Nature* Carolyn Merchant
(1980) calls for a saving of the best that the Scientific Revolution
and the Enlightenment have bestowed upon the world and a rejec-
tion of much of the mechanistic philosophy which came with them.
'The world,' she urges, 'must once again be turned upside down'
(p. 295).

In turning the world upside down we call for a philosophy and
a religion that make room for purpose as an effective causal agent in
the universe. It is now appropriate to bring together in the form of
axioms some of the new emphases discussed in previous chapters.

The first axiom. Nature is organic and ecological
This axiom is postmechanistic. Instead of mechanism and substance being viewed as fundamental, the ecological or organic view
of nature becomes fundamental. We think less of stuff and more of
relations. The most fundamental units of nature are not substances
but events. Modern physics knows this in so far as it recognises that
the basic units of the world take time to be what they are. In so far
as a hydrogen atom can be represented at all by a model it consists
of a central proton with an orbiting electron. If one could imagine
the electron to cease orbiting then the hydrogen atom ceases to
exist. At the heart of the atom event is ceaseless. At the other end of
a scale of complexity is the human being. Since the time of
Descartes it has been popular to think of the human being as a
complex machine. But this is a gross abstraction. A complex
machine such as a computer is an aggregate of individual entities,
namely atoms and molecules. A human being is a composite of
individual entities that have a central government located in the
brain. The parts are not simply added one piece to another. They
are integrated into a centrally co-ordinated system or organism.

The critical difference between the idea of a substance (or
machine) and an organism is that the organism is constituted by its
internal relations to its environment. It is not just pushed and pulled

by external physical forces. We know this is true of ourselves, so why are we so reluctant to apply this understanding to other entities as well? Partly because we are conditioned by our upbringing in the West to make false distinctions between ourselves and the rest of nature. We disenchant the world.

The postmodern worldview takes seriously the proposition that we live in a universe and not a multiverse. It is ecological through and through. The key words in postmechanistic thinking are event (as contrasted with substance), organism (as contrasted with machine), responsiveness (as opposed to inertness), freedom (as distinct from determinism), internal relations (as well as external relations) and purpose as a causal influence for all individual entities in the universe from protons to people.

The second axiom. To interpret the lower in terms of the higher
A postmodern worldview espouses the principle of interpreting the lower levels of organisation in terms of the higher, as well as vice versa. It is therefore postreductionist. In reductionism the complex is interpreted in terms of its most elementary constituents. In biology that means interpreting development, physiology and behaviour, for example, in terms of the behaviour of molecules and eventually of the components of molecules and when that is done claiming a final explanation. So the biological terms to do with growth and differentiation, for example, would eventually be replaced by terms from classical physics.

For some sixty years biochemists hunted for a single molecule or groups of molecules that might be responsible for 'organising' the development of the parts of the embryo such as legs and eyes. They hunted for what they called organisers. They found none. This seems to be because development cannot be reduced to the action of single chemicals. It involves much more complex interactions (Ho & Saunders 1984 p. 10, pp. 267–90, Witkowski 1985). Ultimately the reductionist would like to reduce these problems to what the atoms are doing. This is fine in itself except that the concept of atoms envisaged is that of classical physics. It is a gross assumption to suppose that atoms in my brain have the same properties they have in rocks and mud.

Some philosophers who apply reductionism to philosophy call themselves physicalists, because they regard physics as dealing with things at their most reduced level and they wish to follow suit. The physics they tend to espouse is classical physics. So it is inevitable that they find a world made of machinery. Their analysis is rejected by the new physics.

Analysis of things into their components is a valid approach. A postmodern worldview accepts this, but not as the exclusive approach to understanding. There is a second principle. The traditional mechanistic notion of the constitution of the world out of separately existing parts is turned upside down. The whole organises and even creates the parts. The lower levels of organisation are to be interpreted in terms of the higher. This principle is recognised in recent developments in quantum physics (Bohm 1985b). It has validity over the whole spectrum of individuals from protons to people. The basic principle is this: we understand what is not ourselves by analogy with what we know ourselves to be. We do not really know what atoms are until we know what happens when atoms are organised into brains. No analysis of atoms in mud, let us say, will lead us to suppose that in brains they result in thought and consciousness. The fact that atoms in brains result in thought tells us something about atoms we can find from no other source. Hence the postmodern principle that an atom or electron in a brain is different from an atom or electron not in a brain. We know what a thing is by what it becomes in all its manifestations, not simply those at elemental levels of organisation.

It is manifestly absurd to suppose that the human can be understood solely in terms of what atoms and molecules do in test tubes. Reductionist science breaks down entirely when attempts are made to apply it exclusively to the human being. Science becomes a tyranny, as in much behaviouristic psychology and sociology. It is significant that in these analyses both the guilty self and the responsible self vanish under the scrutiny of reductionism.

The third axiom. To interpret the world in terms of monism as against dualism

A postmodern worldview is postdualistic. The world is not made of two sorts of things, stuff and minds. When mind and matter are separated, as they are in dualism, they can never be put together again at any level. Mind and matter are, rather, two aspects of the one thing. All individuals are seen to be sentient. What are they sentient toward? The answer is what they feel. Or, to put it another way, feeling is a feeling of a feeling. In this view the ultimate processes of the universe are feelings. When we say matter and mind are two aspects of the one thing we are proposing that they cannot be separated. They are like the two poles of a magnet. So it is appropriate for a monistic view such as this to call itself dipolar. But that is very different from dualism. (For further discussion see Birch & Cobb 1981 pp. 98–109.)

The fourth axiom. An ethic for a postmodern worldview is biocentric as opposed to anthropocentric

Ethics is concerned with values. Western ethics has traditionally been almost exclusively concerned with human values. Indeed it could be seen as incurably anthropocentric. A central question is posed to traditional Western ethics. What values should we seek to maximise? 'Our task,' says Cobb (1973), 'is to decide which general statement, from among several alternatives is correct' (p. 312). He proposes the following possibilities: (i) So act as to maximise value for yourself in the present; (ii) So act as to maximise value for yourself for the rest of your life; (iii) So act as to maximise value for all people for the indefinite future; or (iv) So act as to maximise value in general.

The first is hardly to be viewed as an ethical principle at all. It says eat, drink and be merry for tomorrow we die. The second principle is a maxim of selfish prudence. The third is the utilitarian principle of the greatest good for the greatest number of people. But why limit action to human value? This could be a valid ethical principle only if sub-human entities had no intrinsic value. A central argument of this book is that intrinsic value is not limited to human beings. People are not the only pebbles on the cosmic beach. Therefore only the fourth principle is sufficiently encompassing to be acceptable in the postmodern worldview of ethics.

The recognition that every animal is an end in itself and not merely a means to human ends explodes the assumptions of our traditional ethics. What is needed is a new ethics which recognises in every animal, including humans, both ends and means.

The conservation movement of recent years has put great emphasis on the value of non-humans as means, that is their instrumental value to humanity. It has emphasised not only that we are dependent for our food upon non-human life. But, as well, living organisms play a vital part in maintaining the life-support systems of the earth. These are the cycles of nature which result in degradation of wastes and the maintenance of the atmosphere, the water and the soils of the earth. The message of the conservation movement has largely been to look after nature because nature looks after us. This emphasis on the instrumental value of nature has four main arguments. There is the silo argument, for maintaining the existence of all those organisms useful to us; the laboratory argument for maintaining those organisms needed for experimental studies; the gymnasium argument of nature for leisure; and the cathedral argument of nature for aesthetic pleasure.

These are arguments of instrumental ethics. They are rightly used to support conservation programs. But they are not enough. They ignore the intrinsic value of living organisms. As soon as an animal becomes of no more use to humans, as for example when the products now used from whales are superseded by synthetics, then there are no arguments left for the preservation of whales except that we like looking at them. Conservation rests on insecure foundations as long as it does not go beyond an instrumental ethic for its justification. When conservationists try to oppose polluters and developers solely with pragmatic arguments about the value of species and the gene pools of rainforests to human welfare, they have been manoeuvred into fighting on the same ground as their opponents. Their pragmatic arguments for the long-term value of species will be weighed against pragmatic arguments for the immediate needs of human beings. If a judge rules that the arguments of the developers are more compelling and that a flood control dam will provide more tangible benefits to humanity than will an endangered species, to whom will the conservationists appeal?

The fourth principle listed above is that we maximise value in general. The ethical principle that follows is that we should respect every individual for its intrinsic value as well as its instrumental value to others, including ourselves. Its intrinsic value is the richness of its experience (in the case of animals) or its parts (in the case of plants). 'Behold the lilies of the field' is precisely not saying 'Look at those lilies'. The word behold implies a respect, a kind of tenderness which suggests that living things have a livingness akin to ours and an intrinsic value to themselves and to God. Behold means to stand amongst things with a kind of reverence for life which does not walk through the world of non-self with arrogance and unconcern. Behold implies a relationship of the creature to others and to God. It is to respect that relationship. When we break that relationship of integrity we do evil.

The appropriate word for restoration of a broken relationship is salvation. Salvation is an ecological word because it is about restoring a right relationship which has been corrupted. After I had addressed an Assembly of the World Council of Churches on environmental ethics the conference newspaper had as its headline the next day 'Salvation for elephants!' That was appropriate. In an address on this subject Joseph Sittler quoted Saint Thomas: 'Grace does not destroy nature but perfects it'. The 'deep ecology' movement is a modern attempt to seek to enlarge one's sphere of identification with nature 'to care as deeply and compassionately as possible about the fate [of the earth] not because it affects us but because it is us' (Fox 1984 p. 200).

We deal with living organisms appropriately when we rightly balance their intrinsic and their instrumental worth. When the State of Rwanda decided that land on which elephants lived was too valuable for elephants and was needed for cultivation for human food they didn't kill off elephants as pests. They airlifted them to a reserve in another state. Their action suggests that, despite their recognition of elephants as pests, they also recognised, or thought world opinion recognised, elephants to have an intrinsic value and therefore a right to live.

When we try to balance intrinsic value and instrumental value we need an ethic of intrinsic value that goes beyond Albert Schweitzer's 'reverence for life' and other 'egalitarian' ethics which rate all life of equal value. But why rate all life of equal value? If intrinsic value is 'measured' by richness of experience, it follows that creatures such as primates and whales have more intrinsic value than worms and mosquitoes. There is a scale of intrinsic value which presumably bears some relation to the development of the nervous system of the organism. I have no difficulty in applauding the campaign of the World Wildlife Fund to save the chimpanzees of Africa. Nor have I difficulty in applauding the campaign of the World Health Organisation to eradicate the smallpox virus and the malarial parasite.

In the Western world the Christian churches have not been in the forefront of movements to promote the rights of non-humans to life. There has, instead, been a tendency to see nature as none other than the stage on which the drama of human life is performed. The non-human creatures are merely the props, having no value other than their value to us, intrinsic value residing in humans alone. This view has often been taken to be biblical. It isn't. In the Genesis account of nature, God finds goodness in things before, and quite apart from, the creation of Adam. Jesus stressed the divine concern for the sparrows and even the grasses of the field. If a man is worth many sparrows then a sparrow's worth is not zero. Theologians in recent times have been slow to appreciate this. Notable exceptions have been process theologians such as Cobb, Hartshorne and Griffin. Sittler's (1961) address to the Third Assembly of the World Council of Churches was notable for putting Christian unity in the larger setting of the value of nature. But it was largely ignored. Moltmann (1985 p. 31) promotes a similar view to that of process theology when he says: 'if the Christian theology wants to find the wisdom in dealing with creation which accords with belief in creation, it must free that belief from the modern anthropocentric view of the world' (p. 31) and:

> We do not wish to know so that we can dominate. We desire to know in order to participate. This kind of knowledge confers community, and can be termed communicative knowledge, as compared with dominating knowledge. It lets life be life and cherishes its livingness. Christian theology must remember this, its own wisdom, if it wants to make a contribution to the conquest of the ecological crisis of scientific and technological civilisation. (p. 32)

Likewise Gustafson (1984) affirms that the universe does not exist for the sake of human beings and God does not order it solely for us. He, like Sittler, widens the ethical context from the human individual to human communities and then to all sentient life.

The Roman Catholic bishops of the U.S.A. produced in the early 1980s documents on economics and justice. The second one has been severely criticised by Rasmussen (1985) on its exclusively anthropocentric ethic. He argues that the bishops' concept of justice is less comprehensive than that of the Bible: 'In the economy of God, the whole created order is the object of redemption, and justice is rendering whatever is required for the fullest possible flourishing of all creation' (p. 474). To the question—who is my neighbour?—the bishops reply that it is everyone in the world. It is that and more. Is not neighbour all that participates in life? If so the needs of neighbour stretch beyond human needs as does the reach of love. The key concept of life-centred ethics is intrinsic value of all natural entities with a hierarchy of value related to richness of experience.

The fifth axiom. Knowledge cannot be divided into disciplines without loss
The postmodern worldview is postdisciplinary. It seeks to overcome

the tyranny of the expert. There will be disciplines but they will not be separate kingdoms of knowledge. Instead they will be related to some total vision of understanding. This is the subject of Chapter 6.

How does all this bear upon the questions we set out at the beginning of this chapter, namely how a postmodern worldview may illumine the momentous problems of our time: peace, justice and ecological sustainability? We belong to two orders, one which rules, the other is a new creation struggling to be born. One order has its faith in infinite progress through technology. Theirs are the false prophets of Jeremiah (23:17) who cry 'Progress, infinite progress! Peace, universal peace! Happiness, happiness for everyone!' But there is no peace, nor justice nor sustainability nor happiness for everyone.

There is more to enlightenment than the knowledge science, technology, economics and politics bring. This the Enlightenment failed to recognise. It had a faith in the possibility of achieving a simple harmony between self-interest and general welfare. The followers of the Enlightenment were not immune from invoking high ideals to justify selfish interests. Newbigin (1983) reminds us:

> The human rights which the eighteenth century philosophers espoused were mainly rights of the rising bourgeoisie. Freedom meant primarily freedom to hold property, to trade and to travel. It was not freedom for workers to organise trade unions, for blacks to vote, for aboriginal peoples to retain their lands, or for women to have equal rights with men. Late in the twentieth century we are still struggling with this unfinished agenda (p. 16).

The heavenly city of the Enlightenment has not arrived. We have with us still 'children of darkness' who are evil because they know no law beyond self. Their wisdom is that they understand the power of self-interest. The 'children of light' are wise because they believe that self-interest should be brought under the discipline of a higher law. Their foolishness is that they underestimate the power of self-interest (Niebuhr 1972 p. 10). We see this foolishness in the fight of Catholics against Catholics, Protestants against Protestants, Muslim against Muslim, Marxist against Marxist, capitalist against capitalist and any one of these groups against any other—all in the name of a lesser loyalty than a higher law that rules over self-interest.

What is this higher law? It is not the authority of any individual, group or institution. It is not any created good at all. These all tend to become idols. It is the source of all good, the source of all creativity. The moral and spiritual resources for a just, peaceful and sustainable global society are pressing daily upon us, seeking entry into life and blocked only by self-interest. There is a way through. Repentance is still possible.

For decades yet there will be frustration and travail as we struggle for release from one order to enter the other. No one can say whether we shall have global holocaust or new creation. New creation, if it comes, will be from commitment to the source of new creation itself.

In 1986 the head of the Soviet Union, Mikhail Gorbachev, invited the world 'to enter the third millennium without nuclear weapons'. His invitation is strangely reminiscent of the 'Choose Life' statement which the U.S. and Soviet church leaders framed in Geneva in 1979 when they anticipated 'the bi-millenary anniversary of the coming to the world of our Lord and Saviour, Jesus Christ, the Prince of Peace'. And they asked: 'How shall we meet that day? In what state shall we present our planet to the Creator? Shall it be a blooming garden or a lifeless, burnt out, devastated land? Therefore choose life.'

CHAPTER 6

Dismantling the Tower of Babel

Now as they moved eastwards they found a plain in the land of Shinar where they settled. They said to one another, 'Come, let us make bricks and bake them in the fire'—For stone they used bricks, and for mortar they used bitumen [slime]— 'Come,' they said 'let us build ourselves a town and a tower with its top reaching heaven. Let us make a name for ourselves.'

Genesis 11:2–4 (Jerusalem Bible)

The radical split between knowledge and commitment that exists in our culture and our universities is not ultimately tenable. Differentiation has gone about as far as it can go. It is time for a new integration.

Robert N. Bellah (1970 p. 257)

T he Israelites, according to the story in the eleventh chapter of Genesis, were well on the way to getting a mighty tower built. There seemed nothing too hard for them to do. The sorry end of the story is well known. They no longer spoke one language and so could no longer understand one another. They stopped building the town which was called Babel and the great tower they had planned at its centre.

In commenting on this story Koestler (1982 p. 685) suggests that the magnitude and complexity of the offending tower involved specialists of all sorts, each with a special terminology and set of beliefs. So it was quite impossible for the engineers to understand what the priests were talking about, for the brick makers to share the architects' vision, for the philosophers to agree on the function of the tower and for the conservationists and poets to overcome their revulsion against such a monstrous desecration of the pastoral environment close to the shores of the Mediterannean.

The higher the tower grew the more violent became the disputes between the builders. Eventually all communication broke down. Whatever purpose they may have started with vanished into thin air.

Koestler suggests that the parable of the tower is like a sequel to the Fall. The latter represents the human moral predicament, the fate of the tower representing the human intellectual predicament. 'We seem to be compelled to shape facts and data, as we know them,' says Koestler, 'into hard bricks, stick them together with the slime of our theories and beliefs. And thus we continue to carry bricks to Babel' (p. 685).

Today we have a crisis of knowledge. It is not simply that knowledge doubles about every decade. We can cope with that because with the increase of knowledge we discover new general principles that tie together previously disconnected facts. The crisis of knowledge is not a crisis of quantity. It is a crisis of experts. The dominant model of knowledge today is that knowledge can be divided into compartments called disciplines such as physics, economics and so on. The idea of a discipline is that the information in it is relatively independent of that in other disciplines. The people who are trained in disciplines are called experts. The general idea has been that if society had well-trained experts in all the disciplines the experts would guide us to the truth and right action. It hasn't worked out that way.

There are two reasons. On the one hand, knowledge cannot be subdivided into separate compartments without losing something essential—the unity which no segment can grasp. The result is that not only do experts from different disciplines fail to understand one another, but the experts within disciplines also disagree. We build a tower of Babel when we suppose that knowledge is like a jigsaw puzzle. The bits and pieces are the bits of knowledge that the disciplines give us. When we try to fit them together they don't fit. They don't form a complete picture at all. That's what happens when we opt for the substantialist (substance) prejudice in the field of knowledge. Knowledge is not a substance. It cannot be treated as such without great distortion. This is precisely the intellectual dilemma so powerfully symbolised in the parable of the tower.

There is a second reason for the failure of our knowledge to lead us into the truth and right action. It has to do with our moral predicament symbolised by the Fall and alluded to on page 154. The Enlightenment gave us knowledge with commitment to the false god of inevitable progress. It is easy with hindsight to understand why it drove a wedge between rational understanding and religion. The Christian religion of the eighteenth century contained a full wardrobe of questionable assertions about nature and history that could be either disproved or rendered improbable by Enlightenment rationalism. The Christian religion of the time put road blocks in all the wrong places. The Enlightenment view of man threw out the baby with the bath-water. Religion seemed to become peripheral or vestigial. With its demise came the break between knowledge and commitment to values other than those to do with self-centred progress. There was reason to become increasingly disillusioned with a world built on utilitarianism and science alone.

It is not really possible to separate the human intellectual predicament and the human moral predicament. The division of knowledge provides a fertile field for the seeds of hubris to germinate and grow. The physicist or the biologist is accountable to no-one other than the lords of their own subjects. Anyone who has lived in a university knows the political rivalries between disciplines. The head of a department who returns to his staff meeting with the news that he gave way to the department of general studies when needs of all departments were scrutinised will be regarded as having let the side down. The fragmentation of knowledge itself confounds our moral dilemma. It is probable that the tower of Babel housed a bunch of experts who not only couldn't talk to one another. They grew to dislike each other as they indulged in self-glorification.

The fragmentation of knowledge has its far-reaching implications. It has produced destructive conflict between individuals, disciplines, ideologies and nations. It has helped to plunge the world into the global crisis of management in which we seem unable to utilise the world's resources without massive environmental deterioration. As we attempt to save ourselves we are in danger of losing the world. The problems of global management are all connected. You can no longer do only one thing. Resource shortages, unemployment, inflation, environmental deterioration, population explosion and even crime are all interconnected. This network of problems won't be solved by any one expert or any number of experts. It is one problem and has to be tackled as one. Experts can't do that because they have tunnel vision. What is needed is a panoramic view.

Bernard Shaw said in *The Doctor's Dilemma*: 'the professions are a conspiracy against the laity'. He wasn't referring only to the medical profession. There is a difference between an expert and a thinker. An expert confines his thinking within arbitrary boundaries. A thinker sets no boundaries to his thinking. That is why the philosopher Heidegger said 'Science doesn't think'. The expert doesn't think across boundaries. Sometimes the expert tries to cross boundaries in what is called interdisciplinary studies. But this approach usually consists in allocating parts of a whole to what are considered to be appropriate experts. We end up where we began.

Experts provide us with a wealth of information. They load the table with countless pieces of the jig-saw puzzle. How to put them together when they don't fit? That's our problem. Hence T. S. Eliot's questioning in Choruses from 'The Rock':

Where is the life we have lost in the living,
Where is the wisdom we have lost in knowledge,
Where is the knowledge we have lost in information?

Knowledge is lost in a sea of beliefs from a multitude of disciplines. The general purpose of the modern university is lost amid the incoherent variety of special purposes that have accumulated within it. The call of the postmodern worldview is for fewer beliefs and more belief.

'There is only one subject-matter for education,' said Whitehead (1949), and that is Life in all its manifestations. Instead of this single unity, we offer children—Algebra, from which nothing follows; Geometry, from which nothing follows; Science, from which nothing follows; History, from which nothing follows; a Couple of Languages, never mastered; and lastly, most dreary of all, Literature . . . Can such a list be said to represent Life, as it is known in the midst of the living of it? The best that can be said of it is, that it is a rapid table of contents which a deity might run over in his mind while he was thinking of creating a world, and had not yet determined how to put it together. (p. 18)

We might indulge in some such fantasy ourselves. I am the last adult left on earth in charge of a huddle of children who will be the fathers and mothers of all mankind. All knowledge has disappeared along with all my contemporaries in the nuclear Armageddon. All books, all drugs, vehicles, factories, pots and pans and other relics of civilisation have been destroyed or buried irretrievably under a thick layer of radioactive dust. I am the sole repository of the accumulated wisdom and experience of humanity from pre-Sumerian times to the holocast. I feel the responsibility acutely as I reflect that whatever I fail to pass on to my little band of orphans will be lost for ever. Which should come first, Sophocles or safety matches? That is the central problem of education; not how we should teach but what we should teach. Will it be a list of disciplines or is there some way of making the subject matter life in all its manifestations? A modest approach to this problem is to consider some of the disciplines, how breaches between them frustrate purpose and how healing can be initiated.

Science and religion

In the modern tower of Babel science and religion occupy two separate floors. They didn't come into existence that way. Indeed they had a close relationship in the rebirth of science in the sixteenth and seventeenth centuries. Copernicus, according to some sources, was an abbot. The great scientists of the sixteenth and seventeenth centuries were in the main disciples of Luther, Zwingli or reformers in Great Britain. Newton, Harvey, Boyle and a dozen others were deeply religious men. Moreover, they did not keep their science and their religion in separate mental compartments. According to White (1968 p. 101) natural theology was the motivational basis for late medieval and early modern science. He claims that every major scientist from about 1250 to about 1650, four hundred years during which the modern scientific movement was taking form, considered himself also a theologian. There were, besides men, a number of women scientists right into the fifteenth century. During that century, for example, Maria di Novella, at the age of twenty-five, became head of the department of mathematics in the University of Bologna. But for several centuries after the Reformation science was the province of men (Alic 1986).

The history of the rift between science and religion in the West from the mid-seventeenth century on is long and complex (White 1960, Barbour 1966). The gulf widened enormously with Enlightenment rationalism in the eighteenth century. Many of the claims of orthodox Christians about the universe and living organisms were shown to be false. Before Newton the planets were held in their elliptical paths by the hand of God. Newton found they were held in their orbits by gravitation. Until the middle of the nineteenth century each species was held to have been separately created by God over a few days. In 1859 Darwin tells us that species transformed one from another by evolutionary descent over millions of years.

God, as causal agency in the world, was pushed out of the universe depicted by science. Science had no need of an interventionist God. The interventionist God inevitably retreats before the advance of science. The gaps where God could be thought to act became narrower with each scientific advance. When science decided it had no need of God, theology decided it had no need of science. The partition of the fields between science and religion was complete.

After the triumphs of Darwinism in the nineteenth century, science and religion reached a gentleman's agreement not to trespass on each other's territory. Various efforts were made to define the territorial boundaries. A common one was to say science deals with what and religion deals with why. So to the question—what is the nature of nature?—religion has nothing to say. That was the realm of science. To the question—what does nature tell us about God?—the answer was nothing. The division between science and religion had gone about as far as it could go. Science and religion were seen as essentially contrasted activities. From the theological side the separation became quite explicit in neo-orthodoxy, particularly as exemplified by Karl Barth and Emil Brunner. For them science and religion are different domains and should never be mixed. Theology deals with a transcendent God who is radically unlike the world which science studies. God stands 'before and above' the world. This is classical theism *sensu strictu*. The domains of science and religion are different and so are their methodologies. Science advances by human discovery. Religion advances by revelation perceived as a direct intervention of God to provide information.

Besides the view of the relation of science and religion as contrasted activities (classical theism), Barbour (1966 p. 115) identifies two others. One is the view that attempts to derive theology from science; the other sees them as parallel activities. Examples which Barbour gives of deriving theology from science are the natural theology that argued for the existence of God from the design of nature and the creationists' argument today for the existence of God from their misunderstanding of the second law of thermodynamics. I incline to classify these examples as misleading attempts to find parallels between science and theology since, in both cases, God is predicated on other grounds and science is brought in to support this claim. A clear-cut example of deriving theology from science is Burhoe's (1973) interpretation of science from a Unitarian background. He identifies God with natural selection.

The view that sees science and religion as parallel activities is exemplified by the theologian Raven (1953a, 1953b), to whom I referred earlier; the mathematician Coulson, particularly in *Science and Christian Belief* (1955); and biochemist and theologian Peacocke (1979, 1984, 1986). The most consistent and impressive attempt to include science and religion within a unified view is 'process theology', which has a long tradition (see Chapter 4) and which in modern times derives much of its inspiration from A. N. Whitehead.

Recognising the futility of territorial boundaries between science and religion Whitehead (1942) said 'It is fashionable to state that religion and science can never clash because they deal with different topics. I believe that this solution is entirely mistaken. In this world at least you cannot tear apart minds and bodies' (p. 53). So important is the healing of the rift between science and religion that Whitehead (1933) said: 'When we consider what religion is for mankind, and what science is, it is no exaggeration to say that the future course of history depends upon the decision of this generation as to the relations between them' (p. 224). As a result of artificial territorial claims of science and religion, both are impoverished. There are wider truths and broader perspectives to be explored in a postmodern worldview. That will require 'a deeper religion and a more subtle science' (Whitehead 1933 p. 229).

What could be the elements of a more subtle science and a deeper religion? I have already emphasised how science has tended to abstract from reality by dealing exclusively with external aspects of things and with external causes that push and pull. But in addition to external aspects there are inner aspects, and in addition to external causes there are internal causes. The more subtle science will be willing to take account, in Bohm's language, not only of the explicate order but the implicate order of things. 'Science', said Whitehead (1966),

> can find no individual enjoyment in nature: science can find no aim in nature: science can find no creativity in nature; it finds mere rules of succession. These negations are true of natural science. They are inherent in its methodology. The reason for this blindness of physical science lies in the fact that such science only deals with half the evidence provided by human experience. It divides the seamless coat—or, to change the metaphor to a happier form, it examines the coat, which is superficial, and neglects the body which is fundamental. (p. 154)

The disastrous separation of body and mind set in train by Descartes is one example of this blindness. What Whitehead said was inherent in the methodology of science does not have to stay that way. He called for a more subtle science that did not neglect half the evidence of the senses. Some suggestions in this direction have been made in Chapters 2 and 3 for a new dialogue of science with faith.

Religion in the West has tended to preoccupy itself with the internal aspect of life and, moreover, one sort of life—human life. It has recognised the inner aspect of being a human, but its dominant tradition has denied or ignored the inner aspects of the rest of the creation. A deeper religion will explore the whole world with the perspective it has of the human. Furthermore, it will not regard the exploration of the outer as irrelevant but will find a more complete perspective in dealing with the question—what is the nature of what is? And that includes God.

In addressing British scientists Baillie (1951 pp. 11–15) told them he had long been in the habit of regarding as the most import-

ant single passage in the whole literature of Western philosophy
Plato's report in the Phaedo of Socrates' autobiographical reminis-
cences as he sat in prison awaiting death in 399 BC. Socrates says
that when he was a young man he had a consuming interest in
natural science, always seeking into the causes of things, and asking
such questions as whether organic growth is due to fermentation
caused by variations of temperature, and whether thought and
memory can be explained in terms of the brain. In the pursuit of
these studies he said he seemed to forget or to unlearn many important things he had formerly known quite well. And that led him
to have an idea of another possible approach. One day he heard a
man reading a book by Anaxagoras, in which it was said that the
ultimate cause of all things is mind. Socrates was delighted with this
idea. If things are ordered by mind, then they will be ordered for a
purpose. So we need to study purpose as an ordering principle. He
then got hold of the book for himself and read with great eagerness.
But his hopes were grievously disappointed:

> He seemed to me to be exactly like a man who should begin by
> saying that I, Socrates, do all I do by mind, but who, when he
> went on to assign a cause for each of my actions, should say,
> first that I am sitting here now because my body is composed
> of bones and muscles, and that the bones are hard and divided
> by joints, while the muscles can be tightened and relaxed and,
> together with the flesh and the skin which contains it, cover the
> bones; and that therefore when the bones are raised in their
> sockets by the contraction or relaxation of the muscles, I am
> now able to bend my limbs;—and that that is the cause of my
> sitting here [in prison] all huddled up. In the same way also he
> would explain why I am saying this to you: he would speak of
> voice and hearing and air and a myriad other causes of that
> sort, and would altogether forget to mention the real cause,
> which is quite simply that, since the Athenians have thought it
> right to condemn me, I have thought it right and just to sit here
> and bow to their sentence. For, by the dog, I am inclined to
> think that these muscles and bones of mine would long ago
> have been in Megara or Boethia, prompted by their own
> opinion of what is best, if I had not thought it better and nobler
> to submit to any penalty the state inflicts, rather than run away.
> To call these other things causes is too absurd. Had the con-
> tention been merely that without the aid of bones and muscles

and the rest I could not carry my purposes into effect, that
would have been true enough. But to say that I do what I do
because of them and not because my mind knows what is best
is a very loose and careless way of speaking. (quoted by Baillie
1951 pp. 12–14)

The two types of causation which Socrates was so careful to
distinguish are mechanical causation (from the external environment) and purposes (internal relations). That is causation by ante-
cedent events and causation by ends or purposes. The problem of
the relation between science and religion is the respective rights of
these two kinds of causes and the relation between them. What has
been blocking any healthy relationship between science and religion
is the substantialist prejudice, that is to say substance thinking. It
recognises only external or mechanical causation. Science does it by
concentrating exclusively on the explicate order. Religion does it
when it recognises mechanical causation as the way in which God
acts in the world and in human life.

The physicist who at one time spoke of electrons as particles,
existing in independence of any relations they have to their environment, was guilty of substance thinking. The theologian who asserts
that God is independent of the world and unrelated to it is guilty of
substance thinking. The perfection of God is supposed to have that
kind of character. That is to make God a substance. But if the world
is dependent upon God and if God is influenced by the world, then
God is not a substance. The substantialist paradigm in both science
and theology paved the way for the territorial division of substances.
And in this process the scientists' substances always appear more
real than those of the theologian. As the schoolboy said in his essay
on science and religion: 'The difference between science and religion is that science is material and religion is immaterial'! Physics
has now come to recognise that there are no substances. That is
something theology, and as well other sciences, could learn from
physics.

You cannot divide the world up into parts and think. Science
and religion in a postmodern worldview will be concerned with the
whole of the world. Each will bring a different perspective and
emphasis needed by the other. God is not to be conceived as the
creator of substances. God is not before the creation. God is causal
within the creation. God's mode of action is not through external
causation. God does not have to compete with earthquake or tem-
pest. God's action is through internal relations that constitute

entities—'the still small voice within'. Science and religion may use different models to explain the world. And that is fine so long as we recognise that all models are abstractions. Each is like a map. For some purposes all I need as a map is a street directory map. For others I need a geological map or a map of the vegetation of the area, for other purposes I need a map of the world. Each one is an abstraction of the landscape. Such incomplete maps can be useful, provided we recognise their incompleteness.

As science and religion move away from their substantialist presuppositions they may come to find new depth in each other's endeavours. As T. S. Eliot wrote in 'Little Gidding':

We shall not cease from exploration
And the end of all our exploring
Will be to arrive where we started
And know the place for the first time.

An objective of theology is to bring science and religion closer together in a 'deeper religion and a more subtle science'. While doing that there is need to preserve distinctive aspects of science and religion. About the only definition of science that seems acceptable to scientists is that science is what scientists do. When philosophers of science probe into what they think scientists do they come up with a wide variety of ideas. Science seems extraordinarily difficult to define. There is science according to Francis Bacon, science according to Karl Popper, Thomas Kuhn, Imre Lakatos and Paul Feyerabend. (See, for example, Charlesworth 1982 and Chalmers 1976.) Scientists, for the most part, leave these discussions to philosophers of science. They incline to a pragmatism—to learn what science is you become apprenticed to a scientist. At least that is how departments of science in universities operate. The diversity of views as to what science is suggests that it is many things to many people. There are indeed 'varieties of scientific experience', which is the title of an important paper by Ravetz (1981). Yet there must surely be some common strands that run through these diverse experiences.

There was no problem in contrasting science as a method of finding out about things with the dominant model of knowledge at the time of the renaissance of science in the sixteenth century. The story is told that in the University of Paris the philosophers once disputed among themselves as to the number of teeth in a horse's mouth. It was argued that the number could not be a multiple of three because that would imply disrespect to the Trinity; nor could it be a multiple of seven, for God created the world in six days and rested on the seventh. Neither the authority of Aristotle nor the ingenuity of the schoolmen could resolve the problem. It was finally settled by a young man who opened the mouth of a horse and counted the teeth. The doctors of the university were not convinced by this novel and unintellectual procedure. But the opening of the horse's mouth is the beginning of science.

The beginning of science is observation. One may dispute what it is that is observed; nevertheless observation remains an essential part of science. Second is experiment. The word has the same root as experience. Indeed, experiment is a way of manufacturing experience. When Bacon looked at a piece of amber he could make a list of properties such as colour and weight. When he decided to rub amber with a cloth he was increasing his experience, for he found that it then had electrical properties. Thirdly, the formation of hypotheses or conjectures usually precedes experimentation. Hypotheses are tested by means of experiments, that is experience derived from carefully designed manipulations. Hypotheses are in this way refuted or validated. Experimental testing must be open to repetition by one's peers. It counts for little, if anything, to claim to have an experience which cannot be repeated. The scientific knowledge so obtained may be put together in a general theory that usually comes from the pooling of the knowledge and experience of many scientists. However much philosophers may dispute the role of induction and deduction, there stands the centrality of observation, experiment, hypothesis, testing and repeatability.

So far I have given an indication of the method of science. The next issue to raise is the domain of science. Is this method applicable only to certain areas or is the method of science applicable to all areas of knowledge? Can it only give valid information about physical objects such as horses' teeth, or is it widely applicable? There is a diversity of opinion about this. Neo-orthodox theologians exclude science as a methodology for theology because of their claim that theology gets information in quite a different way, namely by a process called revelation. Call it what you will, the insights of Jesus or Paul were based on their experiences. They pleaded with their contemporaries to pursue such experiences for themselves. The interpretation of these experiences led to all sorts of affirmations and disputations down the ages.

My own conclusion is similar to that of Wilber (1984), which he reaches after a much longer argument than I have given here:

> All domains contain certain features or deep structures that are
> open to scientific investigation, because all domains are open to
> experiential disclosure. There is religious experience just as
> certainly as there is psychological experience and sensory ex-
> perience. In that sense, we can speak of the science of religion
> just as legitimately as we speak of the science of psychology,
> biology or physics. (p. 20)

This is the German *Wissenschaft* which includes theology as a
science (Pannenberg 1976 pp. 228 *et seq.*).

On the basis of experience from a variety of sources a religious
person and the theologian formulate a theory which, like any theory
dealing with complex issues in science, is a matter of weighing one
experience against another, together with much subjective judgment. There are rules in this game such as consistency and harmony. In no domain is measurement the ultimate way of judging the
validity of complex concepts.

This latter point is very important. Scientists who have a substance or mechanical view of the world exclude from their domain
psychological and subjective categories. The preferred categories
are those that can be weighed and measured. Hence Whitehead's
(1933 p. 69) criticism that science saw nature as a dull affair that
was scentless, soundless and colourless. 'Only that which is mea-
surable is real', said Galileo. It becomes increasingly incredible to
common-sense that the only things that have any importance,
namely feelings and qualities, are the things to be omitted from
reality. The real is unimportant. The important is unreal.

The originators of the renaissance of science did not have a
materialistic view. Their successors under the influence of
Descartes did. A subtler science to which we need to return excludes no categories of experience at all. Science as it is practised
has both virtues and vices, successes and failures, and its practitioners work from a variety of metaphysical bases. The Cartesian base
is a substantialist metaphysic. This was not the original metaphysics
of science. It is rejected by those who reject the substantialist paradigm. This includes those who opt for dialectical materialism. Two
biologists, Levins and Lewontin (1985), reject Cartesian reductionism in favour of dialectical materialism. Cartesian reductionism,
they say, has failed to give satisfactory approaches in ecology,

evolution, neurobiology and developmental biology. Their book discusses how dialectical materialism has influenced their biology. On pages 151–3 I refer to scientists who have rejected the substantialist metaphysic for a more mentalist metaphysic. The point is that what a scientist does depends a good deal on his or her metaphysical views of the world. There are many ways of playing the game of science.

Science, as a particular set of ways of experiencing and knowing, in principle excludes no domain. What then is religion? It too is concerned with human experiences and the interpretation of these experiences. In the view I am suggesting it does not have access to any ways of knowing that are not available to the scientist. There are no short circuits. The mind that is involved in religious concerns is not a different mind from the mind involved in scientific issues. Some theologians have claimed that the reverse is the case. Some attach a special meaning to the word revelation, making a distinction between the revelation of God in everyday events and in nature and special revelation which refers to special acts of God in history. This leads on to the notion of two sorts of history, secular and sacred. The position taken in this book and in process theology in general is that there is no distinction to be made between general and special revelation. When something of great significance happens it is made possible by a history of events that makes for the fullness of time. God acts in one way which is the way of persuasive love. I find no evidence to suggest that God acts as a manipulator on special occasions.

The medieval theologian claimed, as do also present-day fundamentalist Christians, that the writers of the Bible wrote inerrantly through special revelations vouchsafed to them. It is as though God dictated the whole record verbatim. The Bible was not written this way, as any scholar of history knows. Furthermore, the record in the Bible has to be interpreted. Interpreters differ. This was a problem for Martin Luther when he sought to replace the authority of the pope with the authority of the Bible. He recognised that the Bible was not self-explanatory. It had to be interpreted. Even Peter says 'in the writings of our beloved brother Paul there are some things which are difficult to understand' (1 Peter 3:16). Martin Luther appointed Philip Melanchthon as his interpreter of the Bible. Soon there arose other Protestant theologians who had different interpretations from those of Melanchthon. By what authority then does religion speak if the truth is not infallibly revealed in a book or in the pronouncements of a person?

The critical answer to this question for Protestantism is—by no authority. To what then does one appeal amidst a clash of views? There is only one answer. The appeal is within to human experience. And for any one person that means that person's experience and that person's interpretation of experience. Jesus was asked by the priests and scribes by what authority he did all the things he did and spoke what he spoke (Luke 20:1–8). He turned the question on them and asked by what authority did John the Baptist speak? The question was a shrewd one since they demanded that all authority be vested in them, yet they knew that the people thought John's authority came from God. They answered that they did not know. 'Neither will I tell you,' said Jesus, 'by what authority I do these things.' Tillich (1955) comments: 'The way in which Jesus refuses to answer is the answer' (p. 80). Jesus, instead of answering, points to the acting and speaking of John. Here is the rise of an authority without ritual or legal foundation. But the priests and scribes deny the possibility of 'an authority guaranteed by its inner power' (p. 87). Jesus is saying to the authorities: look at John, see for yourselves what he does. And John says the same to Jesus. In the tremendous painting by Matthias Grünewald in the Prado Museum in Madrid, John points to Jesus on the cross. The picture centres on the exaggerated finger that points to the truth for him. The finger is saying, my experience breaks into me from that source.

Now you may say that is all very fine so far as it goes; science and religion get their information by the same mental routes. But science goes on in laboratories where experience is manufactured, religion has quite different practices—praying and worshipping that go on in such places as churches. If by praying one means a direct telephone line to the source of truth, then nothing like that goes on in laboratories. But if by praying one means putting oneself in a frame of mind that is receptive to understanding, and if by worship is meant ascription of worth to that which is worthy, then that too goes on in the best laboratories.

The distinction between science and religion has more to do with their domains. The biologist who studies the physiology of a porpoise has a different experience from the physicist who studies electrons. The domain of religion has to do for the most part with other sorts of experience such as the sense of being forsaken, forgiveness, caring for, having courage, sensing an at-one-ness with the universe and many others, including what some call mystical experience. The word religion has the root meaning of binding together, which may be a deeper experience for the religious person than for others.

Implicit in what has just been said is that religion is a transforming agency. There are some sorts of knowledge you can only have by being transformed in the process. Religious knowledge is of that sort. The experience of forgiveness is to feel forgiven and to forgive others. The experience of being forsaken is to feel a void that may lead on to a new fullness of life. The experience of courage is, in some circumstances, simply to be. We need courage to be in the face of despair. At-one-ment, the reverse of alienation, is to find the whole universe friendly. I do not want to suggest that none of these experiences go on in laboratories. A deep empathy with nature is part of the dialogue a scientist has with what is studied. The success of Jane Goodall's (1971) scientific study of chimpanzees in the wild was dependent upon the rapport she established with her subjects and evidently also the rapport they had with her.

There are no real battles between genuine science and genuine religion. There will always be battles when one or both are bogus; when dogma replaces interpretation based on experience, or when certain experiences are excluded *a priori* as, for example, when the mechanist excludes anything that cannot be weighed or measured. Bogus in this context means dogmatic, non-experiential, and non-testable (Wilber 1984 p. 51).

An analysis of the religious views of the founders of the great theories of modern physics (relativity and quantum theory)—Einstein, Schroedinger, Heisenberg, Bohr, Eddington, Pauli, de Broglie, Jeans and Planck—reveals that all were non-materialists sympathetic to a spiritual view of the world and in the case of Schroedinger to mysticism (Wilber 1984). Was their metaphysics and their spiritual sensitivity derived from their physics? The answer seems to be that it came from beyond physics (metaphysics). Their understanding of life led them away from materialism to a view they found to be consistent with their physics. For example, Heisenberg said: 'If we want to go beyond physics however, and begin to philosophise, then the worldview that can most easily explain modern physics is that not of Democritus, but of Plato' (quoted by Wilber 1984 p. 32). Likewise Eddington said: 'The new physics gives strong grounds for an idealistic philosophy which, I suggest, is hospitable towards a spiritual religion' (Wilber

1984 p. 169). Schroedinger's view of life was deeply religious. And in relating his religious convictions to his science he said: 'No personal god can form part of a world-model that has only become accessible at the cost of removing everything personal from it' (Wilber 1984 p. 89).

The interrelations of one's science and one's metaphysics are doubtless difficult to disentangle. These examples suggest that their understanding of science guided these physicists in their choice of a metaphysic. The reverse can also be true. The biologist C. H. Waddington (1969 pp. 72–81) was convinced that a scientist's metaphysical beliefs have a definite influence on the work he does, both in the type of problems he sets himself and in the manner in which he tries to solve them. Waddington once told me that he became a developmental biologist as a result of having read all the philosophical works of A. N. Whitehead as an undergraduate in Cambridge University. And his approach to the subject of developmental biology was greatly influenced by his understanding of the Whiteheadian notion of the coming together of many events into one unified event.

The relation between science and metaphysics or religion which these scientists found is very different from the proposition that the fastest route to making religion obsolete is to hitch it to the latest fad in science. That also can happen when the new wine of science is poured into the old bottles of religion. As discussed in Chapter 7, the creative relationship between religion and science is a two-way process involving the transformation of both.

What has blocked the creative relationship between science and religion has been the substantialist paradigm. As soon as scientists break out of that, religious questions are asked. The domain of concern widens. The evidence for this is in the life and work of the founders of the new physics and its modern representatives such as David Bohm. One of these physicists, Heisenberg, said we have to avoid the cleavage of the world into its objective and its subjective sides and think more subtly about the relationship than we have been accustomed to do (Wilber 1984 p. 42).

In biology we see the same breadth of concern when the substance paradigm is broken in the thought and work of Waddington already mentioned. One of the architects of modern evolutionary theory, Wright (1953, 1964) was greatly influenced in his understanding of the gene by his Whiteheadian metaphysical views. And because of this he was unable 'to escape from the problem of the relation of mind and matter' (1964 p. 111). Another architect of modern evolutionary theory, Dobzhansky, had a less explicit metaphysic than Wright but he was greatly influenced by his early upbringing in the Russian Orthodox Church. He rarely involved himself in church practices. But he could not leave his science untouched by his deep conviction that humans were truly free and that life made sense only in terms of commitment to concerns of ultimate worth. How, he asked, did this freedom evolve (Dobzhansky 1956)? How did the urge for commitment to concerns of ultimate importance become so strongly tied to human life (Dobzhansky 1967)?

I had the good fortune of working in the same laboratories as Wright in the University of Chicago and Dobzhansky in Columbia University in New York when they were both in their prime. Our discussions were as much philosophical as they were scientific. In Chicago, Wright and I became regular visitors with Charles Hartshorne of the philosophy department, himself at one time an assistant of A. N. Whitehead. In New York, Dobzhansky and I had a number of memorable discussions with both Paul Tillich and Reinhold Niebuhr. Needless to say our more mechanistic colleagues regarded these as somewhat aberrant, if not bizarre, activities! Two neuro-physiologists, Sperry (1977, 1983a, 1983b) and Young (1978, 1987), ask religious questions as a result of breaking out of the substantialist paradigm. Sperry has been deeply influenced by the role of consciousness as a cause and the role of values in human life. Young, like Dobzhansky, emphasises the importance of free choice in life.

> Great things are done when men and mountains meet;
> This is not done by jostling in the street.

So said William Blake in 'Gnomic Verses,' i.

Ecology and economics

The relationship between science and religion has been crucial for humankind for some four centuries. Every generation has reaped a bitter harvest as the tension between them remains unresolved. I have indicated what seem to me the opportunities of this generation to resolve some of the more destructive relations of the past and find creative openings for the future.

There is a sense in which the unhappy relation between ecology and economics has been with us, not just for centuries but for ten millennia. It began with the Agricultural Revolution which brought with it the beginning of villages and towns and the loss of much virgin lands. This inaugurated major changes to the face of the earth as a consequence of human activity. The Industrial Revolution much later accelerated the process of change and added to the burgeoning population on earth. Later still came the revolution in hygiene and medicine that was responsible for the greatest increase in rate of population growth in the history of the world, with its attendant strain on the resources of the earth.

The needs of peoples of the earth today depend upon three related systems: the production system, the economic system and the ecological system. The production system is the industries to do with farming that produce food and secondary industries that produce material goods such as steel. The economic system is the framework of arrangements within which industries operate. It is supposed to manage the total productive effort. The ecological system is the life-support system on which all life depends. It includes the ecological cycles that maintain the composition of the atmosphere and the oceans and those that are responsible for the degradation of wastes. Logically the economic system ought to be designed to conform to the needs of the production system and the production system ought to be designed in relation to the requirements of the ecological system. It is logical to ask in this order: what are the needs of the peoples of the world for production goods? How can we manage things to produce these needed goods whilst maintaining the integrity of the ecological base of production?

In reality the relations of the three systems are the other way round. The global environmental crisis tells us that the ecological system has been disastrously affected by the design of the production system, which has developed with almost no regard for sustaining the ecological system. For example, the growth of secondary industries and their use of fossil fuels has led to the imminent exhaustion of fossil fuels and the pollution of the atmosphere with excess carbon dioxide and other gases. The effects of the latter could be disastrous in the long term for agricultural production. The faulty design of the production system has been imposed by the economic system which invests in factories that promise increased profits. The goods are not necessarily those most needed. Advocates of economic growth don't care what is produced. They are as happy to see a factory for speedboats set up as a factory to produce cheap bread, and little concern is shown for efficient use of resources and the maintenance of a healthy environment.

In capitalist countries, if not in others also, what the poor urgently need is more cheap housing, bread and public facilities such as schools, medical services and transport. The economic system ensures that we produce 95 cents' worth of expensive things to be bought by the already well-off for every five cents made available to do the things that most need doing. Baking a bigger cake according to market forces is said to be the efficient way to proceed. We do not need more speedboats, computer games or revolving restaurants on top of city towers. But those are the sorts of things we get when we allow a bigger cake to be baked. Market forces will always devote most of the available resources to supplying those with 'effective demand' with what they want rather than to producing what most humans need. That is one reason why most of the world's resources flow into rich countries to produce so many unnecessary items when they could be producing what millions of poor people need. It is why so much land and capital in the Third World is put to producing luxuries for export. It is why in the 1980s the flow of goods was from 'south' to 'north'. When agribusiness turned its attention to producing food in Third World countries for the inhabitants, their products went into the mouths of the middle and rich classes, not those of the poor. The reason was simple. The poor couldn't afford to buy food: the demand was there; the purchasing power wasn't. Injustice became further compounded.

Away back in 1930 the economist John Maynard Keynes pointed to the demoralising consequences of economic affluence. In his essay on the 'Economic Possibilities for our Grand Children' he recognised the possibility that human beings in the future could be freed from the struggle for subsistence, but he was not optimistic. On the contrary, he said, 'To judge from the behaviour and the achievements of the wealthy classes today in any quarter of the world, the outlook is very depressing' and he added: 'If the economic problem is solved, mankind will be deprived of its traditional purpose . . . must we not expect a nervous breakdown?' (quoted by Abrecht 1972 p. 178). A large part of the affluent world is now experiencing a large measure of freedom from the struggle for subsistence, but there are many within that world who are not and many more outside that world who can hardly survive. Furthermore, the world is also experiencing the crisis of the spirit which Keynes predicted. To that is to be added the environmental crisis.

What confronts us is not a series of separate crises in industry, economics and ecology but a single basic defect that lies deep in the design of modern society, be it in capitalist, socialist, developing or developed countries. The problems may, in theory, be more amenable to correction in the centrally controlled economies but this does not seem to be the case in practice. We are all in the same boat concerning relations between the production, economic and ecological systems. Paul Abrecht, who was at the time director of Church and Society in the World Council of Churches, on a visit to East Berlin spoke with the director of the economic planning office in the East German government. The limits-to-growth debate was then raging in the West. He asked the government planner if the German Democratic Republic was also concerned about ecological constraints on economic growth. 'Limits to growth?' he replied, pointing to the television set in his office. 'There's the villain! Most of our people can now watch television from West Germany and they see all the goods available there and expect us to make them available here. So our government must match the West.' When Abrecht asked whether he believed that a television picture from a Western consumer society was stronger than his country's ideology he simply laughed. A churchman from another Eastern European country said to Abrecht: 'In our country Marxism is asleep. Our economy develops according to quite other theories.'

Too often a particular economic system rather than commonsense governs our lives, be it in East or West. Keynes was well aware of this when he wrote in 1936: 'The ideas of economists and political philosophers, both when they are right and when they are wrong, are more powerful than is commonly understood. Indeed the world is ruled by little else' (quoted by Ehrlich, Ehrlich & Holdren 1977 p. 843).

The proper object of economic activity, says the economist of sustainable societies Daly (1973), is to have enough bread, not infinite bread, not a world turned into bread, not even vast storehouses full of bread. The infinite hunger of humanity is exacerbated by the madness of producing more and more things for more and more people. More is not better, especially when the process of getting more destroys the life-sustaining systems of the world. Daly believes in assessing the basic needs of humanity, in devising economic systems that will look after those needs while attending to the health of the environment at the same time. Economists are always asking—what is the health of the economy? They would better ask

— what is the health of the environment and the people living in it?

There are limits to the growth of industries producing material goods. Our task is to see to it that such growth as is necessary fulfils legitimate human needs. That could mean de-development in rich countries in order that the poorer countries have their fair share of the resources of the earth. And in doing that we have to learn how to get more from less. The principle is that the rich must live more simply that the poor may simply live. Today 75 per cent of the world's population live in developing countries; by the year 2000 some 79 per cent will be living in those countries. Bangladesh is the poorest country in the world. With 97 million people it is the eighth-largest country in the world. By the year 2000 at least 53 million people will be added to its population, even allowing for some decrease in birthrate. The world has not solved the problem of how to feed and house the poor people of Bangladesh or anywhere else in the world, though it knows well how to make the rich richer. Increased production of itself will not redress distributional injustice. The rich can no longer continue to hide behind the slogan 'let 'em eat growth'.

For those who want a world of peace, justice and sustainability, existing institutions tend to frustrate individual purposes. The question I am asked more than any other when I speak to high-school students about these things is—but what can I, as an individual do? The modern world is showing that we can do a lot. The mismatch of economics, ecology and politics has brought into being a new emphasis on grassroots movements which see the need for a wholeness that is missing in conventional wisdom. In the assessment of Rector Soedjatmoko of the United Nations University, virtually all the significant social and political movements in the last two decades have begun from below. 'Governments,' he says, 'tend to become prisoners of their own experts. The grassroots movements sweeping across the political landscape force governments to re-examine the advice of their experts and to send them back to the drawing boards to look for other solutions' (quoted in *Development Forum* 13 (2) 1985 p. 15).

Grassroots movements have led to the formation of new political parties as witness the 'Greens' in the German Federal Republic and the Ecology Party in Britain. In March 1983, supported by two million votes, twenty-seven members of the Greens took their place in the Bundestag. The Ecology Party in Britain would have a significant representation in the British Parliament if there were proportional representation in the franchise. For the first time in Australia, state elections in Tasmania in 1989 brought five 'Greens' into parliament, which resulted in them having the balance of power with the prospect of a major change in direction in environmental issues in that state.

The power of public opinion was the force that created departments of environment in practically every country in the world and led to worldwide conservation programs culminating in the worldwide Conservation Strategy of the United Nations Environmental Programme. When the Club of Rome met thirty heads of state some years ago, the then Prime Minister of Canada, Pierre Trudeau, said that most of the heads of state present agreed with the call of the Club of Rome for a new approach to the interrelations between economics, ecology and politics. But he added, 'We don't have the political will' to proceed on that path. Convinced as they may have been by the need for a new direction, they did not have the grassroots support. To proceed along those lines would be political suicide. We tend to think of the politician in the democratic state as a leader trying to persuade the public. The tables are turning. Now the politician is waiting for a lead from the public, together with their support, before taking the initiative. Grassroots support provides the political will.

During the 1960s Rachel Carson awakened the world to the dire consequences of chemical pollution associated with modern industry. A decade later E. F. Schumacher, a forward thinking economist, challenged the 'bigger is better' mode of technological thinking in his book *Small is Beautiful* (1973). He has a significant following in the movement toward an appropriate technology for a sustainable society. In the U.S.A. Paul Ehrlich aroused a nation as well as much of the world to the needs of zero population growth if we were ever to surmount the ecological crisis. He realised that the log jam in so much of our thinking was our inability to relate economics and ecology. He brought a new thinking in this realm in his books, particularly *Ecoscience* (Ehrlich, Ehrlich & Holdren 1977), *Ark II: Social Response to Environmental Imperatives* (Pirages & Ehrlich 1974), *The Machinery of Nature* (Ehrlich 1986) and *New World New Mind* (Ornstein & Ehrlich 1989).

Further examples of the disastrous consequences of the fragmentation of knowledge by the disciplinary approach to the two already given could be multiplied. Another obvious example is modern medicine. Curative medicine has been dominant over preventive medicine. Specialist medicine has tended to drive out general medicine. And the psychological and spiritual aspects of health and disease have taken a back seat. Yet there is no clearcut division between the sick body, the sick mind and the sick soul. When I am sick I want to be made whole and that involves me as a whole person. A doctor in New York, well known for his work in a clinic for sexually transmitted diseases, remarked 'every time I stick in my needle I feel: penicillin is not enough!' Acute stress, or more precisely certain ways of reacting to stress, can affect or in some cases even cause the onset of diabetes, arthritis, asthmas, the common cold, herpes, AIDS and cancer (Locke & Colligan 1986). It is now known that stress inhibits the immune response of the body and we become, as a result, more susceptible to viral and bacterial diseases. Some of the links between emotions and health are known. They involve the base of the brain, the nervous system and hormones (Hall & Goldstein 1986). Medicine is more than plumbing and pill-popping. Medical schools throughout the world face problems presented by the disciplinary approach. Many of them are experimenting with ways to see health as wholeness. But to do that medicine needs to recognise the insubstantial basis of its theory which alternates between a dualistic and a materialistic position. Some practitioners have recognised this deficiency and have begun to develop a process theory of medicine (Ford 1986).

The examples I have given of the tower of Babel fallacy are enough to indicate that religion in the postmodern world will become relevant in so far as it can once again find dialogue with all the disciplines and help to transform their divided house into some sort of whole. The tower of Babel is in shambles. We may be able to rebuild if we start from the new foundations of a postmodern worldview.

CHAPTER 7

New Wine in New Bottles

Religion will not regain its old power until it can face change in the same spirit as does science. Its principles may be eternal, but the expression of those principles requires continual development.

A. N. Whitehead (1933 p. 234)

Progress in truth—truth of science and truth of religion—is mainly a progress in the framing of concepts, in discarding artificial abstractions or partial metaphors, and in evolving notions which strike more deeply into the root of reality.

A. N. Whitehead (1930 p. 117)

Neither do men put new wine into old bottles; else the bottles break, and the wine runs out, and the bottles perish; but they put new wine into new bottles, and both are preserved.

Matthew 9:17 (Revised version)

The preceding chapter was primarily concerned with the predicament arising from regarding knowledge like a substance to be neatly divided into parcels called disciplines. This chapter is concerned with some ways of bringing divided disciplines together again. It commences with religion and science and proceeds to the relation between religion and culture as a whole.

The good news is that new wine is fermenting in both the vats of science and those of religion. Neither the new science nor the new religion can be contained in the old formula of a legal–mechanistic universe; that is, the image of a universe running according to rules laid down by an external law-maker. It has become evident to more and more people that science cannot live with an interventionist God. Nor can religion. As yet the message hasn't got across to today's world. The principles of the Christian religion may be eternal but the expression of those principles needs continual development. The truth may have been delivered once and for all to the saints. It is not delivered to us that way. Even today's preachers and theologians who claim to be recipients of the truth so conveniently delivered once and for all, so long ago, are not as uninfluenced by history and culture as many of them seem to suppose. Whitehead (1947 p. 96) surmised that if the leaders of any ecclesiastical organisation at present existing were transported back to the sixteenth century, and stated their full beliefs, historical and doctrinal, either in Geneva or in Spain, then Calvin or the Inquisitors would have been profoundly shocked and would have acted according to their habits in such cases.

If science and religion are to remain alive their formulations cannot remain static. New wine cannot be put into old bottles. The image, of course, is to the ancient wine bottle which was a wineskin made of leather. New wine simply bursts the old wineskins.

This is not a matter of making religion conform to each new model or discovery in science. It is a mutual matter. Science can be on guard to keep its concerns wide. Religion can point out the abstractions and false metaphors of science. Science can be a winnowing fan to religion, blowing away the husks to reveal the kernels. The encounter of religion with science compels it to purify its thinking about God from views of power that are sub-Christian. Together, both can discover the unity of nature. For if knowledge is one then each new discovery will involve some reshaping of the rest. As biology, for example, moves forward on its frontier at the molecular level, religion has a new way opened up for it also, just as evolutionary biology opened up a whole new province for religious thinking about creation.

The scientific understanding of the origin of species through evolution made nonsense of the origin of species by special creation. It does more. It says to religion: re-think your concepts of how God acts in nature. The 'creationists' of today want to reject the new wine of biology. To accept it would involve them in a reconstruction of their religious formulations which they are unwilling to face. They happily accept the new wine of the big-bang concept of the origin of the universe because they think it fits into the old bottles of a literal understanding of the first chapter of Genesis. But it doesn't.

It is a mistake to suppose that the writers of the Bible in a pre-scientific age were giving a scientific account of the universe. They had other images. They knew nothing about concepts of the 'big bang' or 'continuous creation' of modern cosmology. The writers of Genesis were probably not evolutionists. They didn't write about evolution. So it is pointless to stretch their metaphors to an evolutionary context. But they had insights that an evolutionist can respect. And if we are convinced that evolution is an appropriate way of thinking of the cosmos, we can certainly gain insights from the Bible that can be translated into that context. Teilhard de Chardin sought to do that. So too does process theology. Some insights of religion will remain valid no matter what science discovers.

There are other religious ideas people have held and still hold that have become irrelevant with an understanding of science. The interventionist God is one such concept. This makes life for some people confusing. They want to keep their beliefs like canned sardines that don't change. A living faith is like a living fish. It cannot be canned without losing its life. But it is much more difficult to deal with squirming living fish than canned fish.

Religion and culture

Science is but one part of culture. I have concentrated thus far on the confrontation of science and religion because the greatest intellectual task for religion today is a new dialogue with science that could transform both. The principles involved in such a dialogue apply as well to other aspects of culture besides science.

In the history of Christian thought there have been periods in

which great attempts have been made to find a synthesis of religion
and culture. In the nineteenth century G. W. F. Hegel and Friedrich
Schleiermacher had the greatest influence in this respect. Both
taught at Berlin University in the beginning of the nineteenth century. Tillich (1967 p. 387) regards Schleiermacher as the father of
modern Protestant theology. Hegel's influence extended not only
into religion but also into the political transformation of the world in
the twentieth century. Marx, Nietzsche and Kierkegaard are not
understandable apart from Hegel's influence upon them. In the
twentieth century A. N. Whitehead is the great synthesiser. But
there have been as well periods in which religion was sundered
apart from culture, science was separated from religion and religion
was separated from metaphysics. Karl Barth and his followers in
this century said there can be no synthesis. There is no point of
contact between God and man. God is in his heaven and man is in
the world. This is the situation of religion against culture. A sorry
situation it is for both religion and culture. Religion becomes irrelevant to the life of the world.

If religion is not to be divorced from the rest of life and culture
it has to grow. The religious task is not simply a case of trying to
experience and understand what the founders of the faith bequeathed. It is to make it relevant to our time and culture. And if
culture has something novel and positive to contribute to the dialogue, religion cannot remain uninfluenced. Culture is continually
changing as science, art and education develop. A living religion
evolves with these changes.

Christianity is both a protest against the contemporary world
and an effort to transform itself and the world. There is always new
wine being fermented in the vats of culture. How is religion to
appropriate these new insights? Tillich saw religion, not as a special
function of human life, but as the dimension of depth in all its
functions (Tillich 1959 p. 5). Nothing is to be excluded. But, he
asked, if religion is present in all functions of life, why has humanity
developed religion as a special sphere among others, in myth, cult,
devotion and ecclesiastical institutions? He answers—because of
the tragic estrangement of human life from its deepest possibilities.

According to the visionary who wrote the last book of the
Bible, there will be no temple in the heavenly Jerusalem. There will
be no secular realm. So there will be no religious realm. There will
be no division into sacred and secular at all. The very existence of
religion as a separate realm is a result of our tragic estrangement

from the depth of life's possibilities. When that estrangement is overcome, as envisaged in the book of Revelation, religion as such is no longer necessary. It follows that religion becomes less necesary the more it enables culture to find its real depths. The secular is then swallowed up in the sacred. But while religion exists, if it despises the secular realm it forgets its own emergency character and creates its own ghetto.

When the Christianity of any age seeks to discover the dimension of depth in contemporary culture it will itself be transformed to the extent that it succeeds. That will depend upon a readiness to re-examine all its theology in the light of both the questions and the discoveries of the day. Only in this way can theology hope to be a living influence in the church and the world. The dialogue between science and religion in the past has resulted in no more than a truce on the battlefields. It should have quite another purpose—that each be transformed, one by the other. A healthy relation of faith and culture requires that we constantly rethink faith in terms of the rest of our understanding of reality.

In the first centuries of Christian history the church appropriated a great deal from Neoplatonism, which was its chief competitor in the Hellenistic world. It was both a gain and a loss. It was a loss when its assimilation was uncritical. To a large extent the conversion of the pagan intelligentsia required the assimilation into Christianity of what this intelligentsia found most convincing in its classical heritage, its poetry and its science. In making this point Cobb (1982 p. 6) says that Basil of Caesarea declared that in pagan literature Christians could find something that 'keeps the soul alive'. The victory of the church over paganism was in part due 'to the rule that the Christians assimilate pagan ideas while the pagans do not appropriate Christian ones' (Momigliano 1963 p. 87, quoted by Cobb 1982a p. 6). Even Christian leaders who fulminated against this sort of assimilation accepted much of classical culture. Tertullian was the outstanding example. Yet he was selective in his denunciations. Ever since there have been exclusivists who denied any truth outside their religion. Others have struggled to make their faith relevant to all truth. St Thomas Aquinas was deeply indebted to Islam. His recognition of rational theology in Islam influenced the development of his conception of the power of reason to attain much knowledge of God (Cobb 1982a p. 8).

The church was deeply influenced by the culture of the

Enlightenment in the eighteenth century. On the one hand the Enlightenment cast off the dead hand of authority. On the other hand it presented the case for the modern worldview as mechanistic and bound inevitably to progress on the wings of science. The church never came to terms with the Enlightenment. There were for it both gains and losses. The church gained in so far as it accepted a critical attitude to dogma. This began around 1750 when G. E. Lessing led the fight against a stupid orthodoxy which stuck to traditional interpretations. This critical approach was carried on by a succession from D. F. Strauss, Friedrich Schleiermacher, Johannes Weiss, Albert Schweitzer, Rudolf Bultmann and many others. They were not, of course, the first critics of dogma but they carried through systematically the criticisms of an earlier age by people such as Fausto Socinus of the sixteenth century, perhaps the first 'modern' process theologian.

As a result of the Enlightenment reason took on a new role. 'Have courage to use your own reason—that is the motto of the Enlightenment', said Kant. It was because of the rationalism of the Enlightenment that we no longer have witch trials. In its principle of harmony the Enlightenment laid the foundations for democracy as against authoritarian rule. It was the conviction that in spite of the fact that each one decides now for himself about government, a common will or harmony will somehow result from it all. It is the belief in education to develop the potentialities of every individual so that a stable society will result. The people of the Enlightenment created public schools that had not existed up to that time. The church accepted a role in this also.

The sense of moral discipline so strongly developed in Calvinism included the discipline of work which took on the connotation of working for the transformation of nature for the sake of humanity. The Protestant work ethic was reinforced by the Enlightenment. This was both good and bad. It led to exploitation of labour and it has never been readapted to this age of increasing leisure (see Davis & Gosling 1985).

In its encounter with the Enlightenment the church lost when it surrendered the public or secular sphere of life to control by the assumptions of the Enlightenment. At least for Protestantism this led many to retreat into a religion of the soul (Newbigin 1986). The church lost when it accepted from the Enlightenment a reinforcement of the idea that God made the world and left it to follow its own laws. Science and religion became two separate domains.

Science dealt with the secular realm while religion had to do with a God who transcended that realm. God was removed from nature. And, as Tillich (1967 p. 422) points out, when God is removed from nature, God gradually disappears altogether, because we are nature. If God has nothing to do with nature, he finally has nothing to do with our total being. For many that is precisely what the Enlightenment did. They rejected the supernaturalistic God and became atheists.

Today there is a longstanding, but urgent need for Christians to reassess their inheritance from the Enlightenment, to consolidate what was gained and to free themselves from the negative consequences. The need deepens with each passing day.

It is the contention of the historian of religion Marty (1986) that religion in twentieth-century America was essentially shaped by its encounter with modernity. He traces the diverse ways in which American religion embraced, rejected or cautiously accepted the modern world with both gains and losses.

Part of the culture of the modern world is a plurality of religions. The most common response of Christians to other faiths has been to assume those who are different are for that reason inferior: they lack the saving truth of Christianity. An alternative position is to see Jesus as one saviour among many. In *Beyond Dialogue* Cobb (1982b) sees the former as turning Christ into an instrument of our arrogance and the latter as abandoning the universal meaning and truth of Christ that is central to Christianity. He asks if there is another option and points out that neither the Roman Catholic Church nor the World Council of Churches has accepted either horn of this dilemma. Both are working to avoid imperialism and relativism. Both are committed to dialogue. Dialogue assumes that the partner is worth listening to as well as addressing. But dialogue that goes no further than that stagnates. For if we are to hear the truth in an authentic way we shall be transformed by that truth, no matter what its source is. Cobb (1982b p. 21) draws attention to a statement from a World Council of Churches consultation on dialogue with people of living faiths in 1971 which said 'Dialogue thus involves the risk of one partner being changed by the other. It implies a readiness to receive an enrichment and enlargement.' But Cobb adds that this radical conception of dialogue has not been taken up in subsequent WCC discussions. The WCC promotes dialogue, but it has not yet moved beyond it.

Cobb (1982b) believes that from major forms of Buddhism

there is a challenge to Christians in the Buddhist concept that every belief in God is a form of clinging that blocks the achievement of the ultimate goal of Nirvana. He is likewise convinced that Buddhism can help the Christian to remove from the image of God elements of substance thinking (the substantialist prejudice) which would be a gain for the expression of Christian faith.

The history of the relationship of Christianity to the faith of Islam has mostly been one of confrontation. Today, more than ever, there is need for dialogue. The gulf may indeed be deep and wide between Christianity and fundamentalist Islam, but bridges have long existed between Christianity and Islam that could be opened up again to the mutual benefit of both and to the world (Cragg 1964).

Politics is a part of culture. Religion can seek to discover new depths in this aspect of life. Hence the new movements of 'liberation theology' and 'political theology'. Liberation theology originated in the Third World where it finds its deepest expression in the midst of poverty and political oppression (Boff 1985). Political theology goes back to the Stoics; it was an expression of those religious practices which served the needs of the state (Cobb 1982b p. 2). Solle (1971) holds the view that 'no one can be saved alone' (p. 56). This echoes the emphasis of Reinhold Niebuhr in the postwar years that we cannot seek personal salvation in separation from the salvation of society from injustice. Solle followed her statement with a call for 'the indivisible salvation of the whole world'. This could be a goal of political theology.

Much of the history of the World Council of Churches and the ecumenical movement that led to its formation has been concerned with social and political thought. Abrecht (1984) is one of many ecumenical leaders who judge that no ecumenically organised reflection on theology and social ethics has matched the quality and thoroughness of the 1937 meeting of the WCC on 'Church Community and State in Relation to the Economic Order' and its report of that title. Preston (1983) attributed much of its impact to the presence and influence of William Temple and Reinhold Niebuhr. They achieved a meeting of theology and social ethics that was trail-blazing. The ethicists who were to follow in more recent times have supposed that the issues of social ethics were so complex that only specialist ethicists could deal with them. Christian ethics split off from theology. Once it established itself as a separate discipline it largely ceased to re-examine its assumptions, as so often happens with disciplines. The results, as Cobb (1985 p. 128) points out, have been disastrous. This compartmentalisation has been deeply contrary to the fundamental Christian understanding brought to ethics by Temple and Niebuhr. Liberation theology and political theology may eventually help to heal that breach.

A second fundamental requirement of the fruitful relation of Christian faith and social issues is emphasised by the Indian ecumenical leader M. M. Thomas (1984). No religious or ideological dogma, he argues, can acquire relevance in this dialogue 'unless it shows a capacity to redefine and integrate within its framework the deepest aspiration of liberation which that culture has aroused in humankind . . . in order to do that religions including Christianity [also] need to be redefined' (p. 320). This argument was made in criticism of Newbigin (1983) and is relevant to Newbigin (1986), who emphasises Christian religon as dogma which confronts culture to change it but is not itself changed by that culture. The dialogue of religion with culture, be it with science or social issues or any other aspect of culture, is a two-way affair. To be effective it has to involve a two-way transformation, that of religion and that of the cultural elements concerned. When religion discovers the element of depth in culture it is itself transformed as well as transforming culture. That is authentic dialogue. Niebuhr was sceptical of anything more than ephemeral social gains in this process because the resolution of one problem seemed to lead to another arising which was just as difficult. Niebuhr serves as an antidote to false optimism. But today both liberation theology and political theology work in the real hope that ultimately a more just and a more peaceful world is possible. If we did not have that hope most of us would give up the struggle.

The contemporary movement of feminism calls for a response from religion. Indeed, much of it is a criticism of religion. Male domination is characteristic of all the major religions. All were founded by men and what they are today has been shaped by men. Jesus was a man. He chose men only as his disciples. He referred to God as father. Many churches today refuse to accept women as clergy. Does Christianity have to remain this way? Conservatives say yes. But if the movement of feminism points to a real disorientation of Christianity and if then Christianity is to find the element of depth in the movement of feminism, it must inevitably itself be transformed. So there are those, such as Cobb (1983b) and McFague (1987), who call for a reorientation of Christianity away from its dominantly male image. That is to assert that Christianity is a living movement that can become what it has not yet been. That is the meaning of any genuine encounter of religion with the new elements in culture.

Another aspect of modern culture which the church has not come to terms with is sexual behaviour. Many of us were brought up with what we understood to be the one Christian view of sex: it is fine within the bonds of marriage but not otherwise. This code has little relation to what goes on in the wide world outside. A 1980 survey in a wide range of countries showed the proportion of adolescents reported to have experienced premarital intercourse varied from about 35 per cent (in France) to 80 per cent (among Kenyan males). For example, in the United States in the range 17–21 years of age some 77 per cent of males and 69 per cent of females had experienced premarital sex. In Australia, in the range 15–20 years of age the figures were 58 per cent for males and 47 per cent for females. In Kenya the figure for males up to age 19 years was 80 per cent. In Norway by age 19 some 57 per cent of Christian males and 72 per cent of non-Christian males had experienced premarital sex (Senderowitz & Paxman 1985 p. 8).

The moral teachings of the churches are out of step with cultural patterns of sexual behaviour of youth. This does not mean that the church is wrong and modern youth is right. It does mean there is a gulf between attitudes. The church is not monolithic in its attitude today. Yet the official attitude of most churches reflects the simple moralism of sex within marriage alone. Others in the church are working for a more sympathetic and deeper view. This is well brought out in a debate within the General Conference of the United Methodist Church in the U.S.A. on moral sexual behaviour expected of Christians and whether standards should be stricter for clergy than for lay people. The conservative view was put in an essay by Kirkley (1984). The broader questioning view was put by Cobb (1984), who concluded that the church was ready to think but not ready to legislate. Kirkley held to the *status quo*. One argued that the contemporary culture, particularly of youth, may be discovering a meaning of sex with positive elements that should be explored by religion. The other had nothing to learn from the changing culture.

Included in the change in cultural values concerning sex are contemporary attitudes to homosexuality. According to Coffin (1982), it is probably the most divisive issue in the U.S.A. since slavery split the church. This is because the once unmentionable has become unavoidable, because of cultural changes toward homosexuality. The history of the church is largely one of exclusion of those who are practising homosexuals, whether that refers to 'one night stands' or lasting loving relationships. The 'homosexual problem' is really a 'heterosexual problem', just as the 'woman problem' is basically the problem of male sexism. It is the problem of the attitude of heterosexuals to people who are different. Coffin refers to four stances toward homosexuality: a rejecting–punitive position, a rejecting–nonpunitive position, conditional acceptance, and unconditional acceptance. The Jerry Falwells of the Christian 'moral majority' adopt the rejecting–punitive stance. The appropriate questions to put to them is—can a sexual bigot be a Christian and should the church ordain homophobes? The rejecting nonpunitive stance condemns homosexual acts but not the homosexual. The person is not to blame for his or her orientation but is to blame for homosexual acts. The stance of conditional acceptance is that all rights should be accorded homosexuals, including ordination, but they draw the line with public displays of gay affection and they would not be happy with a gay spouse in the vicarage. Coffin argues for the stance of absolute acceptance of the homosexual person as the one acceptable Christian attitude. Process theologian Pittenger (1967) argues for a similar position. And so have a number of other clergy, as for example ninety Episcopalian priests from the New York area who met to discuss the matter. 'Christians,' they said, 'must re-think the usual position that has turned homosexuals into modern day lepers' and 'homosexual acts should be judged in each individual instance by whether the participants were expressing genuine love or simply "using" each other for selfish purposes' (*New York Times* 20 November 1967 p. 1).

The stance of absolute acceptance should be based on something more substantial than the oft-quoted proposition which Shakespeare put into the mouth of a rather foolish old man, Polonius: 'This above all: to thine own self be true'. It is too easy to kid oneself about what is the true self. We need to discover what we think we are and then to rise above that. And for that we need an image of the human that goes beyond what we are. For Christians this is what they see Jesus and those who reflect him to be. Homosexuals are neither inferior nor superior to heterosexuals. They are different.

The attitude of absolute acceptance of homosexuals has been put into practice by a small number of churches. Religion in these churches is finding a depth it had not known before that works

towards a transformation of both religion and this aspect of modern
culture. I am familiar with four such churches in the U.S.A. and
Australia: Riverside Church in New York with William Sloane
Coffin as pastor, Judson Memorial Church in Greenwich Village in
New York with Howard Moody as pastor, the Glide Memorial
Methodist Church in San Francisco with Cecil Williams and the
Wayside Chapel of the Uniting Church in Kings Cross in Sydney
which was founded and built under its first pastor, Ted Noffs.
Absolute acceptance in each of these churches means that no person
is excluded from the fellowship on any grounds at all.

The fellowship of these churches includes people excluded by
other churches or who exclude themselves from other churches,
which is really the same thing. Total acceptance of homosexuals
means that no questions are asked and no-one is excluded because
of sexual preference or sexual behaviour. Each person is regarded
as a normal human being seeking fulfilment. These churches believe
it is important that individuals seek fulfilment, not in a ghetto but in
a wider society of people. From time to time each of these churches
has special programs dealing with homosexual concerns, such as
police harassment and brutality. My involvement in the Wayside
Chapel has convinced me that the total fellowship is the richer for
practising absolute acceptance. Some churches, notably Protestant
churches in the Netherlands, have accepted homosexuals into the
ordained ministry of the church.

However, the rejecting stance of most churches has led to the
formation of homosexual churches, which is understandable but
unfortunate. The attempts by these churches to become part of
national councils of churches in both the U.S.A. and Australia, and
doubtless elsewhere, have been rejected. The churches as a whole
are obviously not yet ready to meet the homosexual person with
total acceptance. That is a cultural and religious loss.

In the world today 'success' at any point means being completely
adapted to circumstances which are passing from us. That is the
situation the dinosaurs found themselves in. They flourished so long
as their environment remained static. But they were unable to adapt
to change that was pressing upon them. They became fossils. When
a new kind of society and culture is emerging, it is not likely that the
old will willingly disinherit much, if anything, of itself. It tries to
make a new life out of what is left of the old. It may work desperately to keep the old wine in the old bottles. Or it may try to hold the

old wine in new bottles. It never works. New wine needs new bottles to contain it.

Conformity and resistance to change is tantamount to acceptance of corruption because it is a state of participating in existing corruption and being subjected to it. It was religious conformism that threatened both Jesus and Socrates and brought them to their deaths. Our time has experienced many revolutionary transformations. Today we are reacting against further revolutions and transformations. 'Don't let the world around you squeeze you into its own mould, but let God re-mould your minds from within' is Phillips' (1947 p. 27) translation of Romans 12:2. There is a three-fold directive in this passage: exercise judgment, offer resistance and strive to effect personal and universal transformation. The non-conformist must be prepared to risk ostracism, and in many countries today imprisonment or death, and as well the possibility of being wrong. Those who have transformed the world risked wrong decisions. The greater they were the more conscious were they of the risk. They took upon themselves the anxiety of doubt. One who risks and fails can be forgiven. One who never risks and never fails is a failure in his or her whole being, for their own forgiveness is never sought.

The call for a return to simple basics, be it in religion, morality, economics or politics is a call to retain the outmoded ways of the past. It is a call to reinforce the *status quo* and prevent change. 'The defence of morals,' said Whitehead (1942), 'is the battle-cry which best rallies stupidity against change' (p. 309). He went on to refer to a paradox concerning morals that the champions of morality are on the whole the fierce opponents of new ideals. 'Mankind,' says Whitehead, 'has been afflicted with low-toned moralists, objecting to expulsion from some Garden of Eden' (p. 310). Every advance starts off from some assimiliated system of customs. It would have been no virtue for Adam and Eve to have spent the whole of their lives sitting under fruit trees in the garden. They learned a lot from their expulsion. To have returned later would have been an atavistic step. Fortunately they continued their exploration of life.

The theme of the seventh Assembly of the World Council of Churches in 1983 was 'Jesus Christ, the Life of the World' (Gill 1983). If that be a true statement, then Christians in particular have a unique contribution to make to the problems of the world. It is not simply to reflect the thinking of experts in the various disciplines. Rather it is their task to make their own unique analysis from a perspective unknown to the expert. The theme of that Assembly implied that the whole world—its science, its politics, its art, its economics and its total management—is the field of action for the churches. This role the churches are not fulfilling today. A major reason is that they are contributing to, rather than fighting against, the substantialist prejudice in which knowledge and understanding are divided into territories, some of which are religious and others secular. They have not seen themselves as seeking the element of depth in all these different areas of life. If they were to dig deep wells in the secular realms, is it not possible that they would find a great underground resource of water—a reservoir of the water of life from which all draw? Or to change the metaphor, what we see as islands separated in an expanse of ocean are all connected under the ocean. But we concentrate our gaze on the distances between islands instead of their undersea continuity. We need more imagination to get out of our island mentality and to see the whole as one.

Conclusion

A central affirmation of this book is the presence of the future in life, that human life feeds on purpose. Richness of life depends upon purposes we freely choose. That which animates human life animates alike the rest of the entities of creation. The evidence of science leads to a view of the universe as purposive in the sense that its entities exist by virtue of a degree of freedom which allows them a degree of self-determination. In this postmodern ecological worldview the whole of the universe and its entities look more like life than like matter. The appropriate image is no longer the machine but the organism. This view is counter-intuitive if we concentrate on the thinginess of things. Our failure to see the world in ecological or organic terms is because we tend to reify everything in it. The modern worldview which was born in the sixteenth century and which dominates our thinking to this day tends to interpret everything from the bottom up. We think of the universe in terms of building blocks like bricks and try to put them together into a universe. And what we get of course is a contrivance without feeling, without life. That is the tragic consequence of the modern worldview.

The most important change in the postmodern worldview is to interpret from the top down. It is to regard human experience as a high-level example of the rest of reality. It turns the modern worldview upside down. The dominant tradition of Christianity in the last three centuries has been the opposite. Yet there always has been a stream of thought and life that rejected the mechanistic worldview. We find it in the prophetic tradition in the Old Testament, in the teaching of Jesus and elsewhere in the New Testament and in the writings of the church fathers. It has been retained more by the Eastern tradition of Christendom than by the Western tradition. Today it finds its fullest development in the mode of Christian thought known as process theology. True to its tradition, process theology seeks a close working with contemporary culture in all its manifestations.

Process theology has been a major preoccupation of American studies for the past fifty years. It has been a continuous challenge to the modern worldview derived from seventeenth century mechanism, eighteenth-century rationalism, nineteenth-century positivism and twentieth-century nihilism. That it is less known and less influential outside the U.S.A. is perhaps associated with a plethora of terms that accompanied its modern birth. The terminology is not a necessary part of the baggage of this mode of Christian thought. It is far more dependent upon images from the New Testament and organic images from physics and biology. And it is discovering the value of images in art as well (e.g. Odin 1984).

It is not a way of thought and life simply for an elite, though its appeal is naturally greatest for those whose experience of Christianity is incomplete until they have experienced an intellectual conversion. God speaks to the peasant working in the fields. And God speaks to the more philosophically disposed. Each finds a richness of experience. Each will be the same and yet different. The peasant doesn't demand an intellectual justification. The philosopher does. It is popular these days for theologians living in rich cities to say that most of what they know they have learned from the poor. This is sometimes a sort of inverted snobbery, especially when those who say this spend so little time with the poor. Maybe the poor they meet are more authentic in their lives and really show what courage and dedication mean. I have lived most of my life with students in universities. Most of them are not peasants, though many of them would classify themselves as poor! Most of what I have learned has been from them. They are human beings who seem to me like anyone else who struggles to find meaning and richness in life. What I do know about students is that their inner need is not met by the purely emotive side of experience. They want in their heart of hearts an intellectual understanding of what they experience. Theirs is faith seeking understanding. This is what I understand theology to be all about. I can recall a discussion in which Paul Tillich said that theology was due to Greek philosophers who became Christians and couldn't live as Christians without giving account of themselves in meaningful terms.

The take-home message of this book may be summed up in three words: passion, philosophy, program. Each is involved in the working out of purpose in human life. They are the three elements of religion: intuitive, cognitive and active:

Passion: the only appropriate response to faithful participation in that which matters most is with passion. It is Schleiermacher's 'feeling of unconditional dependence', Tillich's 'with infinite passion' and Jesus' 'with all your heart'. The existential or feeling side of life is intuitive.

Philosophy: the affective side of life seeks meaning in understanding, which is the cognitive and purposive side of life. It is Jesus' 'with all your mind'. Paul admonished Christians 'do not be children in your thinking . . . in thinking be mature' (1 Corinthians 14:20). This is philosophy and theology.

Program: the feeling and the cognitive side of life are sterile until they find an outcome in action. By their fruits you shall know them. This is the practical side of life worked out in a program for life. It is Jesus' 'with all your strength'.

To live is to feel, to think and to act. The call to the full life is to love with all our heart and mind and strength, these three. There is no more emphatic utterance in all scriptures than that. I know of no greater commitment that life can make.

References

Abrecht, Paul R. (1972). The future as a 'religious' problem. *The Ecumenical Review* 24,176–89.

Abrecht, Paul R. (1984). The evolution of ecumenical social thought: Some personal reflections. In *Faith and Faithfulness* (ed. P. Webb), pp. 102–26. Geneva: World Council of Churches.

Agar, W. E. (1943). *A Contribution to the Theory of the Living Organism.* Melbourne University Press.

Alic, Margaret. (1986). *Hypatia's Heritage: A history of women in science from antiquity to the late nineteenth century.* London: The Women's Press.

Andrewartha, H. G. & Birch, L. C. (1984). *The Ecological Web: More on the distribution and abundance of animals.* University of Chicago Press.

Ariga, T. (1959). *An Enquiry Into the Basic Structure of Christian Thought.* Tokyo: Maruzen.

Baillie, John (1951). *Natural Science and the Spiritual Life.* Oxford University Press.

Baker, John A. (1979). Biblical views of nature. *Anticipation* 25,40–6.

Barbour, Ian G. (1966). *Issues in Science and Religion.* Englewood Cliffs, NJ: Prentice-Hall.

Barnett, S. A. (1989). *Biology and Freedom: An essay on the implications of human ethology.* Cambridge University Press.

Barrow, John D. & Tipler, Frank J. (1986). *The Anthropic Cosmological Principle.* Oxford: Clarendon.

Bellah, Robert N. (1970). *Beyond Belief: Essays on religion in a post-traditional world.* New York: Harper and Row.

Berman, M. (1981). *The Reenchantment of the World.* Ithaca, NY: Cornell University Press.

Bettenson, H. (1956). *The Early Christian Fathers.* Oxford University Press.

Birch, Charles (1976). *Confronting the Future. Australia and the world: The next hundred years.* Ringwood, Australia: Penguin Books.

Birch, Charles & Cobb, John B. Jr (1981). *The Liberation of Life: From the cell to the community.* Cambridge University Press.

Boff, Leonard (1985). *Church Charisma and Power: Liberation theology and the institutional church.* London: SCM Press.

Bohm, David (1973). Quantum theory as an indication of a new order in physics. *Foundations of Physics* 3,139–68.

Bohm, David (1977). The implicate or enfolded order — a new order for physics. In *Mind in Nature* (eds. John B. Cobb & David R. Griffin), pp. 37–42. Washington: University Press of America.

Bohm, David (1980). *Wholeness and the Implicate Order.* London: Routledge and Kegan Paul.

Bohm, David (1982). Conversations between Rupert Sheldrake, Renee Weber and David Bohm. *ReVision* 5,23–48.

Bohm, David (1985a). Hidden variables and the implicate order. *Zygon* 20,111–24.

Bohm, David (1985b). Fragmentation and wholeness in religion and science. *Zygon* 20,125–37.

Boulding, Kenneth (1971). The economics of the coming spaceship earth. In

Global Ecology (eds. J. H. Holdren & P. R. Ehrlich), pp. 180–7. New York: Harcourt Brace.

Brown, R. Manbury (1986). *The Wisdom of Science: Its Relevance to Culture and Religion.* Cambridge University Press.

Burhoe, Ralph (1973). The concepts of God and soul in a scientific view of human purpose. *Zygon* 8,412–42.

Burnet, F. M. (1940). *Biological Aspects of Infectious Disease.* Cambridge University Press.

Capra, Fritjof (1982). *The Turning Point: Science society and the rising culture.* New York: Simon & Schuster.

Chalmers, A. F. (1976). *What Is This Thing Called Science?* St Lucia, Queensland: Queensland University Press.

Charlesworth, Max (1982). *Science, Non-Science and Pseudo-Science.*Geelong, Victoria: Deakin University Press.

Cobb, John B. Jr (1959). *God and the World.* Philadelphia: Westminster Press.

Cobb, John B. Jr (1967). *The Structure of Christian Existence.* Philadelphia: Westminster Press.

Cobb, John B. Jr (1973). Ecology, ethics and theology. In *Towards a Steady-State Economy* (ed. H. E. Daly), pp. 307–20. San Francisco: W. H. Freeman.

Cobb, John B. Jr (1982a). *Process Theology as Political Ecology.* Philadelphia: Westminster Press.

Cobb, John B. Jr (1982b). *Beyond Dialogue: Toward a mutual transformation of Christianity and Buddhism.* Philadelphia: Fortress Press.

Cobb, John B. Jr (1983a). God and the scientific worldview. In *Talking with God* (eds. David Tracy & John B. Cobb Jr.), pp. 39–56. New York: Seabury Press.

Cobb, John B. Jr (1983b). God and feminism. In *Talking with God* (eds. David Tracy & John B. Cobb Jr), pp. 75–89. New York: Seabury Press.

Cobb, John B. (1984). Is the church ready to legislate on sex? *Christianity and Crisis* 44,182–5.

Cobb, John B. Jr (1985). Points of contact between process theology and liberation theology in matters of faith and justice. *Process Studies* 14,124–41.

Cobb, John B. Jr (1988). Ecology, science and religion: Toward a postmodern worldview. In *The Reenchantment of Science: Postmodern proposals* (ed. David R. Griffin), pp. 99–113. Albany, NY: State University of New York Press.

Cobb, John B. Jr & Griffin David R. (1976). *Process Theology: An introductory exposition.* Philadelphia: Westminster Press.

Cochran, A. A. (1966). Mind, matter and quanta. *Main Currents in Modern Thought* 22,79–88.

Cochran, A.A. (1972). Relation between quantum physics and biology. *Foundations of physics* 1,235–49.

Coffin, William Sloane (1982). *The Courage to Love.* New York: Harper and Row.

Coulson, Charles A. (1955). *Science and Christian Belief.* Oxford University Press.

Cragg, Kennedy (1964). *The Call of the Minaret.* Oxford University Press.

179

Daly, Herman E. (ed.) (1973). *Towards a Steady-State Economy.* San Francisco: W. H. Freeman.

Daly, Herman E. (1977). *Steady-State Economics.* San Francisco: W. H. Freeman.

Daly, Herman E. & Cobb, John B. (1989) *For the Common Good.* Boston: Beacon Press.

Darwin, Charles (1872). *The Expression of Emotions in Man and Animals.* (Reprint, University of Chicago Press, 1970).

Darwin, Francis (ed.) (1888). *The Life and Letters of Charles Darwin.* London: John Murray.

Darwin Francis (ed.) (1902). *The Life of Charles Darwin.* London: John Murray.

Davies, Paul (1982). *The Accidental Universe.* Cambridge University Press.

Davies, Paul (1983). *God and the New Physics.* New York: Simon & Schuster.

Davies, Paul (1984). *Superforce: The search for a grand unified theory of nature.* New York: Simon & Schuster.

Davis, Howard & Gosling, David (1984). *Will the Future Work? — values for emerging patterns of work and employment.* Geneva: World Council of Churches.

Delbruck, Max (1986). *Mind From Matter: An essay on evolutionary epistemology* (ed. posthumously by Gunther S. Stent). London: Blackwell Scientific Publications.

Dobzhansky, Theodosius (1956). *The Biological Basis of Human Freedom.* Columbia University Press.

Dobzhansky, Theodosius (1967). *The Biology of Ultimate Concern.* New York: New American Library.

Durning, Alan B. (1989). *Action at the Grassroots: Fighting poverty and environmental decline.* Worldwatch Paper 88. Washington: World Watch Institute.

Eastman, T. E. & Fales, E. (1984). Otherworlds, space, superforce and the quantum universe. *Foundations of Physics* 14,89–99.

Ehrlich, Paul R. (1986). *The Machinery of Nature: The living world around us and how it works.* New York: Simon and Schuster.

Ehrlich, Paul R., Ehrlich, Anne H. & Holdren, John P. (1977). *Ecoscience: Population, resources and environment.* San Francisco: W.H. Freeman.

Ehrlich, Paul R. & Sagan, Carl (1984). *The Cold and the Dark: The world after nuclear war.* New York: W. W. Norton.

Ford, Marcus (1986). *Towards a Process Theory of Medicine: Interdisciplinary essays.* New York: Edwin Mellen Press.

Fox, Warwick (1984). Deep ecology: A new philosophy of our time? *The Ecologist* 14,194–204.

Fox, Warwick (1989). *Toward a Transpersonal Ecology: The context, influence, meanings and distinctiveness of the deep ecology approach to ecophilosophy.* Boston: Shambala. New Science Library.

Frankl, V. E. (1964). *Man's Search for Meaning: An introduction to logotherapy.* London: Hodder & Stoughton.

Fromm, Erich (1962). *The Art of Loving.* London: Unwin Books.

Gill, David (ed.) (1983). *Gathered for Life: Official report, sixth assembly of the World Council of Churches.* Geneva: World Council of Churches.

Goodall, Jane van Lawick (1971). *In the Shadow of Man*. Boston: Houghton Mifflin.

Goodall, Jane van Lawick (1986). *The Chimpanzees of Gombe: Patterns of behavior*. Cambridge, MA: Harvard University Press.

Gosling, David & Musschenga B. (eds.) (1985). *Science Education and Ethical Values*. Geneva: World Council of Churches.

Gould, Stephen Jay (1983). Genes on the brain. *New York Review of Books* **30** (30 January), pp. 5–10.

Gould, Stephen Jay (1984). *Hen's Teeth and Horses' Toes*. Harmondsworth, Middlesex: Penguin Books.

Gould, Stephen Jay & Lewontin R. C. (1979). The spandrels of San Marco and the Panglossian paradigm: A critique of the adaptationist programme. *Proceedings of the Royal Society of London*, B **205**,581–98.

Gregorios, Paulos (1978). *The Human Presence: An Orthodox view of nature*. Geneva: World Council of Churches.

Gregorios, Paulos (1979). An Eastern Orthodox perspective of nature, man and God. *Anticipation* **25**,64–8.

Gregorios, Paulos (1980). *Cosmic Man: The divine presence*. New Delhi: Sophia.

Griffin, David Ray (1976). *God, Power and Evil: A process theodicy*. Philadelphia: Westminster Press.

Griffin, David Ray (1985). Bohm and Whitehead on wholeness, freedom, causality and time. *Zygon* **20**,165–91.

Griffin, David Ray (1986). *Theology and the rise of modern science*. Unpublished manuscript.

Griffin, David Ray (ed.) (1988). *The Reenchantment of Science: Postmodern proposals*. Ithaca, NY: State University of New York Press.

Griffin, Donald R. (1976). *The Question of Animal Awareness: Evolutionary continuity of mental experience*. New York: Rockefeller University Press.

Griffin, Donald R. (1984). *Animal Thinking*. Cambridge, MA: Harvard University Press.

Gustafson, James N. (1984). *Ethics From a Theocentric Perspective: Vol. 2. Ethics and Theology*. University of Chicago Press.

Habgood, John (1968). Minds and machines. In *Science and Religion: New perspectives on the dialogue*. (ed. Ian G. Barbour), pp. 300–08. New York: Harper and Row.

Hahn, Lewis E. (ed.) (1990). *The Philosophy of Charles Hartshorne*. The Library of Living Philosophers: Vol. 20. La Salle, IL: Open Court.

Haldane, J. B. S. (1927). *Possible Worlds and Other Essays*. London: Chatto and Windus.

Hall, Nicholas R. & Goldstein, Allan L. (1986). Thinking well: The chemical lines between emotions and health. *The Sciences* **26**,34–40.

Hartshorne, Charles (1941). *Man's Vision of God*. Chicago: Willet Clark.

Hartshorne, Charles (1948). *The Divine Relativity: A social conception of God*. New Haven: Yale University Press.

Hartshorne, Charles (1962). *The Logic of Perfection*. La Salle, IL: Open Court.

Hartshorne, Charles (1967). *A Natural Theology for Our Time*. La Salle, IL: Open Court.

Hartshorne, Charles (1970a). Recollections of famous philosophers and other important persons. *Southern Journal of Philosophy* 8,67–82.

Hartshorne (1970b). *Creative Synthesis and the Philosophic Method.* London: SCM Press.

Hartshorne, Charles (1977). Physics and psychics: The place of mind in nature. In *Mind in Nature: Essays on the interface of science and philosophy* (eds. John B. Cobb Jr & David Ray Griffin), pp. 89–96. Washington, DC: University Press of America.

Hartshorne, Charles (1979). God and Nature. *Anticipation* 25,58–64.

Hartshorne, Charles (1984a). *Omnipotence and Other Theological Mistakes.* Ithaca, NY: State University of New York Press.

Hartshorne, Charles (1984b). *Creativity in American Philosophy.* Ithaca, NY: State University of New York Press.

Hartshorne, Charles & Reese, W. L. (1953). *Philosophers Speak of God.* University of Chicago Press.

Haught, John F. (1984). *The Cosmic Adventure: Science, religion and the quest for purpose.* New York: Paulist Press.

Henderson, L. J. (1913). *The Fitness of the Environment.* New York: Macmillan.

Henderson-Sellers, Ann & Blong, Russell (1989). *The Greenhouse Effect: Living in a warmer Australia.* Kensington, N.S.W.: New South Wales University Press.

Ho, Mae-Wan & Saunders, P. T. (1984). *Beyond Neo-Darwinism: An introduction to the new evolutionary paradigm.* New York: Harcourt Brace Jovanovich.

Hoyle, Fred (1989). Articles of faith. *Nature* 339,23–4.

Humphrey, N. (1983). *Consciousness Regained.* Oxford: Oxford University Press.

Kawai, M. (1965). Newly acquired pre-cultural behaviour of the natural troop of Japanese monkeys on Koshima Island. *Primates* 6,1–30.

Kearney, H. (1971). *Science and Change 1500–1700.* New York: McGraw Hill.

Kingsley, Charles (1930). *The Water Babies.* London: Hodder and Stoughton. (original edition 1863).

Kirkley, Charles F. (1984). Fidelity in marriage and celibacy in singles. *Christianity in Crisis* 44,186–8.

Koch K. (1979). The Old Testament view of nature. *Anticipation* 25,47–52.

Koestler, Arthur (1982). *Bricks to Babel: Selected writings with author's comments.* London: Picador.

Kushner, H. S. (1982). *When Bad Things Happen to Good People.* London: Pan Books.

Leontief, W. W., Carter, A. P. & Petri, P. (1977). *The Future of the World Economy: A United Nations study.* Oxford University Press.

Levins, Richard & Lewontin, Richard (1985). *The Dialectical Biologist.* Cambridge, MA: Harvard University Press.

Lewontin, R. C. (1983). The corpse in the elevator. *New York Review of Books* 30 (2 January), pp. 34–7.

Lewontin, R. C., Rose, Steven & Kamin, Leon J. (1984). *Not in Our Genes: Biology, ideology and human nature.* New York: Pantheon Books.

Linden, E. (1986). *Silent Partners: The legacy of the ape language experiments.* New York: Times Books.

Locke, Steven & Colligan, Douglas (1986). *The New Medicine of Mind and Body*. New York: E. P. Dutton.

Manuel, F. (1968). *A Portrait of Newton*. Cambridge, MA: Harvard University Press.

Marty, Martin E. (1986). *Modern American Religion: Vol. 1. The Irony of it All 1853–1919*. University of Chicago Press.

McDaniel, J. (1983). Physical matter as creative and sentient. *Environmental Ethics* 5,291–317.

McFague, Sallie (1987). *Models of God: Theology for an ecological, nuclear age*. Philadelphia: Fortress Press.

Meadows, D. H., Meadows, D. L., Randers, J. & Behrens, W. W. (1972). *Limits to Growth*. New York: New American Library.

Merchant, Caroline (1980). *The Death of Nature: Women, ecology and the scientific revolution*. San Francisco: Harper and Row.

Merkle, John C. (1985). Abraham Joshua Heschel: The pathos of God. *Christianity and Crisis* 45,493–6.

Mesarovic, M. & Pestel, E. (1974). *Mankind at the Turning Point*. New E. P. Dutton.

Mesarovic,. M. & Pestel, E. (1984). Organic and sustainable growth. *World Futures* 19,233–48.

Moltmann, Jurgen (1985). *God and Creation: An ecological doctrine of creation*. London: SCM Press.

Momigliano Arnoldo (1963). Pagan and Christian historiography in the fourth century AD. In *The Conflict Between Paganism and Christianity in the Fourth Century* (ed. Momigliano A.), Oxford: Clarendon.

Monod, Jacques (1974). *Chance and Necessity: An essay on the natural philosophy of modern biology*. London: Fontana/Collins.

Montefiore, H. (1985). *The Probability of God*. London: SCM Press.

Naess, Arne (1989). *Ecology, Community and Lifestyle: Outline of an ecophilosophy*. Cambridge University Press.

Needleman, Jacob (1988). *A Sense of the Cosmos: An encounter of modern science and ancient truth*. New York: Routledge Chapman & Hall.

Nelkin, Dorothy (1977). *Science Textbook Controversies and the Problems of Equal Time*. Cambridge, MA: MIT Press.

Newbigin, Lesslie (1983). *The Other Side of '84*. London: British Council of Churches.

Newbigin, Lesslie (1986). *Foolishness to the Greeks*. Geneva: World Council of Churches.

Niebuhr, Reinhold (1941). *The Nature and Destiny of Man*. New York: Charles Scribner's Sons.

Niebuhr, Reinhold (1946). *Discerning the Signs of the Times*. New York: Charles Scribner's Sons.

Niebuhr, Reinhold (1972). *The Children of Light and the Children of Darkness*. New York: Charles Scribner's Sons.

Niebuhr, Reinhold (1976). *Justice and Mercy* (ed. Ursula M. Niebuhr). New York: Harper and Row.

Odin, Steven (1984). The penumbral shadow: A Whiteheadian perspective on the Yugen style of art and literature in Japanese aesthetics. *Japanese Journal of Religious Studies* 23(1).

Ornstein, Robert & Ehrlich, Paul (1989). *New World New Mind: Toward conscious evolution*. New York: Doubleday.

Pagels, Heinz R. (1984). *The Cosmic Code: Quantum physics as the language of nature*. Harmondsworth, Middlesex: Penguin Books.

Pannenburg, Wolfhart (1976). *Theology and the Philosophy of Science*. London: Darton Longman & Todd.

Pannenberg, Wolfhart (1982). Spirit and mind. In *Mind in Nature* (ed. R. Q. Elvee), pp. 134–57. San Francisco: Harper and Row.

Passmore, J. A. (1959). Darwin and the climate of opinion. *Australian Journal of Science* 22,8–15.

Peacocke, Arthur R. (1979). *Creation and the World of Science*. Oxford: Clarendon Press.

Peacocke, Arthur R. (1984). *Intimation of Reality: Critical realism in science and religion*. Notre Dame, IN: University of Notre Dame Press.

Peacocke, Arthur (1986). *God and the New Biology*. London: J. M. Dent and Sons.

Pestel, Eduard (1989). *Beyond the Limits to Growth: A report to the Club of Rome*. New York: Universe Books.

Peters, Ted (1985). David Bohm, postmodernism and the divine. *Zygon* 20,193–217.

Phillips, J. B. (1947). *Letters to Young Churches: A translation of the New Testament epistles*. London: Butler and Tanner.

Pirages, Denis C. & Ehrlich, Paul R. (1974). *Ark II: Social response to environmental imperatives*. San Francisco: W. H. Freeman.

Pittenger, Norman (1967). *Time for Consent?: A Christian approach to homosexuality*. London: SCM Press.

Popper, Karl (1971). Sir Karl Popper talks about some of his basic ideas with Bryan Magee. *The Listener* (7 January), pp. 8–12.

Premack, D. & Premack, A. J. (1983). *The Mind of an Ape*. New York: W. W. Norton.

Preston, R. H. (1983). *Church and Society in the Late Twentieth Century*. London: SCM Press.

Pribram, K. H. (1977). Holonomy and structure in the organization of perception. In *Images, Perception and Knowledge* (ed. Nicholas J. M.) Dordrecht, Holland: Reidel.

Pribram, K. H., Nuwer, M. & Baron, R. (1974). The holographic hypothesis of memory structure and brain function and structure. In *Contemporary Developments in Mathematical Psychology: Vol. 2* (eds. R. Atkinson, O. Krantz, R. Luce, & P. Suppes), San Francisco: W. H. Freeman.

Prigogine, Ilya & Stengers, Isabelle (1984). *Order and Chaos: Man's new dialogue with nature*. New York: Bantam Books.

Rasmussen, Larry (1985). On creation and growth. *Christianity and Crisis* 45,473–6.

Raven, Charles E. (1953a). *Natural Religion and Christian Theology. The Gifford Lectures: First series. Science and Religion*. Cambridge University Press.

Raven, Charles E. (1953b). *Natural Religion and Christian Theology. The Gifford Lectures: Second series. Experience and Interpretation*. Cambridge University Press.

184

Ravetz, J. R. (1981). The varieties of scientific experience. In *The Sciences and Theology in the Twentieth Century* (ed. Arthur R. Peacocke), pp. 197–206. Notre Dame, IN: University of Notre Dame Press.

Robinson, John A. T. (1967). *Exploration into God.* London: SCM Press.

Russell, Bertrand (1935). *Religion and Science.* London: Thornton Butterworth.

Russell, Bertrand (1961). A free man's worship. In *Basic Writings of Bertrand Russell 1903–1959* (eds. R. E. Egner & L. E. Denman), pp. 66–72. New York: Simon and Schuster.

Russell, Bertrand (1968). *The Impact of Science on Society.* London: Unwin Books.

Santimere, H. P. (1985). *The Travail of Nature: The ambiguous ecological promise of Christian theology.* Philadelphia: Fortress Press.

Savage-Rumbaugh, E. S. (1986). *Ape Language: From conditioned response to symbol.* New York: Columbia University Press.

Schumacher, E. F. (1973). *Small is Beautiful: Economics as if people mattered.* New York: Harper and Row.

Searle, John (1984). *Minds, Brains and Science: The 1984 BBC Reith Lectures.* London: British Broadcasting Corporation.

Senderowitz, Judith & Paxman, John M. (1985). Adolescent fertility: Worldwide concerns. Population Reference Bureau Publication, **40** (2),51 pp.

Sheldrake, Rupert (1981). *A New Science of Life: The hypothesis of formative causation.* London: Blond and Briggs.

Shinn, Roger L. (1982). *Forced Options: Social decisions for the twenty-first century.* San Francisco: Harper and Row.

Sittler, Joseph A. (1961). Called to unity. *The Ecumenical Review* **14**,181–90.

Solle, Dorothy (1971). *Political Theology.* Philadelphia: Fortress Press.

Sperry, Roger (1977). Absolute values. In *The Search for Absolute Values: Proceedings of the Fifth International Congress on the Unity of the Sciences: Vol. 11* (pp. 689–94). New York: The Intercultural Foundation.

Sperry, Roger (1983a). *Science and Moral Priority: Merging mind, brain and human values.* Oxford: Blackwell.

Sperry, Roger (1983b). Interview with Roger Sperry. *Omni* **5**(ii),69–100.

Stapp, H. P. (1972). The Copenhagen interpretation. *American Journal of Physics* **40**,1098–1116.

Stapp, H. P. (1977). Quantum mechanics, local causality and process philosophy. *Process Studies* **7**,173–82.

Stapp, H. P. (1979). Whiteheadian approach to quantum theory and the generalized Bell's theorem. *Foundations of Physics* **9**,1–15.

Sutherland, S. (1984). Consciousness and conscience. *Nature* **307**,391.

Tanaka, T. (1984). *Hyatology and Whitehead's process thought.* In *Process and Reality East and West* (pp. 7–21). Unpublished collection of papers of the Japanese Society for Process Studies.

Thomas, Lewis (1974). *The Lives of a Cell: Notes of a biology watcher.* New York: Viking Press.

Thomas, Lewis (1979). *The Medusa and the Snail: More notes of a biology watcher.* New York: Viking Press.

Thomas, M. M. (1984). Mission and modern culture. *The Ecumenical Review* **36**,316–22.

Thoreau, H. D. (1908). Walden: Or life in the woods. London: N. M. Dent and Sons. (original edition 1854).

Thorpe, W. H. (1956). *Learning and Instinct in Animals*. Harvard University Press.

Tillich, Paul (1955). *The New Being*. New York: Charles Scribner's Sons.

Tillich, Paul (1959). *Theology and Culture*. Oxford University Press.

Tillich, Paul (1966). *The Future of Religions*. Westport, CT: Greenwood Press.

Tillich, Paul (1967). *A History of Christian Thought: From its Judeo and Hellenistic origins to existentialism*. New York: Simon Schuster.

Trevor-Roper, H. R. (1956). *The European Witch Craze of the Sixteenth and Seventeenth Centuries*. New York: Harper Brothers.

Trigg, J. W. (1983). *Origen: The Bible and philosophy in the third-century church*. Atlanta, GA: John Knox Press.

Waddington, C. H. (1969). The practical consequences of metaphysical beliefs on a biologist's work: An autobiographical note. In *Towards a Theoretical Biology: Vol. 2. Sketches* (ed. C. H. Waddington) pp. 72–81. University of Edinburgh Press.

Waddington, C. H. (1975). *The Evolution of an Evolutionist*. Edinburgh University Press.

Weinberg, Steven (1977). *The First Three Minutes: A modern view of the design of the universe*. New York: Basic Books.

Wheeler, J. A. (1977). Genesis and observership. In *Foundational Problems in the Special Sciences* (eds. Butts and Hintikka), pp. 3–33. Dordrecht, Holland: Reidel.

Wheeler, J. A. (1982). Bohr, Einstein and the strange lesson of the quantum. In *Mind in Nature* (ed. R. Q. Elvee), pp. 1–30. San Francisco: Harper and Row.

White, A. D. (1960). *A History of the Warfare of Science with Theology in Christendom: Vol. 1*. New York: Dover.

White, Lynn T. (1968). *Machina ex Deo: Essays on the dynamism of Western culture*. Cambridge, MA: MIT Press.

White, Lynn T. (1972). Snake nests and icons. *Anticipation* **10**,30–7.

White, Lynn, T. (1975). Christians and nature. *Pacific Theological Review* **7**,6–11.

Whitehead, A. N. (1929). *The Function of Reason*. Princeton University Press.

Whitehead, A. N. (1930). *Religion in the Making*. Cambridge University Press.

Whitehead, A. N. (1933). *Science and the Modern World*. Cambridge University Press.

Whitehead, A. N. (1941). Immortality. In *The Philosophy of A. N. Whitehead* (ed. P. A. Schlipp), pp. 682–700. Evanston, IL: Northwestern University Press.

Whitehead, A. N. (1942). *Adventures of Ideas*. Harmondsworth, Middlesex: Penguin Books.

Whitehead, A. N. (1947). *Essays in Science and Philosophy*. New York: Philosophical Library.

Whitehead, A. N. (1949). *The Aims of Education*. New York: Mentor Books.

Whitehead, A. N. (1966). *Modes of Thought*. New York: Free Press.

Whitehead, A. N. (1978). *Process and Reality* (corrected edition, eds. D. R.

186

Griffen and D. W. Sherbourne). New York: Free Press. (original edition 1929).

Wieman, H. N. (1929). *Methods of Private Religious Living*. New York: Macmillan.

Wilber, Ken (ed.) (1984). *Quantum Questions: Mystical writings of the world's great physicists*. Boulder, CO: Shambhala. New Science Library.

Witkowski, Jan (1985). The hunting of the organiser: An episode in biochemical embryology. *Trends in Biochemical Science* **10**,379–81.

Witkowski, Jan (1986). Reason and silence before beauty. *Trends in Biochemical Science* **11**,52.

Wright, Sewall (1953). Gene and organism. *American Naturalist* **87**,5–18.

Wright, Sewall (1964). Biology and the philosophy of science. In *Process and Divinity* (eds. W. L. Reese & E. Freeman), pp. 101–25. La Salle, IL: Open Court.

Yates, F, (1972). *The Rosicrucian Enlightenment*. London: Routledge and Kegan Paul.

Young, J. Z. (1978). *Programmes of the Brain: The Gifford Lectures 1975–77*. Oxford University Press.

Young, J. Z. (1987). *Philosophy and the Brain*. Oxford University Press.

INDEX